Richard Meier Architect

Introduction by Joseph Rykwert

1964/1984

Richard Meier Architect

RIZZOLI
NEW YORK

*Library of Congress Cataloging in
Publication Data*
Meier, Richard, 1934–
Richard Meier, architect.
Bibliography: p.
1. Meier, Richard, 1934–
2. Architecture, Modern—20th
century—United States.
I. Title.
NA737.M44A4 1984
720′.92′4   83–42911
ISBN 0–8478–0496–8
ISBN 0–8478–0497–6 (pbk.)

Editor: Joan Ockman
Designer: Massimo Vignelli
Design Coordinator: Abigail Sturges

Type in Bodoni by Roberts/Churcher
Printing and binding by
Dai Nippon, Japan

For Joseph and Ana

Contents

Preface

An ongoing conversation I have had with my children, Joseph and Ana, over the past year revolves around the question, "What is your favorite color?" Joseph, almost five years old, immediately responds, "Green," and when asked why, says, "Green is the color of grass, trees are green, green is all around us, it's the color of spring." Ana, who is three and doesn't like to be outdone by her brother, replies that her favorite color is blue, because "the sky is blue, the ocean is blue." Then both of them turn to me and say, "Daddy, what is your favorite color?" Every time we play this game, my response is the same: "White."

"But Daddy," Joseph says, "you can't choose white. White is not a color; white is not in the rainbow; you have to choose a color that *is*, like red or green or blue or yellow." And I explain each time that I think white is the most wonderful color of all, because within it one can find every color of the rainbow.

White is in fact the color which intensifies the perception of all of the other hues that exist in natural light and in nature. It is against a white surface that one best appreciates the play of light and shadow, solids and voids. For this reason white has traditionally been taken as a symbol of purity and clarity, of perfection. Where other colors have relative values dependent upon their context, white retains its absoluteness. Yet when white is alone, it is never just white, but almost always some color that is itself being transformed by light and by everything changing in the sky, the clouds, the sun, the moon. Goethe said, "Color is the pain of light." Whiteness, perhaps, is the memory and the anticipation of color.

Whiteness is one of the characteristic qualities of my work; I use it to clarify architectural concepts and heighten the power of visual form. It aids me in my primary preoccupation, which is the molding of space and light—not abstract space, not scaleless space, but space whose definition and order are related to nature and context, to human scale, and to the culture of architecture. My raw materials are not only volume and surface, light and form, changes of scale and view, movement and stasis. They are also the physical and functional elements of construction themselves. I am deeply concerned with the making of a building, and prefer to think of myself more as a master builder than as an artist; I believe the art of architecture ultimately demands this. The history of architecture provides a constant repository of inspiration for my work as well, because part of the significance of any building derives from the awareness of the past that it encompasses, the way it embodies values of permanence, continuity, and therefore quality. But my allusions and quotations are never literal; the meanings are always internalized in the work, the metaphors purely architectural.

In stating that my fundamental concerns are space, form, light, and how to make them, I mean to accentuate that my goal is presence, not illusion. I pursue it with unrelenting vigor because I believe that today as in the past it is the heart and soul of architecture. Architecture is vital and enduring because it contains us; it substantiates the space we exist in, move through, and use. My work is an effort to redefine and refine this ongoing human order, to interpret the relationship between what has been and what can be, to extract from our culture both the timeless and the topical. This, to me, is the basis of style, of the decision to include or exclude, to exercise individual will and intellect. In this sense, style is something born out of culture, yet profoundly connected with personal experience.

To gain any sense of my involvement, of course, it is necessary to consult the work in this book. The buildings and projects in the following pages represent twenty years of architectural endeavor. They are part of an ongoing career, but they also mark a significant point of transition for me as I reach age fifty. I would like to thank some of the people who have been especially important in the preparation of this book: Joan Ockman, who has been indispensable in writing and editing the manuscript and coordinating the project; Massimo Vignelli, the superb graphic designer, who devoted many hours to the layout; Abigail Sturges, who has been responsible for its materialization; Ezra Stoller, who takes timeless photographs. I should also thank the numerous people who have participated over these twenty years in varying capacities in the work illustrated here, especially my partner Gerald Gurland. My gratitude to you all.

Richard Meier
June 1984

Introduction

Joseph Rykwert

An architect can only get going seriously, so Le Corbusier used to say, after he has passed fifty. If he was right, all the work in this book would show the tentative beginnings of a career, since it represents Richard Meier's work before the half-century climacteric. As you look through it, you will realize that my reference is a paradox, since the work is both accomplished and mature. Moreover, it maintains a consistency of achievement which very few of Meier's contemporaries anywhere (if any at all) can equal. It is this consistency which is perhaps the most immediately striking thing about his work. Because of it, many of his critics as well as his admirers have spoken of Meier as having picked on a style at the outset of his career, a style developed out of the middle manner of Le Corbusier, and stuck to it doggedly—which seems to me to be a complete misunderstanding.

Meier never had such a choice. He did not pick one style from among others: the style chose its architect. "It was I who was adopted by the genius of the language," wrote Joseph Conrad of his "choice" to write in English, "which directly I came out of the stammering stage made me its own so completely that its very idioms I truly believe had a direct action on my temperament . . ."

The parallel is illustrious, but fair. Any "language" which a young architect "chose" in the late fifties and early sixties had to be an alien one. Like Conrad, he had no inherited idiom in which he might address his public. And yet those who selected one style from several alternatives more or less arbitrarily showed it later by their ability to slough off one style and put on another.

Unlike them, Meier has always worked as if no possible alternative existed. Being curious and observant, he has inevitably been aware of distractions and temptations, but he does not allow himself to be deflected. This, you may object, is merely to make a virtue of keeping one's blinkers on. After all, the modernity associated with buildings like Meier's has long been discredited, and the white architecture which was its incarnation along with it. Yet this much-vaunted devaluation has not led to the replacement of the old currency by some equally glittering and more valuable new one. If, as the poet said, new styles of architecture are the token of a change of heart, then things are as they should be. You cannot change a worn-out heart very easily, not even in our times.

For a sensitive and inquiring architecture student in the late fifties of this century there was only one body of architectural work which was backed by a sustained, sometimes enthralling theoretical meditation: Le Corbusier's. That is how it must have seemed on the East Coast of the United States at any rate. Meier, a student at Cornell, had left before the school acquired its present public image. Great exemplars had to be looked for outside the group of his teachers. There was Mies in Chicago, who at that time had already built a great deal and was to build even more in the immediate future. His words sounded pregnant too, and were certainly gnomic, but his teaching must have seemed too schematic, too closed and jealous, to command a questioning and inquiring mind. Gropius, perched at Harvard, had also built and written a great deal: the worst of his later commercial work was still to come, but in fact the existing buildings and words did not really provide an exemplar. Aalto was still a shadowy figure, both geographically and linguistically, even if there was a building of his, a large but untypical one, to hand in Cambridge, Massachusetts. The only native master to rival the European imports, Wright, was too remote in time; and by the fifties his fame was tarnished by the adulation of imitators or courtiers, his current work the production of too large a studio. At the present remove, Wright's work appears much more clearly, and he is a master with whom we must all come to terms: Meier knows that well. But at the fretful beginning of his career there was no skirting around the towering bulk of Le Corbusier's achievement; anyone who attempted to do that did so at his own peril.

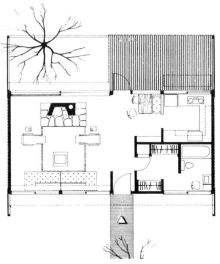

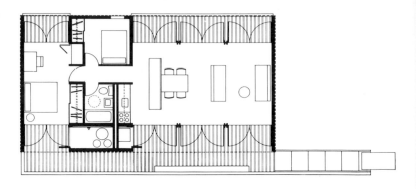

Yet even this work, so well documented and familiar, could not be absorbed directly on the other side of the Atlantic. Practice, usage, and convention would not allow it; anyone who attempted such an integration needed assurance in his native ways before he set out on the enterprise.

Meier's apprenticeship was careful and regular. A year with Davis, Brody & Wisniewski (later Davis, Brody & Associates), already recognized as a leading "good design" practice, was followed by another in the New York office of the gigantic Skidmore, Owings & Merrill. More important were the three following years working for Marcel Breuer. Breuer was then past his main achievement, which was to look at New England clapboard architecture—at what Vincent Scully has memorably called the "shingle style"—with his Eastern European, Bauhaus-trained eyes, and devise a wholly new way of exploiting its judicious mix of light, cross-braced walls and heavy stone or brick underpinning and hearths: a way which also owed something to Wright but was genuinely new and unexpected.

By the time Meier had gone to work for Breuer, however, the shock of recognition was long past, and Breuer was doing mostly public and industrial building, of which the IBM research center at La Gaude in the south of France (on which Meier worked) and the Benedictine abbey of St. John at Collegeville, Minnesota, are notable examples. While working for Breuer, Meier carried out his first independent commission: a beach house on Fire Island, New York. It owes more to Breuer than anything he has done since. With the house for his parents at Essex Fells, New Jersey, however, Meier did something outside the received convention, something quite alien to Breuer's preoccupations. The Breuer Domestic manner (for all its charm) could not move into a major mode, or even into the larger scale, as Meier must have discovered in action. The irresolution irked him. In another context, Vincent Scully had experienced an analogous mood

when writing his *Shingle Style:* he found himself leafing though the early volumes of Le Corbusier's *Oeuvre Complète* "with stupefied absorption. The thin, tense, hyperintelligent forms were apparently the relief I needed from Shingle fuzz, plastic intersections, and infinite spatial variety."

That is very much an architect's perception. But Scully was looking for the teasing antithesis to his Shingle obsession, while Meier recognized this antithesis as his challenge. Haltingly at first, he set about translating the forms of that inebriating intelligence into his native "fuzz." Or at least the native fuzz as it had been interpreted for him by a preceding generation. That is why there is nothing about that early work which could suggest the conscious adoption of a style. From that early house for his parents, the effort is toward something rather different. That small, single-story building has a deep rectangular roof emulating the reveals of the roof and floors at Wright's Falling Water, which had recently made a great impression on Meier. It is not set into materially obtrusive masonry, but placed over walls which project out of the house into the garden to emphasize the unity of inside and outside. Meier found this much-vaunted unity to be illusory. His next building, the renovation of a house in Chester, New Jersey, overstates the separation dogmatically, heavily; it could almost have been Californian. In his parents' house, however, Meier offers a gentle, accommodating reading of Mies, with none of the asperities of the early work of the master or the stilted aggressions of his followers. It is almost a Wrightian reading of the Miesian concern with dispersing interior volume into exterior space. The planar elements with which this is done look unusually (for Meier) substantial and heavy, though the color is unified; their weight is emphasized, as is the simplicity of the geometry, by two cylindrical outbuildings.

In reaction to his parents' house Meier was able to formulate his approach anew. He may have been helped by doing a number of

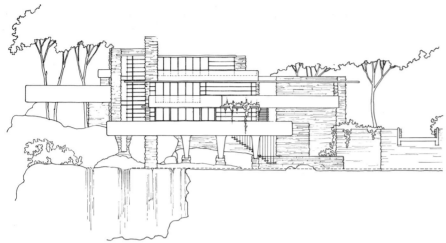

Falling Water, Bear Run, Pennsylvania. Frank Lloyd Wright, 1936. Front elevation

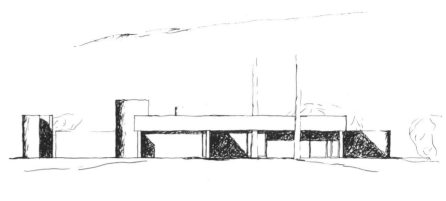

House for Mr. and Mrs. Jerome Meier, Essex Fells, New Jersey. Richard Meier, 1965. East elevation

interiors (one for his friend the painter Frank Stella) about this time. By the time he designed the Smith House at Darien, Connecticut, his approach had matured. In obvious contrast to the work of his exemplars—and the surrounding buildings—the house does not "hug" the earth, but stands tall, tightly packed and vertical—a gesture to the stunning landscape, a mark of settlement. Even the approach is geometricized, a quadrant which comes to a stop at the outbuilding/garage. At forty-five degrees, the path rises to the house, a white wall of siding, pierced by an entrance and carefully placed windows. It is constantly dappled by the changing shadows of the two large trees on either side, and gives no hint of the view over the Sound which is to come. As you open the door, there it suddenly is, through the huge duplex windows of the main two-story living room. You enter that main space through the double wall of smaller rooms—bath and bedrooms, kitchen and utility room on the northwest; the main living space faces southeast and the view. There is an intended reference here to the distribution of the Villa Stein at Garches, with its protecting wall facing the entrance and the vast expanse of glass toward the garden. But this schematic parallel is contradicted by more obvious differences. The entrance wall is pierced not by narrow slits but by a pattern of windows (a shade too deliberate if the aim of art is really that of concealing itself). Facing the entrance is the main fireplace, which serves the ground (below the entrance) and second floors, and rises well above the roof, providing the house with an exterior focus—literally—whose materiality is not annulled by the white paint. The materials are mixed: wood siding, balloon framing for partitions, steel columns on the southern face. The fireplace, unlike Wright's (but like Breuer's), has no part in the structure. The schematic plan, which is echoed by the later houses, demonstrates another difference between Meier's approach and that of some of his predecessors, particularly European ones: it is not so much the plan which generates the general configuration of the house, but rather the section. I say this in spite of Meier's assertions to the contrary, but it

seems to me a genuine formal and methodological innovation of his, even if he is himself slow to acknowledge the shift from plan to section.

In the next, the Hoffman House in East Hampton, which stands on a flat, square site, the monotony of the data challenged Meier to a game of constructing the plan from two groups of two squares each: one set parallel to the site boundary and the road, the other on the diagonal. It is perhaps the last building by Meier in which photographs and plans tell the whole story. The section becomes very much more important in the next, the larger Saltzman House, also in East Hampton, whose huge central windows are as much a display of this new plastic richness as openings to view the somewhat anodyne landscape. Perhaps the unbuilt house at Pound Ridge, New York, designed in 1969, shows this most clearly, since it is also set on a relatively flat site, and interior level differences are entirely a matter of design. In schematic layout, the house is very much like the one in Darien. The entrance is through a double wall containing smaller "private" rooms: bed, bath, utility, and kitchen; the full-height space beyond, facing southeast, is glazed on three sides. The fireplace, however, does not, as at Darien, occlude a view of the landscape. That is done by a cylinder, through which a staircase is glimpsed. The staircase pushes through the glass southern wall. It leads up to the master bedroom which, with its bath and dressing rooms, is suspended in and articulates the huge open space; it has, too, the role of defining the working areas of the house. Only when you relate the master bedroom to the main space do you take in the importance of that cylinder which occluded your entrance view, since it is both a down-duct from the main bathroom and a roof light from above. The height of the main space and the principal bedroom is greater than that of the rooms in the double north wall, and the difference in level is taken up in the horizontal roof-line by two terraces on either side of the entrance space, with its circular staircase, which the arriving visitor sees rising through two floors, proclaiming the importance of the

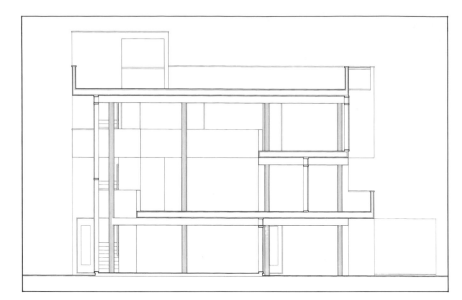

section. The configuration of the entrance wall is much less contrived than at Darien, in spite of the greater complexity of the section. The double north wall becomes a container projecting a half-cylinder to the west and a half-square to the east, both top-lit bays. Because of the continuous horizontal roof-line and the differences in section heights, the bays become important plastic elements, as do, on the glazed south face, the projective half-cylinder of the stairway and the semicircle of the main bedroom balcony. Plastically less obvious though equally important is the way in which the double north wall is not part of the continuous envelope. In spite of the simplicity of the roof line and the openness of the double-walled box toward the duplex main space (which is more than twice as wide), the two rectangles overlap in plan, and the overlap is emphasized by the two projecting bays. The main space is much more complex: at Darien there were two walls, a row of columns, and the glass screen, a progression unencumbered by any vertical insertions. At Pound Ridge there are two walls, three rows of columns, as well as the articulations of the height differences and the spatial insertions.

The Pound Ridge house is the one I most regret that Meier did not build. The flattish site and the simple program imposed minimal constraints, and it therefore exhibited his formal method to the best advantage, a formal method which no longer had much connection with what had been learned from Breuer. Nor is it directly taken from any one other master, not even Le Corbusier. It is a composite precipitate; and the solvent was not an architectural but a pictorial one: Cubism, particularly Synthetic Cubism. The agent which had acted on this solution was an essay by Colin Rowe and Robert Slutzky, which appeared in the Yale architecture periodical *Perspecta* in 1963, and offered an interpretation of the device of transparency in what then seemed quite novel terms. Transparency had been treated somewhat cavalierly in the literature of the *Isms*. Rowe and Slutzky examined this rather loose terminology to establish two main uses of

the word: "literal" transparency, which had to do with the display of overlapping, see-through objects on a picture plane, and with the display of parts of a building through large areas of glass or trellis; and "phenomenal" transparency, which signified overlap and interpenetration as formal conventions, metaphors, in which there were no transparent materials, no see-through bits, but in which primary geometries submitted to variations through shift and rotation to connote spatial complexity. The essay certainly did not "discover" Cubism for the younger architects, yet it mediated it to a whole generation. It appeared at a moment when Louis Kahn's notion of a building within a building, or a building within ruins, began to be canvassed and could, with Rowe and Slutzky's help, be accounted for in terms of the heady, Corbusian formal discipline.

This was the time when Meier graduated from Cornell and Michael Graves went from Cincinnati to Harvard. For a while afterward their ways were parallel. They both moved to New York and began to teach architecture at various schools, Meier principally at Cooper Union, Graves at Princeton. They also shared a painting studio. But while Graves, as it were, became his own painter, Meier, who has continued to work at both painting and collage, always regarded this as an ancillary activity, and has worked collaboratively with a number of painters, chiefly with his old friend Frank Stella.

The reliance which architects of Meier's generation placed on the Cubist model of space was inevitably paradoxical, since Cubist painters were concerned with representation on a plane primarily, and only by extrapolation with sculptural objects. To architecture they had no access; it was not within their cultural realm. Many of them were to accept the white architecture of the twenties as "theirs," in spite of all that Le Corbusier and Ozenfant had written in defense of the iconic object against its dismemberment by Cubist pictorial procedures. The iconic object, which Le Corbusier and Ozenfant then assumed into their own pictorial method (which method they called Purist), was always a commonplace: bottles and glasses, pipes and cigarettes, musical instruments, newspaper and package wrappers, the human face, very exceptionally the rest of the body. Yet it is precisely in the Cubist destruction of the object that the particular manipulation of volume which Le Corbusier was to bequeath to coming generations of architects was learned.

The paradox can be taken further: the Cubist method depended on the movement of the viewer; volume in the new architecture could only be experienced through what Le Corbusier called the *promenade architecturale,* which in fact inverted the Cubist manipulation by becoming a way of making and of reading the three-dimensional object, though derived from the recording of the multiple-viewing eye on a picture plane.

There is another aspect of the Corbusian procedure which is often elided. The "five points," which were accepted by many architects in the thirties, make much of the freedom which the new technology allows the architect. This freedom can only be truly exercised within the constraints of rational composition: composition is rational in Le Corbusier's terms when it is generated by the geometry of proportion. There is very little interest in this proposition nowadays, and it tends to be absorbed in the manipulation of another commonplace which can also be "deduced" from Cubist painting and sculpture: the primary geometrical forms—square, circle, triangle, and their simplest combinations. The method of operating with elementary geometry can be assimilated into modish talk about types and typology, through whose rather open meshes the more complex and elusive proportional problem tends to slip. Yet another reason for this neglect is that talk of proportion and the related matter of number is inevitably about quantity, and therefore distracts attention from the all-important matter of quality. It tends to be conducted either in

terms of obscure and sometimes occult speculation or of hand-me-down perceptual psychology. It is therefore inaccessible to both clients and critics.

Meier himself has been rather ambivalent about this matter. He is prepared to agree that proportional measurements help to correct or check designs, but he is not prepared to speculate about proportion as a generator of form. Insistent on the problem of quality as primary, he prefers to discuss the relation between program and site, the reference to historic type, the modeling of volume by light.

The investment of attention in formal properties and therefore in quality is easier to maintain in work for private clients. Meier very soon moved into industrial and public work, where such justifications are less readily accepted in terms of public spending. This made the consistent development of his formal method, the temperate justification of each step, much more important. The clients who first employed him were inevitably those who had already established a concern with quality in building.

The first public commission to be executed was a large conversion: of the disused New York laboratories of the Bell Company in downtown New York into artists' housing. The huge buildings accommodated over three hundred loft spaces on the edge of Greenwich Village long before loft-living had become fashionable among the New York intelligentsia. After a number of abortive schemes for medical authorities and universities, the next executed project was for public housing in the Bronx, the Twin Parks complex, built between 1969 and 1974. It is the first of Meier's major schemes in which the facing material is the dark brick of the surrounding buildings. In fact, it shows an almost finicky care about continuing and elaborating the urban texture. Although some of the buildings in the context are considerably higher than their immediate neighbors, they do not quite

M.I.T. Senior Dormitory, Cambridge, Massachusetts. Alvar Aalto, 1948.
Typical floor plan

Dormitory for the Olivetti Training Center, Tarrytown, New York.
Richard Meier, 1971. Entry level plan

tower over them. What is more important, the buildings hug the lines of the street very closely and constitute themselves into the perimeter of a public space—a tactic which may seem obvious enough now, but which in the late sixties was still something of an innovation.

The project has its problems. While the attempt to integrate air-conditioning units into the pattern of the fenestration has resulted in some very ingeniously managed rhythms, the effect on the interior walls seems awkward. More important, the relation between the smooth faces of the high blocks and the interior spaces does not allow for any mediation between them. However, the buildings are raised on *pilotis*, and it required both foresight and ingenuity to save some of the space (particularly that on Garden Street) from being eaten up by parking.

Exploring variations of the street pattern in this plan was to introduce a theme of major importance in Meier's later work. The Monroe Developmental Center, designed and built at the same time as the Twin Parks project and finished in a similar brick tile, is almost the opposite in both program and siting. Set on an unwooded piece of flat land on the edge of Rochester suburbia and adjoining the local state hospital campus, it is a single-story building providing housing, education, and therapy for five hundred mentally retarded persons. The housing is all on the perimeter: the whole plan is a square enclosed by two L-shaped groups of housing units. Each unit is a smaller square, with a top-lit circulation area at the center. The residential units are set out in couples which connect to the main circulation squares through staff units.

Inevitably there are special areas for inhabitants who require individual care and various other constraints which a program of this nature imposes. But also endemic to this kind of extensive building is the architectural treatment of the very long circulation areas, which threaten to turn into institutional corridors. Meier has managed to place most of them on the exterior of his built area, so that one side almost always looks to the gardens, and they become a kind of discontinuous colonnade. The joints between the twin housing units and the circulation area are inset in such a way that the passage is always broken around them. But perhaps the most remarkable thing about the Monroe Center is the relation between the overall broken square perimeter and the small, enclosed square of the individual housing unit, modulated by the intermediate square enclosures of the public areas. Without recourse to any twist or rotation (apart from the diagonal siting of one staircase), a great spatial variety is managed within a forbiddingly monotonous context and the plainest of massings.

The period of these major buildings is also one of several important unbuilt commissions. The Health and Physical Education Building for the State University of New York at the Fredonia campus was Meier's first academic scheme. The relatively simple program (services, administration, and three main sports areas, one of them a swimming pool) was complicated by the siting of the building in relation to a ring road which connected the various campus buildings to the outdoor athletic areas. Although the final project selected was carried to full working details, the building has not been executed. A much more important though also abortive scheme was the work which Meier carried out for the North American branch of the Italian Olivetti corporation. Olivetti is a firm which to some extent trades on its patronage of the best design in the world, and the commission marks the recognition which Meier had by 1971 been given as one of the leading young architects in the United States. For Olivetti Meier designed two quite separate programs: the first was for a group of prefabricated buildings, to be erected on some six sites all over the United States, to provide local branch offices and repair shops for the corporation; the second, a modified smaller version in timber, was developed for seven other sites. In the event, none of these were built,

16

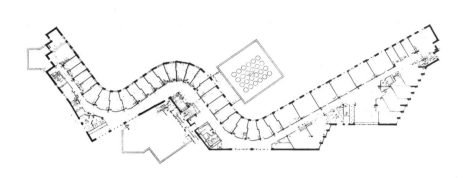

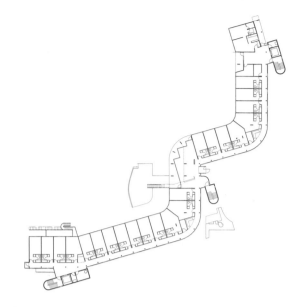

as the Olivetti corporation decided to economize on development.

In both types the layout is simple: two blocks of offices and workshops bisected by a circulation passage; in the larger type the passage is roofed by a glass vault. In both types the formal device is the exposing of the main arrival area—reception and staircase—within a glazed box to which the firm's logo in relief is related. Sited at roadside in suburban industrial estates, there is something glaring and contrary about these designs' refusal to raise the advertising pitch to that of the surrounding buildings. They are compact and spare; their only indulgence is the use of the glass box, lit at night, throwing the company logo into relief.

Both types were to be prefabricated: the first of steel elements and heavier material, the second of timber and light elements. In the larger and heavier type a plan-form appears for the first time that is to become something of a mark of Meier's later work; in this project, however, it is almost a by-product of tilting a square on plan very slightly—some 12½ degrees to the grid of the building—and rounding its corners. Inevitably, this is the glass box.

These Olivetti showrooms are tightly organized, the glass box opening into a central top-lit passage and the grid of plan and elevation allowing for relatively painless expansion. They share this curious and unremarked characteristic with some of Meier's other buildings, that the tight and apparently fixed order, the closed statement, does in fact allow for extension and latitude; even in a compact building like the Smith House at Darien, the addition of a large bedroom on the east side of the second floor has left the building unimpaired.

The other side of the Olivetti commission was two "permanent" buildings. The company wished to provide its training center at Tarrytown, New York, with a dormitory block, and also to build

headquarters in Virginia, near Washington, D.C. The terraced, rather hierarchical office building is set obliquely to the roads and clad in steel panels; its main space is a nearly semicircular showroom which takes up two floors. The effect of the metal paneling and the rather delicate glazing of the larger transparent areas would have made it one of the stateliest of Meier's buildings. The serpentine dormitory block, like the analogously planned student housing at Cornell University, inevitably recalls the plan of Aalto's student housing for M.I.T. in Cambridge, Massachusetts; but apart from the obvious similarities of massing, the buildings are very different from Aalto's and from each other.

The Olivetti housing project exploits the differences in site level by being set with its center on the crest of a hill: this grade is a datum. The fall of the ground provides for two floors below, to accommodate service and recreation rooms. In the middle of the block a many-storied entrance hall makes a caesura in the horizontal run of alternating wall and window, with an unexpectedly jagged profile. As far as possible the plan spares all the trees growing on the site and allows every room a view of the Hudson River. Similar considerations operated at Cornell, where Meier's buildings for undergraduate housing on Cayuga Heights overlook the lake and are sited in wooded parkland. This circumspect dodging of the trees, this angling of views, might seem an irrelevance or feint in an architect so firmly labeled a formalist as Meier is. Nevertheless, they really do determine his forms, or at least his choice of types: which indicates a contradiction between his approach and the way in which it has been received by his critics. They have concentrated on stylistic analysis and on formal derivations, preferring such epidermic reactions to considering how he comes to terms with his problems on the drawing board.

Arguably, the critic looks at appearances, and the architect's struggle

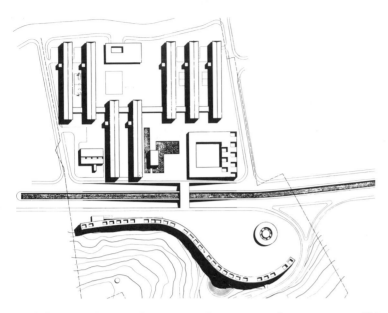

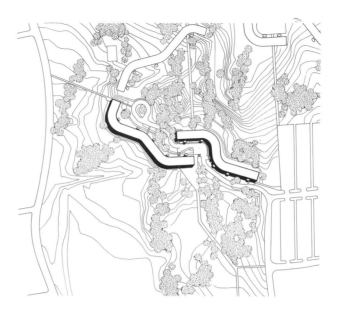

with his problems is his private business and no concern of his "consumers"; still, buildings cannot quite be treated as if they were detachable sections in some ringworm of stylistic development. So with Meier's use of the undulating S-shape or W-shape plan: his almost obsessive concern with relating his building to contours and his respect for trees have led him to apparently willful and even derivative forms. Yet his inventive process is always concerned with an acknowledgment of a programmatic demand. The undulating plans of the Olivetti and Cornell buildings are of course repetitive units in a large-scale form, one of the standard type-problems of the twentieth-century architect. It was Aalto who (on a flat site parallel to the Charles River) first wound his linear block into an S-shape. Aalto may have taken courage from Le Corbusier's Algiers block, the most majestic attempt of the kind; possibly he was inspired only by a predilection for the undulating line, which he displays in the design of small objects as well as large buildings. However, what in Aalto's work is a deliberate search for an idiosyncratic form, in Meier's case is a recharging of an available shape through its formal context: making it therefore *mean* something new.

It does not seem helpful to me to disparage this as a mannerist procedure and insinuate parallels between the generation after Raphael and Michaelangelo, and that after Le Corbusier and Frank Lloyd Wright—and Aalto: parallels no doubt exist, and may be interesting, but never explanatory or justifying. Unless circumscribed by cautionary distinctions, such parallels are likely to be obfuscating. So with Meier's use of the curved building. Compare it with Affonso Reidy's use of the same device in Rio de Janeiro twenty years earlier and you will see that while for Reidy the form is a piece of inert variationism, for Meier it is a "natural" way of approaching certain evident formal problems—used unostentatiously, as an accepted and familiar device whose merit depends on its context and connotations, not on its novelty.

The next important development in Meier's work comes in response to his most substantial commission up to that date: the Bronx Developmental Center. The site is dismal: a stretch of land between some railroad tracks, with dependent (but disused) warehouses on the west and the Hutchinson River Parkway on the east. As at the Monroe Center, the client here was the Facilities Development Corporation for the New York State Department of Mental Hygiene. In Rochester, however, a one-story building was situated in parkland. In the Bronx a four-story building is sited in industrial wasteland. The approach which was right at Monroe was, of course, entirely inapposite here: in fact, most of the tactics Meier had used seemed irrelevant, except the form of cladding with metal panels which had first been developed for the Fredonia sports center two years earlier and was reconsidered as an expedient factory-made finish for the Charles Evans Industrial Buildings a little later. This cladding was in fact an excellent protective skin for a building of this introverted nature in a hostile—or at any rate unwelcoming—environment. It had a characteristic which distinguished it from Meier's other work, in that the pattern of the panel joints gave a harsh, gridlike quality to the walls of the building, particularly since the aluminum skin was left bare.

What immediately modifies this impression, and is operated very skillfully by Meier, is the complex rhythm created by varying the nature of the panels. Inevitably, the production process supposed very few standard elements, and so the rhythms depend on the grouping of these elements as well as on the variations between different windows and mechanical vent openings. Placing the panels horizontally for the most part was a simple but essential move in this formal game: it allowed for a horizontal "layering" of the design that illustrated the use of the building. The grid of the panels helps to make the building lucid and legible; the variations in the relationships of the openings give it a certain rhythmic intensity.

Gávea Residential Neighborhood, Rio de Janeiro, Brazil.
Affonso Eduardo Reidy, 1952. General site plan

Cornell University Undergraduate Housing, Ithaca, New York.
Richard Meier, 1974. Site plan

Bird's eye view of one of the New Communities at Harmony.
Stedman Whitwell, 1825

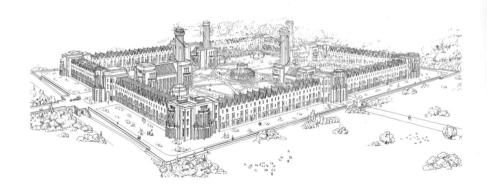

The reflecting and cold exterior surface belies the bright and soft interior, with its variety of colors and its elaborately shaped and layered courtyards. In a sense this building is the inversion of the Monroe Center. There is the same care to group the inmates into family-sized units, but while at Rochester these opened onto parkland, in the Bronx they are stacked vertically (three such units on each floor) on four floors. The units are L-shaped. There are four of them, and they are paired, being connected with service spaces and classrooms, which provide a transition area between the open courtyards and the privacy of the housing units on the east of the building, toward the highway. The entry is through the long westward block, which faces the railroad and the car park and contains administration, therapy, cafeteria, and other spaces of public use. Between the two blocks lie the terraced gardens. On the north the two blocks are connected by an open link, at the center by a glazed one, and at the south end by the sports block, which includes a closed swimming pool. There is therefore a double layering in the plan: the transition from private to public is east to west, from open to closed space is north to south. In the northern courtyard, there is also an important transition element—a miniature square house, which is intended to prepare residents for a domesticated life in the outside world. In the interior there are two very memorable public rooms, the swimming pool and the cafeteria. Because of the omnipresence of steel, the ship analogy is emphasized more heavily than in previous schemes, though it is familiar enough from the work of earlier masters. Moreover, the building has sharply different elevations to each of its four directions.

This syndrome was to become more important in the buildings which followed. Perhaps the most extreme example of it is the Atheneum in New Harmony, Indiana. It was designed while the Bronx Center was being built, and has—unlike the Bronx—a spectacular site on an artificial knoll overlooking the banks of the Wabash River, which

floods in springtime, leaving the building reflected and isolated.

The program demanded a propylaeum for an abandoned utopia. The town of Harmony was founded by Georg Rapp, a German social reformer and prophet of the second coming, who took his followers from Germany to Pennsylvania in 1803, and on to Indiana in 1815, where they farmed some 30,000 acres. But they proved restless, and he moved them back to another Pennsylvania site in 1825. The site and buildings were sold to the Welsh social reformer Robert Owen, who renamed it New Harmony. A grand new communal building was designed by Stedman Whitwell, an English architect, and partly built. A number of teachers and assorted sages were transported to the settlement by Owen's associate, William Maclure, in a specially designed boat, the operation being called the "Boatload of Knowledge." In fact Owen abandoned the experiment after three years and returned to Britain because of money and personal difficulties. But Maclure and some members of his family remained— some of their descendants still live there—and during the nineteenth century the town had its importance in the intellectual and scientific life of the Middle West. The community has recently had a resurgence, and receives many visitors, for whom an information and orientation center has long been needed.

Of Meier's buildings this is certainly the most complicated. The main approach up the hill leads the visitor to a blank panel, which faces him across the path, and admits him at forty degrees to the orthogonalities of the building, insofar as the visitor can detect them. Walking up to this rather overwhelming white wall, he will see a cut appear in it at ground level, and in the cut the entrance porch, so that he has to move around the blank panel to make his entry. As he looks up, however, he will see that the panel is one side of a triangle, and that above rises the prow of an acute angle.

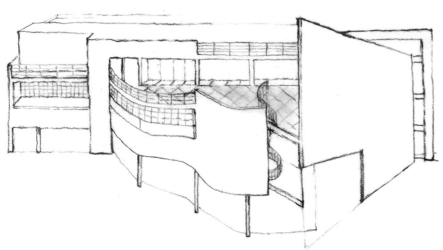

Now, acute angles are very difficult to do in architecture, as has been shown by the National Gallery of Art in Washington (for instance), with which the New Harmony Atheneum is always being compared. Except that Meier uses his acute angle cunningly, to suggest the prow of a boat: the wall on approach can be read as a sail, and as you enter the image is taken apart and reassembled for you, so that the angle the wall makes and the undulating screen around the foyer again suggest the prow and a wave. Such pictorial nudges and hints are not alien to architecture.

But the panel also acts as a detached facade, behind which the plan curves. The curve is cut by the path through the building, which lies at five degrees to the main structural grid—and to the interested observer this is made explicit on the exterior by the jointing of the paving and by the ramped path, which goes down to a belvedere that also acts as a projection of the main entry into the town. The interior path rises between the major volumes in the building, the auditorium on one side and the undulating foyer with its exhibition spaces on the other. Light filters into the interior spaces through the interstices of the various irregularities, and through others the visitor gets controlled glimpses of the town.

The two external staircases take up the play of obliquities. The slope of the exterior ramp is reflected by another high blank panel, which is parallel to the column grid, while the ramp, parallel to the panel in elevation, is at five degrees to the grid in plan, making the visitor conscious of the shifts and nudges in a rather strident if marginal way as he leaves the building.

The formal devices of the shift in the grid, the use of facade panels, and the juxtaposing of contrasting shapes are used to harmonize, divert, and startle the visitor as he moves through the building. It is for that very reason complicated—and pictorial, in fact the only building of Meier's where the plan and the building have strikingly similar pictorial qualities.

The houses built during this period, in the seventies, also achieve a new level of accomplishment. The small Shamberg House at Chappaqua, New York, develops a miniature version of the Pound Ridge volume, though with the addition, and it seems to me improvement, of a much more articulated glass wall. The Douglas House at Harbor Springs, Michigan, with its double-flue external fireplace, steep site, and tight organization on five levels, is an elaboration of the Smith House at Darien, though again, with a very much calmer and yet much more elegant glass wall, perhaps too closely related to the internal grid of the house. The entry, because of the sharply sloping site, is at the top level, onto the roof. From the entrance hall, shielded with a glass hood curved to that shape which had appeared in plan in the Olivetti building, and derived from the displaced square, you look down the two levels of the living room and catch a glimpse of the dining space below. The obliquities of the staircases become a new formal element which is used with a nautical abandon only complete assurance can give.

The series of projects which then followed established Meier's stature as one of the leaders of world architecture. They were for public buildings: the seminary at Hartford, Connecticut; the administrative headquarters for the Renault company, outside Paris; and new museums for Atlanta, Georgia, and Frankfurt, West Germany.

Of these only the seminary is completed and occupied at the time of writing. Hartford is an old town, and its seminary well known. In recent retrenchments, the Gothic buildings in which the seminary was once housed were handed over to the University of Connecticut, to become its law school. The seminary redefined its role, no longer that of a training college for the Presbyterian ministry, but a higher institution

20

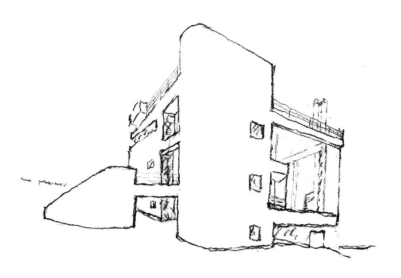

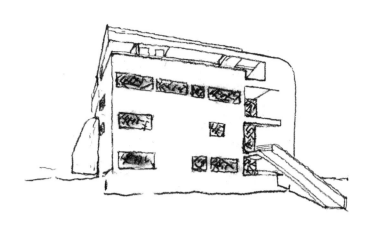

for theological studies without any denominational restriction.

Meier's preoccupation with filtering light through the complexities of his volumes and his constant use of reflecting white forms, suggesting a dogged search for purity, made him a very sympathetic architect for the project. The site selected was a few yards from the old building, a slightly wooded suburban corner plot; it therefore imposed the need for three (if not four) facades. The building is a long, three-story block, approximately L-shaped, and parallel with the street on its long side. Its orthogonality is broken at one end by the undulating glass walls of the library, and at the other, at the foot of the L, by the rounded corner of the assembly hall and the hood of the chapel apse. The body of the building lies between these public spaces—the "learned" area of the library, and at the other end the main meeting room, which backs into the small chapel. The chapel was not part of the original program, but was Meier's gloss on it; ironically it has become an emblem of the institution. Although it is not a conventionally sacred, delimited space, it dominates the whole organization discreetly.

A visitor approaching the white building from Hartford will first become conscious of the eroded corner with the undulating glass reading-room wall: if he approaches at night he will see this almost as a beacon. In the distance he will glimpse the old Gothic college. But he will also be made aware of the layering of the new white building, since he will obliquely catch a view of a square courtyard behind a spur wall—like the narthex of an early church. And he will scry something like an entrance there. As he draws level with the spur wall, it will become a rather more complex screen. On the inside it carries one of Meier's typical nautical stairs. But outside, facing the approach, the main entry is a construction of planes, and is flanked on one side with a non-door (an opening as high as the entrance, but too narrow to afford passage) and on the other with a square opening, as it

were, a non-window. Above the entry the wall is indented and has a balustrade like that of the stairway behind; this balcony or crenellation reads almost like an open-air pulpit. At the other end of the wall, there is another, much smaller non-window. In the middle, the wall rises dramatically to bend into the hood over the end of the chapel, while yet another square projects out of the wall to make the shallow apse on the interior, with its blue skylight. In the layering of planes, the entry canopy and this projective square are outermost; then comes the line of the spur wall and chapel; then two blank walls, the projections over the reading rooms and over the entrance; next the framing element, which is both a lengthwise structure and a cornice. The last plane is that of the building's actual skin and of most of the glazing. The structure protrudes between these two last layers, and the glazing itself provides a hierarchical ordering, through the density of its mullions.

The hierarchy is quite straightforward vertically: public rooms at ground, semipublic at the second level (class and seminar, voids over the taller spaces), and private (offices and study cubicles) at the top. The main part of the L-shaped organization, the upright, is along the major street, and contains all the accommodation except the chapel and the meeting room. The orthogonality of the building is broken once in section, by the chapel hood, and twice in plan, by the reading-room wall and the angle of the meeting hall, which echoes the section of the chapel in plan.

The Atheneum and the Hartford Seminary are both clad in the same material, a white, porcelain-finished steel panel. The resemblance of these steel-framed buildings to earlier wood ones obviously has little to do with material, and everything to do with formal intention.

These panels are also the material chosen for the three other buildings I mentioned, designed at the same time: they seem to have become a

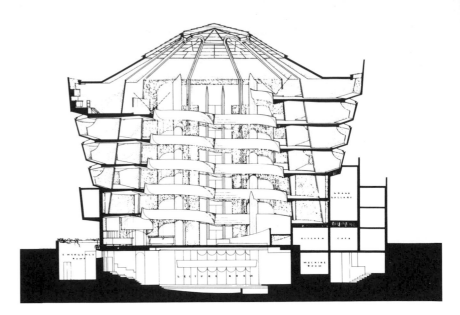

definitive, typical finish for Meier. Of these three two are under construction at the time of writing, and the third, the new office center for Renault at Boulogne-Billancourt, on the Seine, is a victim of recent economy cuts. The Renault project occupies a triangular site, between the river and a motorway, and the strategies of contrasting and shifted grids which Meier has explored elsewhere are here invoked on a much enlarged scale. The eight-story office block becomes the industry's public face, turned toward Paris; but the internal structure of the Renault works imposes another grid. The program in scale and complexity is the largest Meier has had to deal with to date. It would have been fitting to see the transatlantic reinterpretation of some of the themes which originated in Paris return here to shape one of the major achievements of French industry.

The way in which a whole gamut of different geometries may be caught in Meier's "typical" network is shown in the two museums which are under construction at the time of writing. The one in Atlanta, Georgia, is the more obviously "plastic" of the two. It is on a corner site between the bulk of the Memorial Arts Center and a Gothic church. The main approach is through a cubic entrance pavilion to a split ramp—one part ascending and one part descending—which leads the visitor past a series of incidents to the quadrant glass wall of the main hall of the museum. The ramp is the diagonal of the site and turns into the radius of the circle implied by the quadrant. The incidents on the way punctuate the ascent: there is a wall through which the entrant passes and which continues up into the hood over a lecture theater, much as the entry at Hartford became the chapel hood, though of course translated into an entirely different context here; on the other side of the ramp a little further along there is a low building with an undulating wall (containing an entry over a restaurant), reminiscent of a similar device at New Harmony, though again displaced in context and therefore assuming another implication, of projecting out of the quadrant as if it were its tongue.

The quadrant itself fills the space between the two arms of the L in which the administration and the smaller exhibition galleries are housed. The main public circulation is over another ramp which rises parallel to the outside wall of the top-lit and brilliantly glazed quadrant. Between the outside wall and the ramp is more gallery space. The configuration of the quadrant hall recalls unavoidably and intentionally the Guggenheim Museum (for which Meier has recently arranged a reading room and to which he has paid both verbal and formal homage). He was evidently fascinated by the changed function of the museum type, which has become a sacred space of the latter twentieth century, and for which the Guggenheim has created a unique and highly charged form—perhaps too highly charged. The movement which the elevator up and the spiral ramp down create in the Guggenheim is antipathetic to the rather random path of the spectator and to the leisurely absorption of works of art. That is why Meier has separated stairs and elevators from the ramp, which becomes the dominant formal device of the main volume, but which is not itself an exhibition space: all gallery surfaces for moving about and display, including all those opening off the ramp, are parallel to the ground, horizontal.

The complexity (or perhaps more justly, the rich layering) of the internal volumes, achieved through the kind of hierarchical patterning which Meier has done so well in the past, becomes more crucial in Atlanta, because the program calls for a building whose formal qualities become part of the spectators' experience. The play with grids and the complexity of the space are welded together by an overall structure and by the use of the porcelain-panel facing. And at Atlanta more than elsewhere, Meier has compacted this building of typical shapes on which I have remarked in his previous work: there is the hooded lecture room, the undulating entrance hall, the form of entry, the shifted grids. The reference is not, as may be suspected by a superficial observer, self-reference. On the contrary, it shows

The High Museum, Atlanta, Georgia. Richard Meier, 1983. Perspective section

Solomon R. Guggenheim Museum, New York, New York. Frank Lloyd Wright, 1946–1959. Cross section

Meier attempting an exposition of the traditional forms of modern architecture. These forms are in no sense canonical, they have no fixed meaning, nor even a clearly circumscribed range of reference; they are merely types: shapes and formal devices which have a refractive power dependent on their context, and which state the architect's place with reference to the past, pay his debts.

Increasingly, too, in spite of all the nautical overtones, Meier has made another move: into what might be called "noble" materials. The porcelain walls of Hartford and the Atheneum rise in both his museums from granite bases. It is almost as if he was deliberately echoing a Cézannian move in architecture—turning the nautical style of the old masters into the permanent art of the museums.

In the other civic building of the period, the Museum for the Decorative Arts in Frankfurt, Meier has for the first time made geometry a springboard for his design. He won a limited international competition with this project; he was certainly the only one of the entrants to look for a geometrical foundation in the site itself, whose most obvious feature was the *biedermeierisch* Villa Metzler, a white cube of a building in which the collection was originally housed. He has again used an L plan-shape: here to frame the old villa, with which his own buildings form a square. It is both a much more ambitious and a more serene approach to an old building than that which he adopted when he was completing the Villa Strozzi renovation in Florence, where, inversely, he inserted the rectangle of his rather cut-up building into the L provided by the surviving nineteenth-century walls.

Because of the irregularities of the street pattern at Frankfurt, Meier has exploited a shift, of 3½ degrees, to distribute the plan with the maximum of incident within a square which is sixteen times (four times four) the area of the Villa Metzler. He has deliberately echoed the cubical form of the old villa, its roof, and even its segmental eaves

in the plan-forms of his building.

The program at Frankfurt does not call for the sort of grand statement which was appropriate in Atlanta. Both the collections and the context demand a domestic scale. And in spite of the considerable bulk of Meier's building, and of its subtlety, he has attained this scale, and has managed to make very good sense of the surrounding public gardens, so that his intrusion in the city is inordinately discrete as well as plainly beneficial.

In speaking of his buildings, Meier is concerned to insist on his interest in light and its manipulation, and on his almost obsessive commitment to the white color of his walls. Looking at these buildings in the context of the situation of the early eighties, what strikes me most is their tonic character, their critical stance toward the shoddy and slipshod in our built environment. To make their critical statement explicit, the white color is inevitably an excellent device, which in most contexts separates the building from its ground. The porcelain panels, too, have an unscathed aspect, which makes the building a luminous object, even under a gray sky.

But these are all negative considerations. What is more important is the positive stance of which these negative virtues are only a reflection: Meier's fidelity to program and context. Rising above that is his ability to mold and decline elementary forms into complex volumes, and to combine them in such ways that their very context elevates them to the power of metaphor.

Smith House

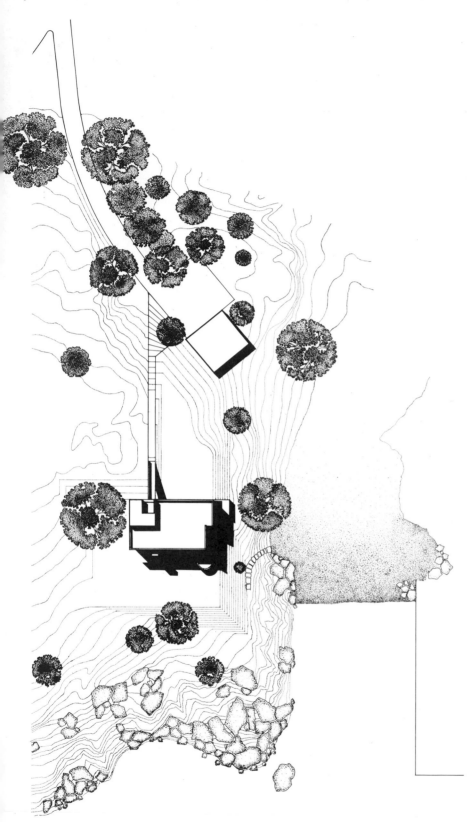

Darien, Connecticut
1965–1967

The Smith House, situated among rocks and trees on a 1½-acre site, overlooks Long Island Sound from the Connecticut coast. A dense cluster of evergreens stands at the entrance to the property. Behind, the land clears and rises to the center of the site, then drops sharply to the rocky shoreline, falling away on one side to a small, sandy cove.

This natural layering creates a formal progression as one moves from the entrance road down to the shoreline, and determines the major site axis. The house is set perpendicular to this axis, slightly below the crest of the hill. As the site plan indicates, the approach, entrance, and views are organized to cross the contours of the site, thereby affording an impressive prospect of the landscape and water. Access to the house is uphill, while the primary view looks down toward the water. The intersecting planes of the house respond to the rhythms of the slope, trees, rock outcroppings, and shoreline.

The angle of the garage to the path leading to the front facade and the curved wall to the right of the door help to draw one into the house and through to the open rear facade. The front facade is treated as an opaque screen that must be penetrated. The view that greets one upon passing through the entrance is celebrated on the rear facade, where the surfaces of the glazing catch light and color from the land, sky, and water. The masonry fireplace in the living room, directly opposite the entry, appears to be a solid drawn from the front facade and continues a visual line of movement through the transparent glass plane above it.

27

Site

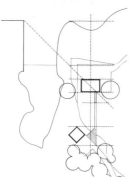

Program

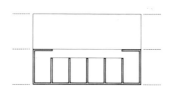

Structure

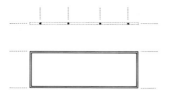

Entry

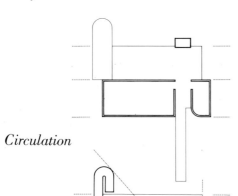

Circulation

Enclosure

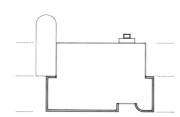

Northwest elevation

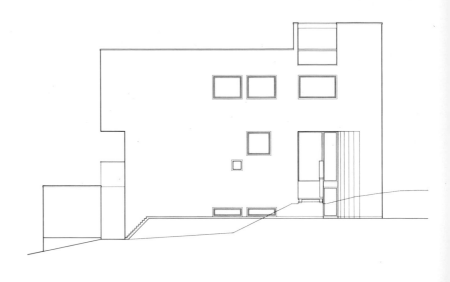

Lower level plan

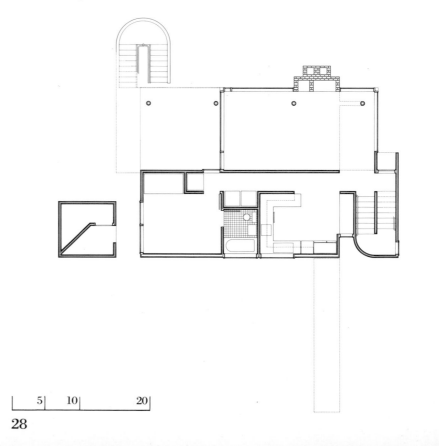

5   10   20

28

Southeast elevation

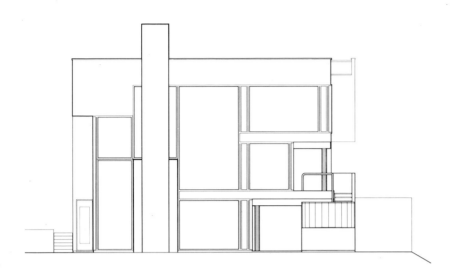

Longitudinal section

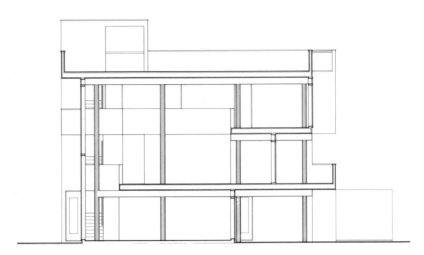

Entry level plan

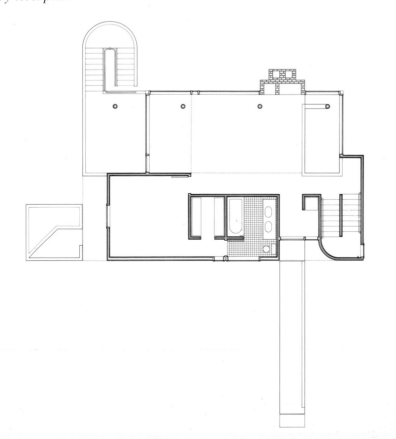

Upper level plan

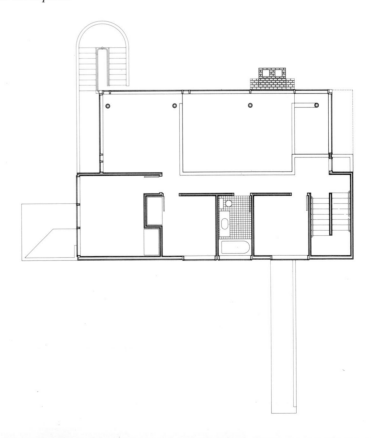

Cross section

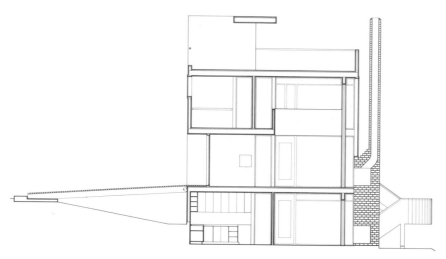

This house has often mistakenly
been thought to be made of
concrete. It is wood construction.
The chimney is brick, and there are
interior steel lally columns.

The spatial organization of the house, as of many of the projects following, is based on a programmatic separation between public and private areas. Every person in the household is intended to have a private space for sleeping, bathing, and retirement. The private part of the house is located on the entry side and faces land, woods, and road. It consists of a series of closed, cellular spaces organized on three levels. The public spaces where the family meet and entertain are at the rear of the house, overlooking the water. They are composed of three platforms within a single, three-sided glass enclosure.

The vertically organized zones of private and public space are structured by two different systems. On the private side of the house, the wood stud-walls are load-bearing. On the public side, the structure consists of round steel columns, independent elements that also mark the spatial grid. The exterior materials—vertical wood siding and glass—serve to express the contrast between the closed and open spaces inside. The complementarity of solids and voids in strong juxtaposition creates a spatial dialogue in both plan and elevation.

The internal circulation system of the house reinforces the organizational and formal themes. Horizontal circulation links the private with the public areas. Vertical circulation occurs via two diagonally located stairways, one an enclosed stair within the private zone, the other an exterior stair serving the public zone. This corner placement of the circulation creates a secondary, diagonal relationship with the site as the viewer descends along the line of the hill, projecting the house beyond its physical boundaries toward the indented cove. The effect of the balconied spaces cascading through the three-story vertical elements enhances this reading.

The white form of the Smith House is not only rooted in a New England tradition of the house as a compact, self-sufficient entity, but also expressive of a strong and extroverted attitude toward its site: beyond its internal function as a shelter, it is an object that acts as a prism to the natural scene around it.

Hoffman House

East Hampton, New York
1966–1967

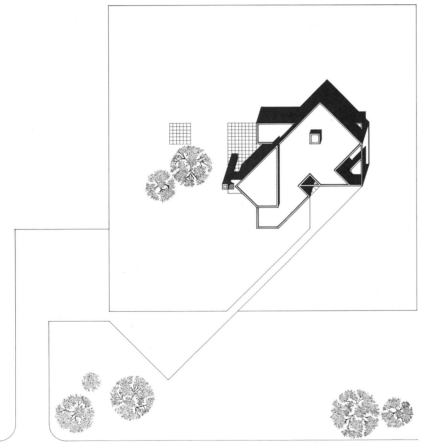

An ordinary site—a flat property fronting a public road on the south—allowed a certain freedom of design in the Hoffman House. The house, in effect, defines the site by its presence. Viewed from the road, it appears as a three-dimensional abstraction of interlocking geometries. The road serves as the generator of two sets of double squares in plan, one set orthogonal, the other rotated forty-five degrees at the entry point; this produces two interlocking forms, one parallel to the road, the other diagonal to it. The spatial interplay of the diagonal and orthogonal organization, centering about the point of intersection of these two systems, is the basis for the design of the house.

The intersecting wall planes facing the road frontage serve as an opaque screen that conceals the living space from passing traffic. To the west, the fireplace with its free-standing chimney pulled out from the glazed corner of the house—a solid responding, as in the Smith House, to the axis of the entrance—effectively allows the whole 2½-story living room to be surrounded by light. This living room is a triangular space defined by columns supporting a balcony, which acts as a canopy to the main seating area. Light enters this space from three sources: the main glazing and two clerestory windows set above the second-story bedrooms.

By virtue of the interpenetrating angular geometries, all of the major spaces in the house take on a dynamic quality, providing a complex spatiality within a minimal overall envelope.

Program

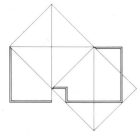

Structure

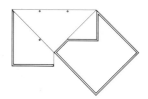

Entry

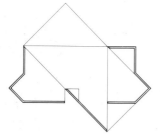

Circulation

Enclosure

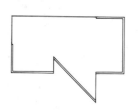

Ground level plan

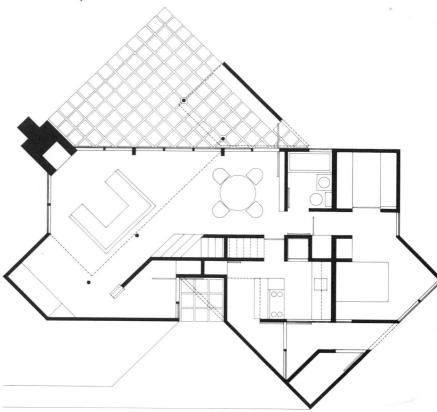

Upper level plan

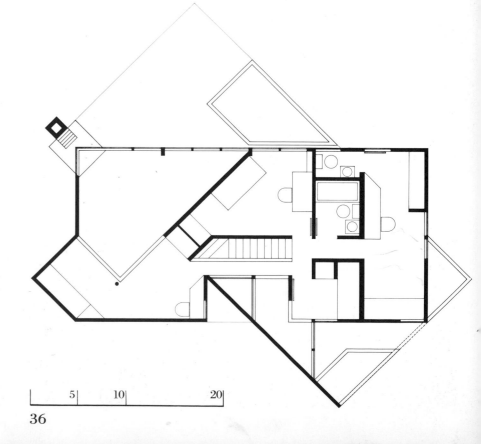

5   10   20

36

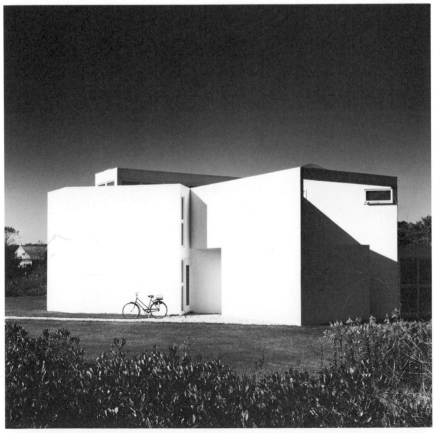

Saltzman House

East Hampton, New York
1967–1969

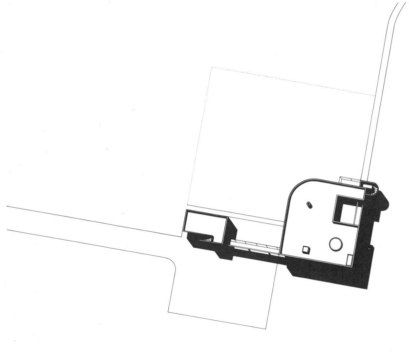

Slightly inland from the Atlantic Ocean on three acres of flat land near the tip of Long Island, the site for the Saltzman House has few distinguishing characteristics—a windmill by the shore, an adjoining potato field, and the shoreline itself, which is not visible at ground level. The parallel relationship between the front edge of the property and the shoreline determined the siting of the house, which is elevated to permit views of the sea and along the open coast to Montauk Point. From a distance, the cubic composition appears to flatten into a two-dimensional shape against the background of land and sky.

As in the Smith House, the organization of the plan is based on a programmatic separation of public and private areas. Here, however, the two zones interpenetrate to a greater degree. The public space opens up like a funnel in plan as the building rises, so that the integrity of the closed private zone, located along two adjacent sides of the cubic volume of the house, is partially eroded on the second level, and disappears entirely on the third. The view to the ocean is dramatically revealed as one moves upward.

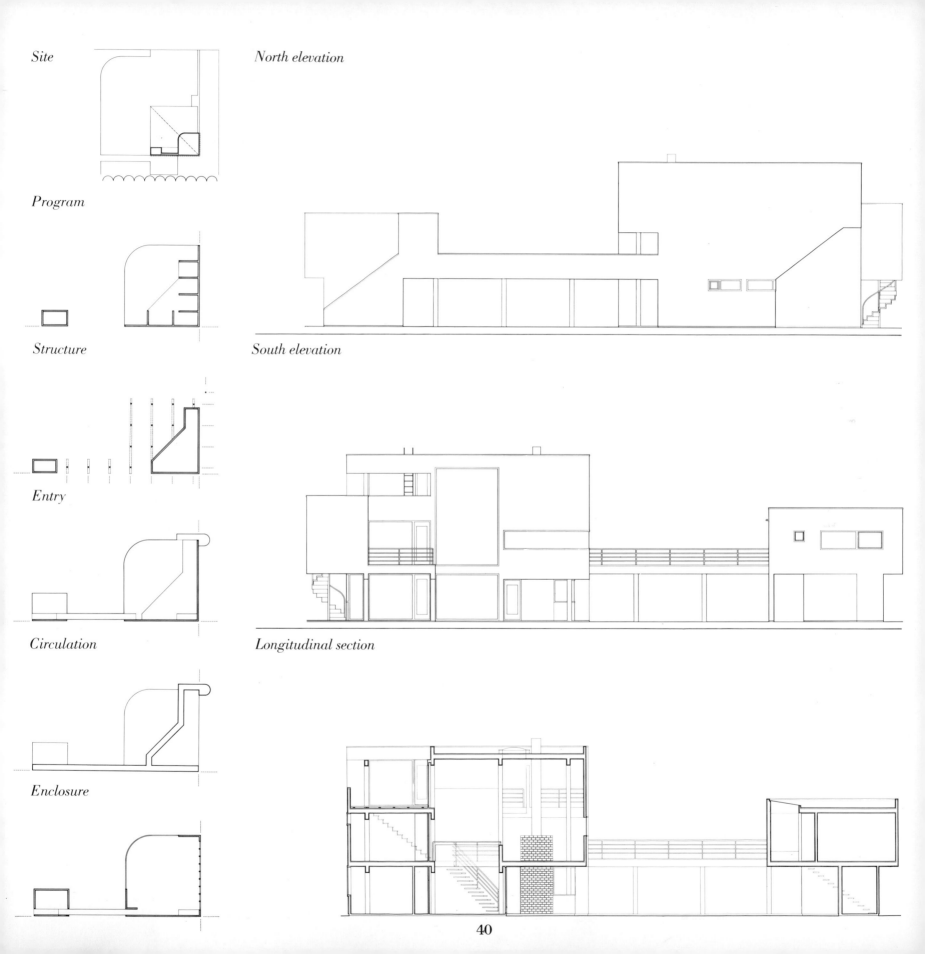

Site

North elevation

Program

South elevation

Structure

Entry

Longitudinal section

Circulation

Enclosure

40

Ground level plan

Middle level plan

Upper level plan

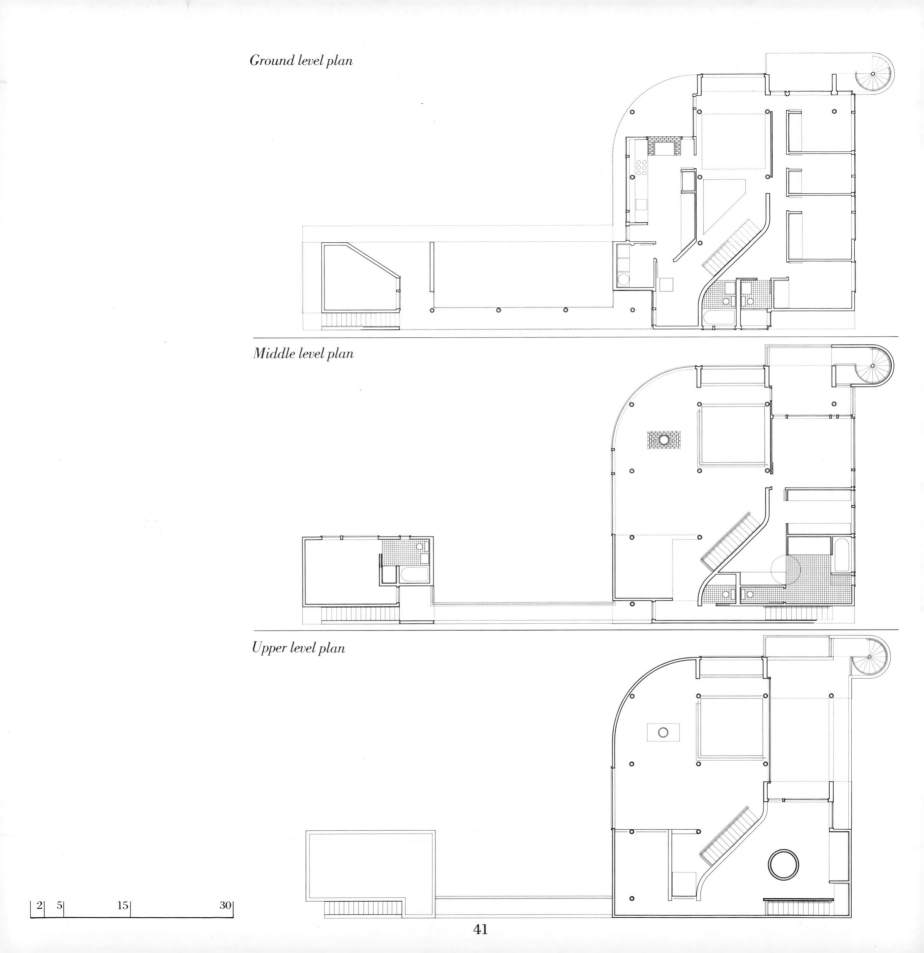

| 2 | 5| | 15| | 30| |

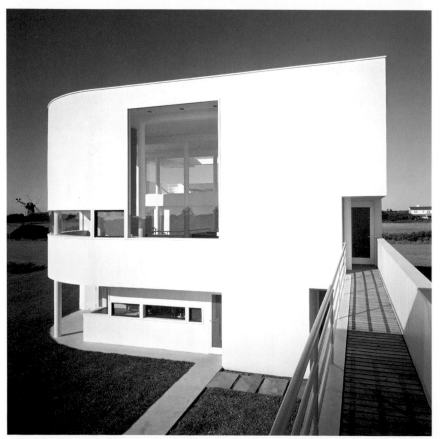

For better or worse, this house sparked a new type of "summer house" in the Hamptons which seems to have multiplied all over the eastern Long Island horizon. In retrospect, the issue seems to be less one of style than of how congenially buildings in an open landscape relate to their sites.

Two circulation systems pass up and through the building. The first originates in an outside stair attached to a small guest house, and becomes a bridge linking the guest house to the main house at the second level; it continues via interior stairs along the side of the house, connecting the second level to the third. The second circulation system, serving the upper level, rises diagonally across the center of the house, the seam between the public and private zones. Both systems find their compositional conclusion in an exterior spiral stair at the corner diagonally opposite the entry.

Structurally similar to the Smith House, the Saltzman House employs wood load-bearing walls in the private zone and round steel columns in the public zone. The system of enclosure—vertical wood siding painted white and perforated with ribbon windows and large expanses of glazing—is more elaborate than that of the Smith House. The stretched and rounded corners created by the diagonal plan relationship and the eroded appearance at grade level suggest the interior complexity of this house, implying its more dynamic organizational system, and reflecting the interlocking and asymmetrical distribution of the public and private spaces.

House in Pound Ridge

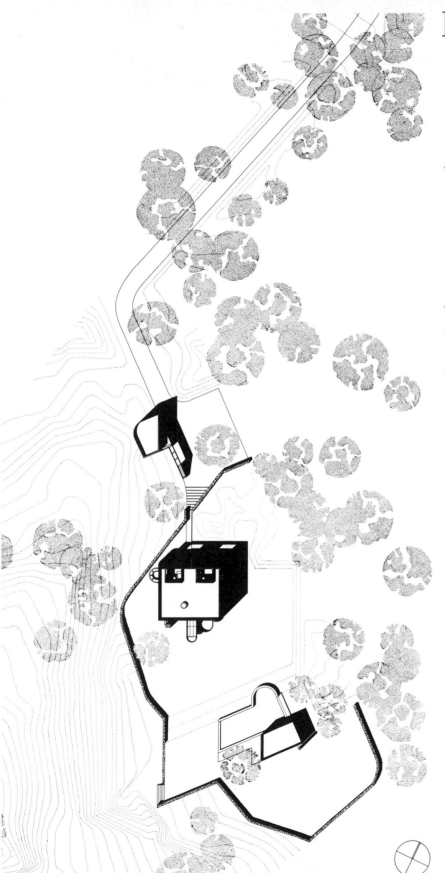

Pound Ridge, New York
1969

The House in Pound Ridge, an unbuilt project, is designed for a rocky, wooded site, an interior lot open at the center and surrounded by trees, joined to the road by a long and narrow right-of-way. The pattern of open and closed spaces traces a natural path through the landscape. Approached by the right-of-way through an avenue of trees, the slope of the land rises gradually. It continues to rise to the east, while falling to a steep ravine on the southwest.

A series of existing rubble stone walls is used to delimit the cleared section of the land and to define the sequence of the house and its outbuildings. The right-of-way ends outside the compound at a caretaker's cottage and garage. Behind this, steps lead through a break in the old wall, a point of transition from a rugged to a more manicured landscape. At this point, the garage, the north corner of the main house, and the pool house at the southeast end of the site together describe a sight line through the property and the trees.

The house is entered through a solid frontal plane. Inside, this plane reveals itself to be a thickened "wall" containing kitchen, utility space, and, on the second level, guest bedrooms with private roof decks above. A spiral staircase giving access to the guest bedrooms is exposed on the facade by a two-story cut-out with curved glazing. Except for the view from this stair, the outlook from this side is not extensive. Most of the light enters through small windows punched in the wood bearing-walls or through the skylights.

47

Site

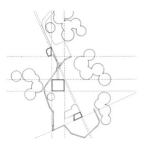

Program

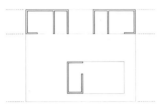

Structure

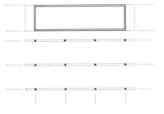

Entry

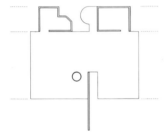

Circulation

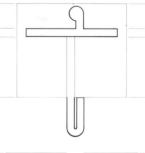

Enclosure

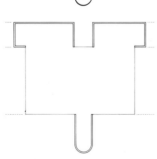

Longitudinal section through living area

| 2 | 5 | 10 | 20 |

Ground level plan

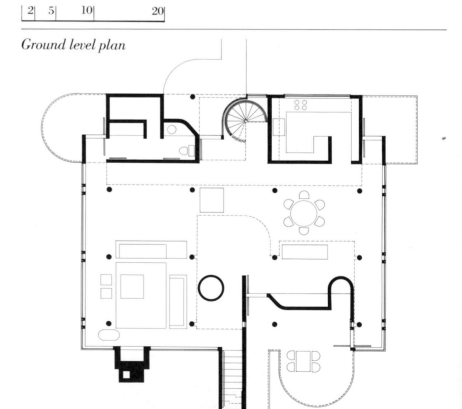

48

Longitudinal section through guest bedrooms   *Cross section through master bedroom*

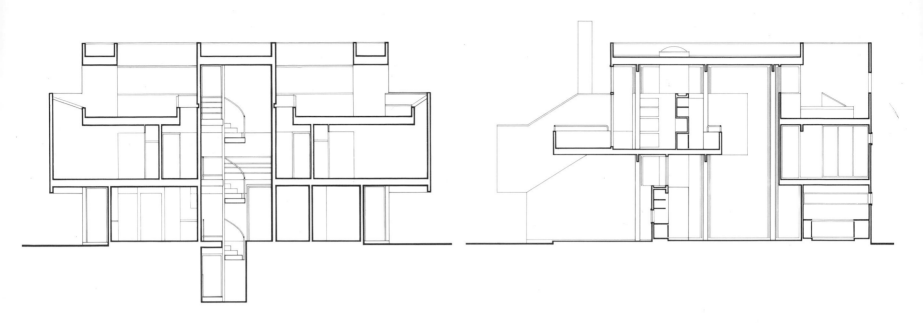

Upper level plan   *Lower roof plan*

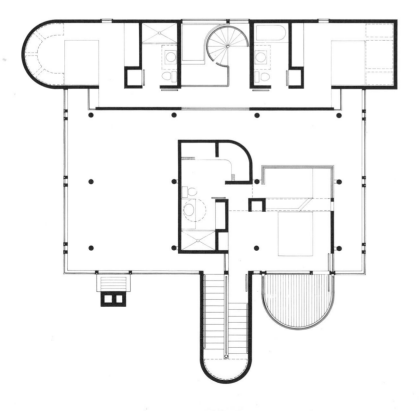 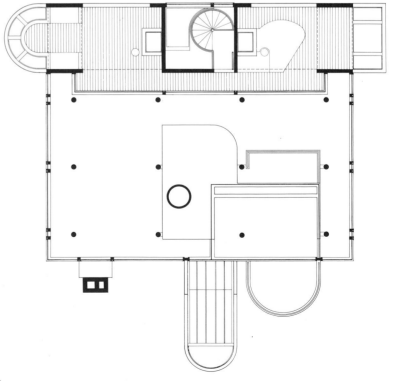

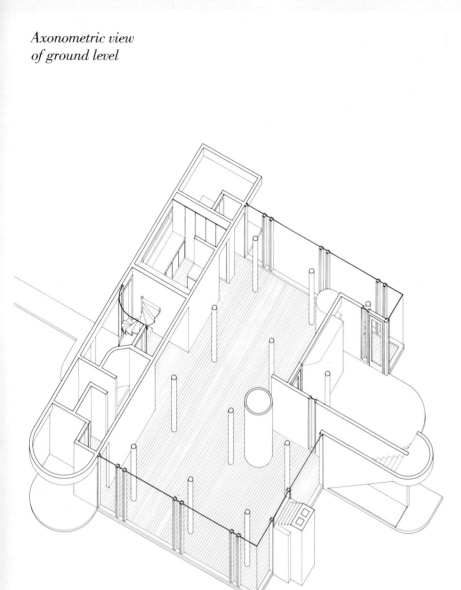

*Axonometric view
of ground level*

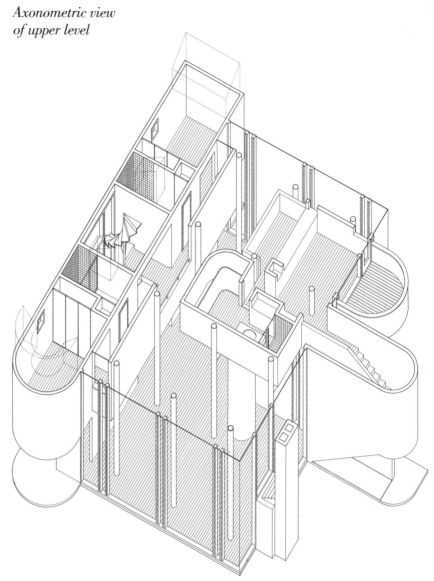

*Axonometric view
of upper level*

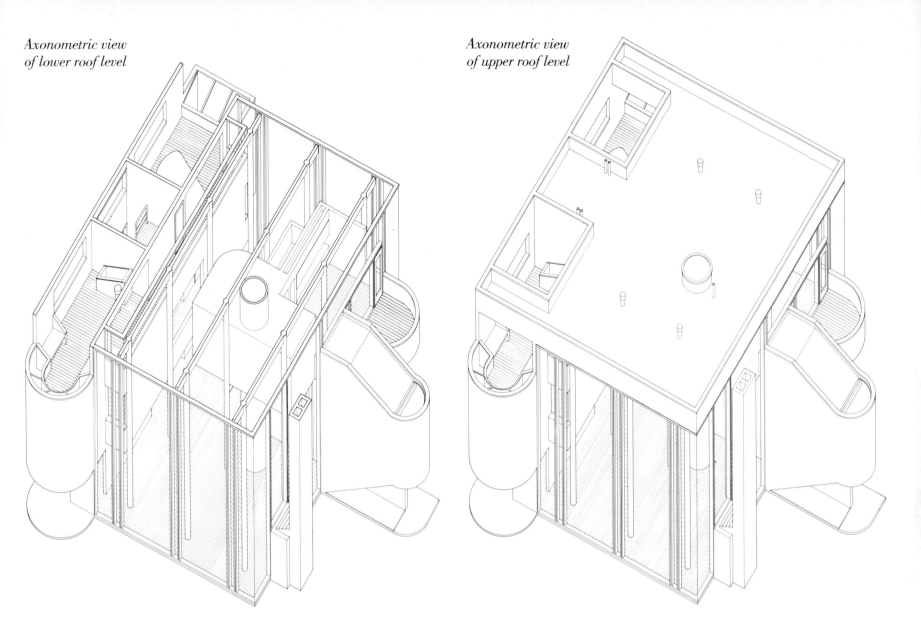

*Axonometric view
of lower roof level*

*Axonometric view
of upper roof level*

To the solid front zone of the house is attached a transparent three-level glazed pavilion facing the rear of the site and containing living and dining areas at ground level. The master-bedroom module floats asymmetrically above, anchored to the ground by a top-lit garret staircase that provides access to it. The solid volume of this stair projects beyond the glazed enclosure of the pavilion and, as in the Smith and Hoffman houses, the extension at the rear is meant to answer the inset at the entrance. The master bedroom cannot be reached directly from the guest rooms in front; the open side of the house must be crossed at ground level, an arrangement which maintains the privacy of the owner's suite. This distribution of the private areas in the house defines the basic parti: a broken T-shaped volume superimposed on a glass box.

From the glazed zone of the house there is a 270-degree view, through the window walls and the grid of round steel columns to a natural wall of trees beyond. The large expanses of glass, interrupted only by the projecting staircase, the chimney, and a balcony from the master bedroom, bring the exterior environment within, while the dense woods outside filter and modulate incoming sunlight. Throughout, the architectural organization is designed to enhance the sensuous experience of the natural environment, allowing for a multiplicity of views, perspectives, and reflections.

The main cubic volume of this house is less site-specific than that of most of the other houses designed at this time. It is a kind of ideal type for a wooded site. Fifteen years after it was designed it still retains its applicability.

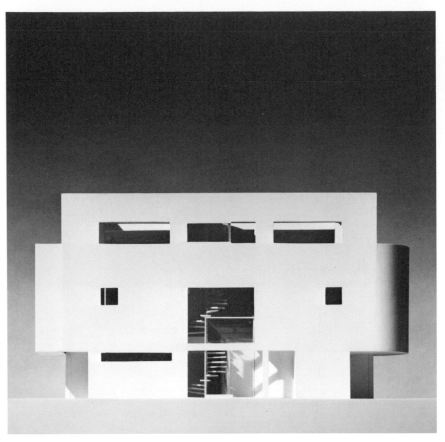

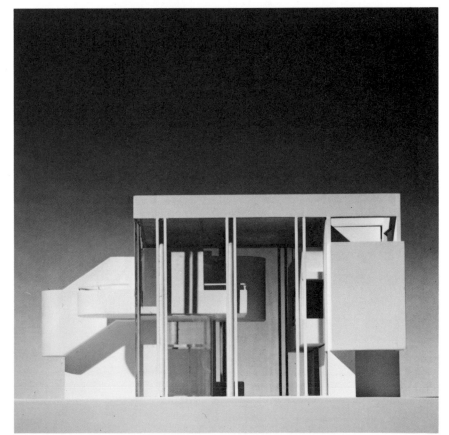

House in Old Westbury

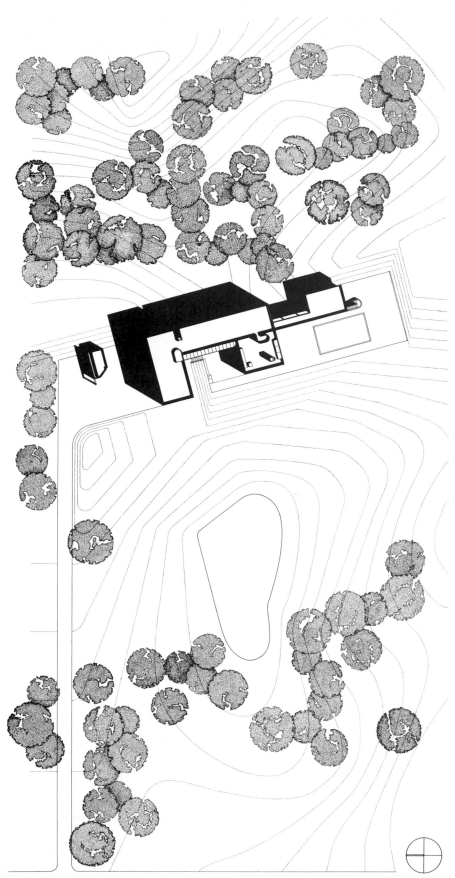

Old Westbury, New York
1969–1971

Although only an hour's drive from New York City, the Long Island site of this house is secluded and rural. The house is situated at the top of a meadow deep within a wooded property. The land slopes down gently across the meadow to a pond on the western edge of the site, and through a dense barrier of trees to the public road beyond. The house is oriented to allow morning sunlight into the bedrooms, and to provide a pastoral view across the meadow to the pond, which drains the ground around the house of floodwater and provides a reflective focus to the dialogue between house and site.

Invisible from the road, the house is approached obliquely, by way of a driveway that runs perpendicular to the road, then turns seventy-five degrees to meet the house on its major axis. As the program for this house, for a family with six children, included an unusually large number of bedrooms (eleven) and almost as many bathrooms, and at the same time required a clearly defined relationship of public and private spaces, the circulation system became the major organizing element in the design.

A free-standing steel column, adjacent to a small gatehouse and located on the structural grid, is a signpost indicating the beginning of pedestrian movement. From here, the front facade with its high portico on the entry side screens the bulk of the house from view, while a glazed cut-out around the doorway allows a glimpse all the way through the house along the axis of the circulation spine, which penetrates the entire length of the building. A curved wall next to the entry and protruding into the portico helps to guide one into the house. Just inside, a third-floor skylight admits a column of natural light, bisecting the axis of the circulation spine. This motif establishes a theme for the rest of the house: the infiltration of light from many different directions.

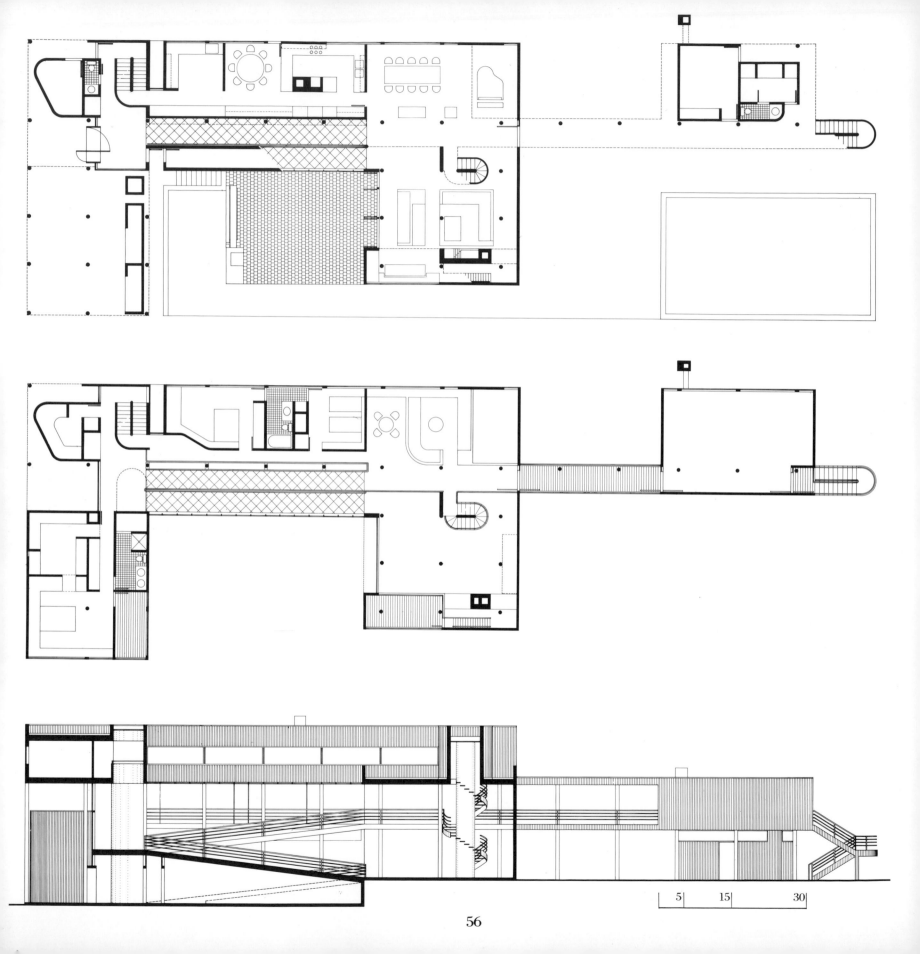

5 15 30

Ground level plan
Middle level plan
Longitudinal section

Axonometric view of interior stair
of living room

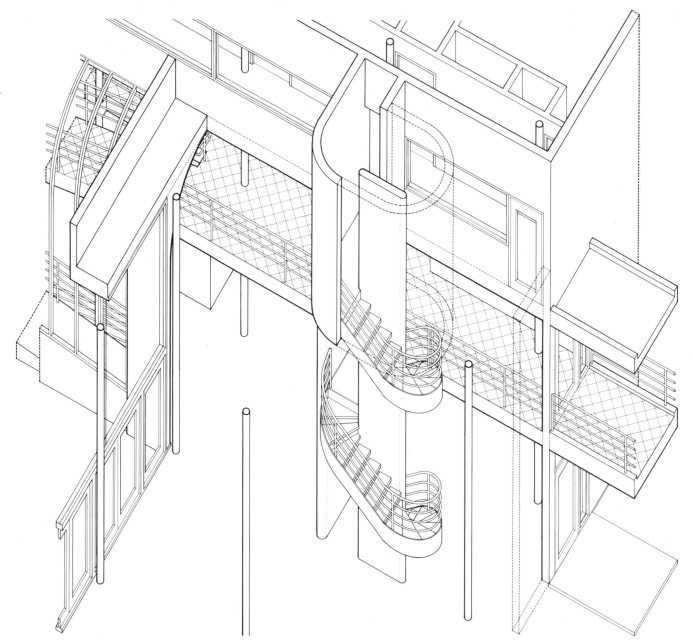

While this house seemed to be unique in terms of its program and scale at the time it was designed, it has since changed hands successfully without major modification, which goes to show that such a "one-off" design is more susceptible to adaptation than one might initially imagine.

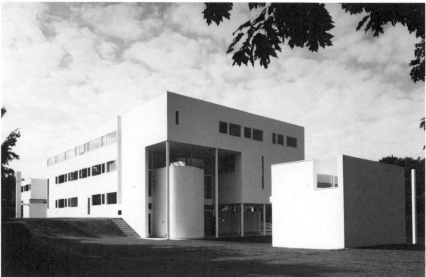

In a house as large as this one, a clear and simple path of circulation is of primary importance. With the exception of the master-bedroom suite, all the bedrooms as well as the service spaces are organized into a series of single-level spaces on the sheltered, wooded side of the house, directly off the main circulation axis. In contrast, the public spaces are freely planned in volumes of varying heights, and located on the side facing the meadow and pond. Three different circulation elements—zigzag ramp, free-standing stair, and enclosed stair—allow for different kinds of vertical movement within the two zones of the house.

The zigzag ramp, echoing the natural incline of the site, lends continuity to the interior, affording a gradual system of movement from floor to floor. Passageways and stairs become events encountered at the landings of the long traverse, which, as it crosses and recrosses the levels, progressively unfolds the interior volume of the house. This promenade is enclosed by a glazed arcade on one side, opening up views to the pond and meadow and making the space transparent to the outdoors, while protecting it from the elements.

The living and the dining areas are linked to the third floor by a helical steel stair that winds kinetically through three stories, continuing past the family room on the middle level. It emerges as a solid volume on an open roof terrace at the level of the third-floor bedrooms.

In earlier houses, the open spaces were structured by a grid of free-standing columns, and the enclosed spaces by wood bearing-walls. The intention to articulate the difference between public and private spaces by means of their structural enclosure is similar at Old Westbury, but here the steel columnar grid is privileged throughout as the primary system. On the exterior surfaces, the alternation of wood and glass allows a nuanced expression of the nature of the spaces within and of the disposition of the private and public functions. In the living room, a deep wall containing a fireplace located back to back with a minor stair leading to the family room embodies an aspect of this dialectic between open and closed spaces that occurs on a larger scale throughout the house.

Beyond the particular requirements of the family for whom it was built and the scope of its program, this house represents a development from the previous ones in terms of the complexity of the design strategies employed in it. Space, circulation, light, and scale are engaged here in an unified but elaborate composition. The systems of movement—the interaction of ramps, stairs, and passageways—provide a constantly changing experience for the inhabitants and a multiplicity of choices and spatial discoveries.

It seems to be a truism that one never gets anything built without some struggle. It took months of determined effort to convince the fabricator of this helical stair that it would be structurally feasible.

Shamberg House

Chappaqua, New York
1972–1974

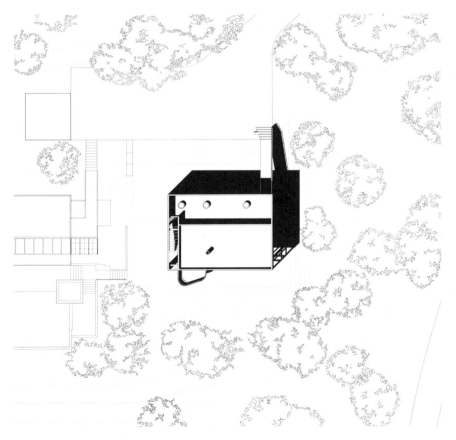

The Shamberg House is located adjacent to an existing cottage and swimming pool, on a heavily wooded hillside with a sweeping view of Chappaqua, New York. It is built on a relatively level rock shelf between the pool and the access road, which curves around the property, containing the house. The existing cottage remains as a guest house for the owners' adult children, and the new building serves as a year-round family gathering place.

A variation of the Pound Ridge parti, the Shamberg House consists of a volume of glazed public space that is intended, as at Pound Ridge, to complement a thickened "wall" of small enclosed spaces containing the private functions. Because it was designed for only two people, this house has a simpler structure than some of the earlier ones.

On the front, the major formal gesture is an entry bridge which starts half a story below grade level—an approach that emphasizes the tautness of the solid front wall by its plunge into a recessed foyer. On axis with the entry is a balcony overlooking a two-story glazed living room and a view of the wooded hillside below the house; from this transitional space one can best appreciate the contrast between the two vertical zones of the house, the one articulated as solid, the other as void. The balcony gives onto a serpentine stair to the lower level, which weaves together the two discrete spatial parts.

To the right of the balcony, the entry-level plane of circulation continues along a corridor serving the spaces behind the front facade, to an interior bridge leading to the owners' bedroom, which is cantilevered over the living-room space. Movement through the bedroom culminates in an exterior balcony, a diagonal response to the entry bridge. Beyond the interior bridge, the corridor ends in a perpendicular exterior stair—an access from the bedroom to the swimming pool below the house—which is accommodated in a shallow space that extends the structural grid by part of a bay but is open to the sky. This ninety-degree turn of the circulation route and the cut-outs on the otherwise solid side facade express the end of the system of movement.

Another set of concerns is reflected on the two more open facades. In this house, for the first time, the paired vertical mullions of the rear window wall are slipped off the columnar grid, producing a tension between the structural system of the columns and the hung system of enclosure. Freed from aligning with the structural elements, the mullions now take on a more subtle formal articulation, gesturing vertically in the direction of the protruding balcony, and relating horizontally to the height of the second-floor balustrade and the fascia above. In this way the glazing on the rear facade becomes a transparent projection of the interior facade behind it. The layering of solid and transparent spaces continues to be expressed in similar fashion on the largely glazed east facade, reinforcing the relationship of complementarity between diagonally opposite corners of the building. As the recessing of the entry at the northeast corner finds its response in the projective balcony at the southwest corner, so the solid, planar articulation at the northwest corner relates conversely to the open glazing on the southeast. The superimposition of this diagonal corner relationship upon the house's orthogonal system of layering gives the architecture a rotational energy.

Personal experience is always a factor in design. After a semester spent as architect in residence at the American Academy in Rome, the opportunity to reinterpret a Baroque staircase in this house was inviting. Perhaps this same experience reveals itself in the curved shelf of the mantelpiece and a few other details.

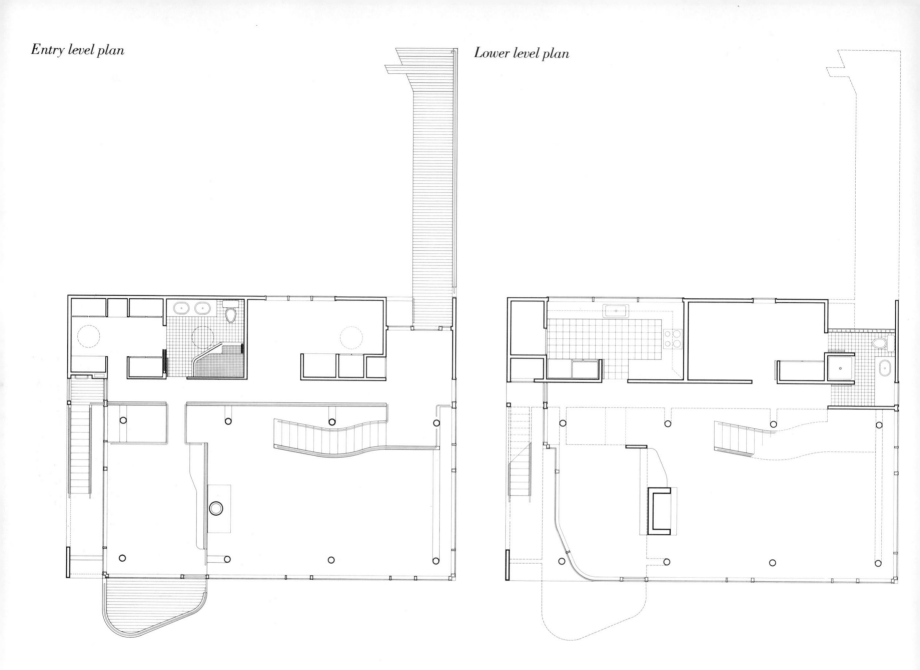

Entry level plan

Lower level plan

| 2 | 5 | 10 | | 20 |

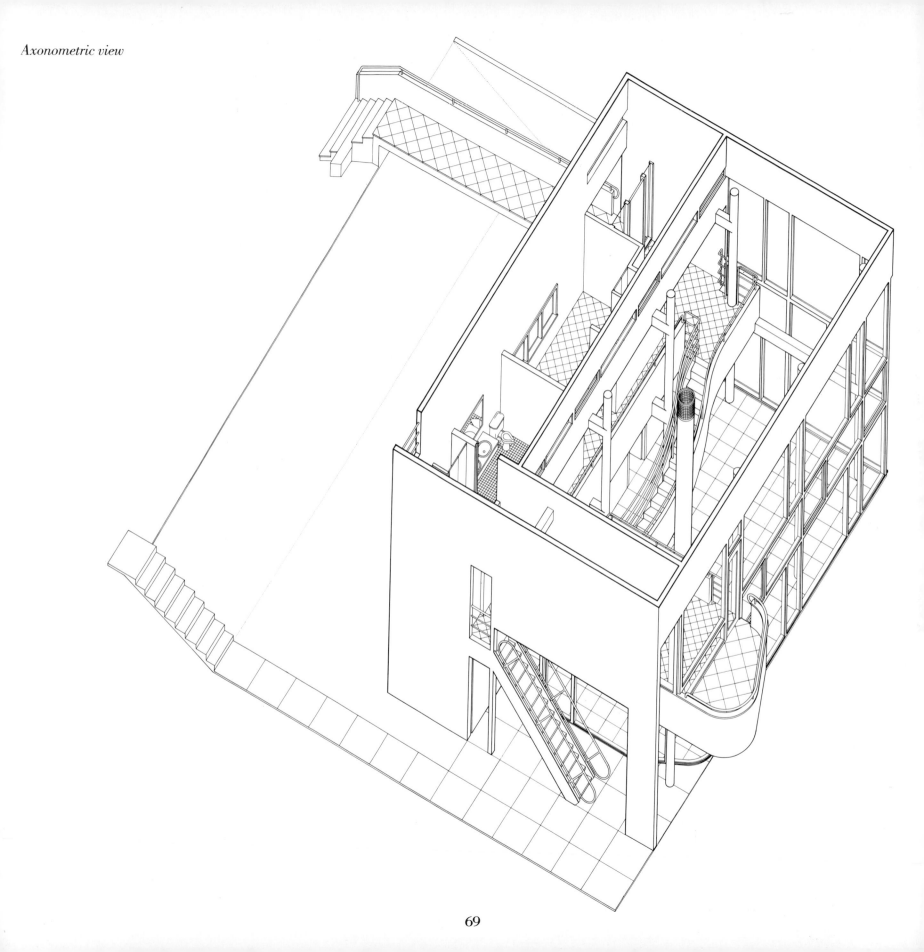

Axonometric view

Douglas House

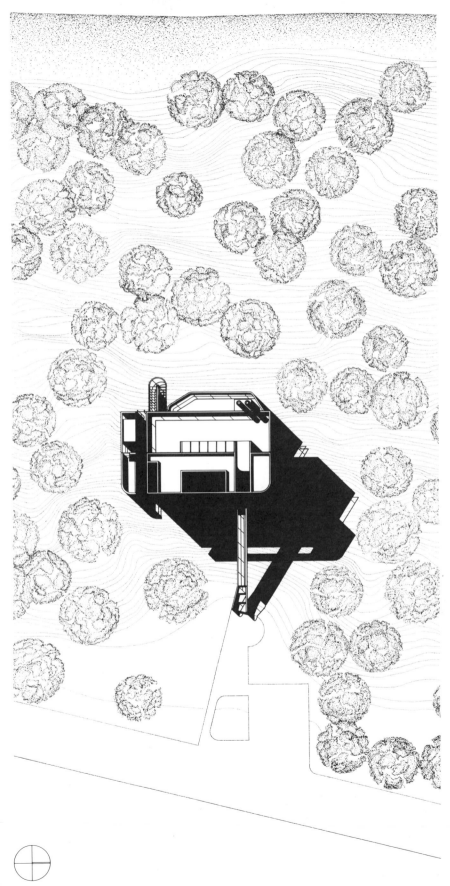

Harbor Springs, Michigan
1971–1973

The Douglas House is magnificently situated on a steep and isolated site that slopes down to Lake Michigan and is protected by a thick cover of conifers. So steep is the fall of the land from the road down to the water that the house appears to have been dropped into the site, a machined object standing in the midst of a natural world. The dramatic dialogue between the whiteness of the house and the blues and greens of water, trees, and sky allows the house not only to assert its own presence but also to enhance, by contrast, the beauty of the landscape.

In many ways the Douglas House completes a cycle that begins with the Smith House. As in several of these houses, the entry is treated as an extension beyond the limits of the building. Here, as the sharp downhill grade of the land requires the house to be entered at roof level, it takes the form of a flying bridge that seems to shear off the top of the frontal plane. The only parts of the house visible from the road are the roof and top floor; not until one crosses the bridge does one perceive the five stories and 4,500 square feet of living space contained within the volume below. A lower bridge directly under the upper one provides circulation from the living-room level back to the ground and ultimately leads, via a stair, a catwalk, and a ladder, to the beach below.

Once inside the entry vestibule, the view opens down to both the living and the dining levels, and out to a large roof deck overlooking Lake Michigan. This deck, like other elements in the house, suggests the metaphor of a land-based ship. As in the Smith House, the living-room fireplace is located in plan directly opposite the entry, but in this case two stories below; at roof level its stainless-steel smokestacks act as a foil to the entry and frame the view. The curved skylight on the inside edge of the roof deck also acts as a buffer between the entry and the view of the lake.

Entry level plan

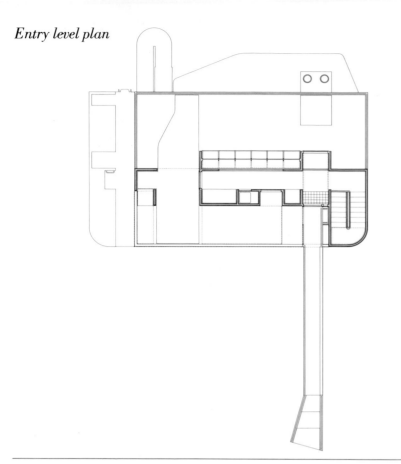

Upper level plan

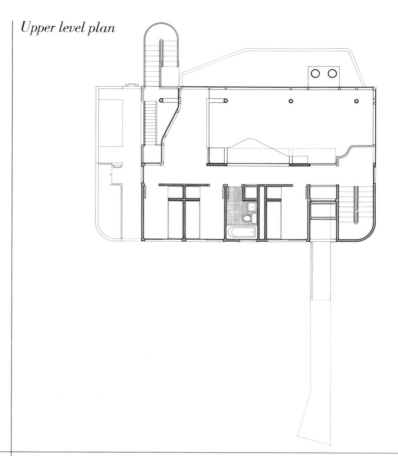

Middle level plan

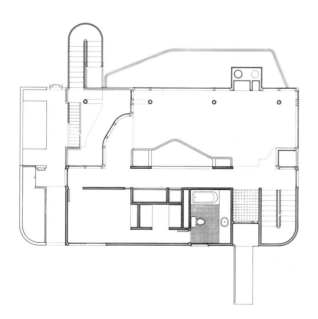

Lower level plan

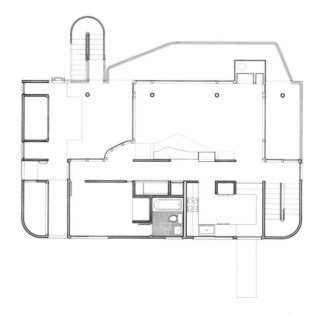

| 5| | 10| | 15| | | | 30| |

South elevation

North elevation

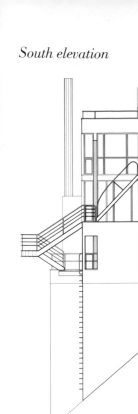
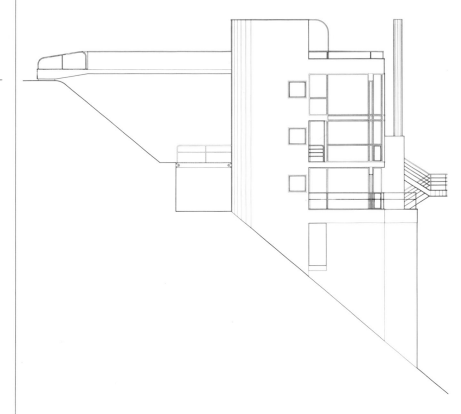

West elevation

East elevation

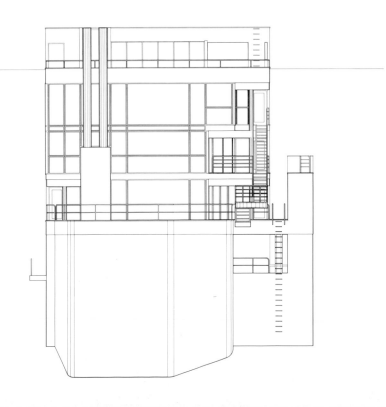
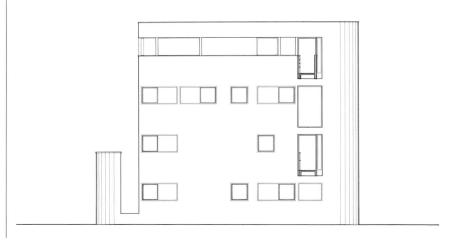

Longitudinal section

Every building project has its own "personality," which in a sense reveals itself in the course of design. In this case, after an initial design proposal was rejected by the developer, who didn't want a "white" house built on his site, a much more exciting site was found, which was largely inspired by the evolving form of the house. It is fair to say that in this case the house generated the site.

Cross section

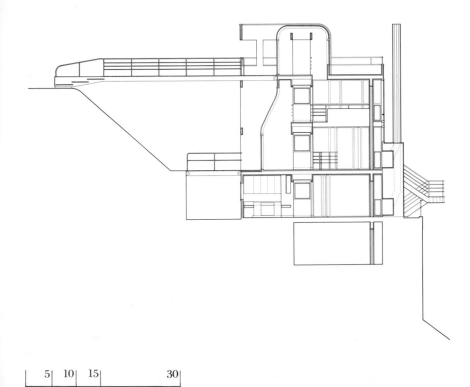

5| 10| 15| 30|

Shortly after the completion of construction, the length of shoreline surrounding the house on both sides came to be designated, quite appropriately, as national seashore, which prohibits any future development nearby. This ensures the house's superb and spectacular isolation for years to come.

The idea for the central slit that admits toplight into the house was suggested by the natural illumination found in Italian and southern German Baroque architecture.

As in previous houses, the separation between public and private spaces is expressed by solid and glazed walls respectively. The public side, the west, provides a lake view from all floors. The east side, facing the road, is the private zone, having smaller fenestration, and containing bedrooms and service spaces on all three levels. The curved skylight of the roof deck illuminates the center of the house; light penetrates the interior all the way down to the dining level, to which it travels through a curved cut in the living-room floor plane. This shaft of light unifies all the levels vertically, and by its location on the shear line reinforces the separation between the public and private sectors of the house.

Horizontal circulation takes the form of four open corridors, stacked one above the other. This inflected strip of circulation, unlike its linear counterpart in the Smith House, affords a real spatial interplay between the public and private parts of the house, between openness and closure. In this sense it truly functions as a mediating element. The wall flanking the corridors on the west is eroded by horizontal strip-openings, which not only open the corridors to the west view and refract light coming from the skylight above, but make the circulation wall a visual element in the public space. On the east side, the bedrooms and service spaces open onto the corridors in a straightforward manner, while on the west side the public spaces are entered both directly and by way of a stack of curved landings diminishing in size from top to bottom. On the upper level, this landing space, which projects over the double-height living-room volume below, serves as a study. Its form is echoed in a bulge of the corridor wall in front of the interior stair.

The interior stair runs from top to bottom of the house, beginning adjacent to the entry vestibule, and is the major means of vertical circulation. Diagonally opposite it in plan is a second vertical system, an exterior steel stair connecting the upper-level bedrooms to the main living level. From here, a cantilevered stair takes over, in which the ship motif is again evident in pipe railings and other details. A ladder continues downward to a recessed space—a porch on the mechanical level—and ultimately descends to a path leading to the beach below.

Circulation stops at the lake shore. As one looks back up at the house, the various levels can be traced in the mullions of the glazing, which project the cross-section of the house onto the transparent rear facade plane.

The Douglas House carries on the architectural investigation begun with the Smith House and comments upon it. Architectural works are not isolated inventions, nor are they simply variations on a theme. Rather, each successive construct is informed by all those that came before, and uses this information to discover its own uniqueness.

Suburban House Prototype

Concord, Massachusetts
1976

Ground level plan

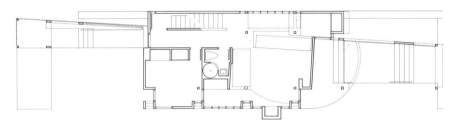

Middle level plan

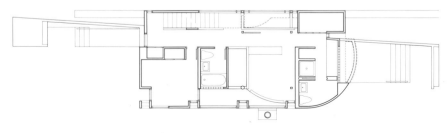

Upper level plan

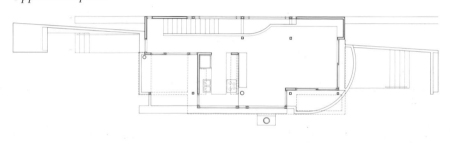

5│ 10│ 20│

This project involves a prototype for suburban middle-income housing. The model photograph and plans show one version of the house designed as a single-family unit. The axonometric drawings show more generalized versions designed as repetitive multi-family units for the surburban block or development. These units are rotated spatially in several ways to share party walls, and serve for one family, two families, or four families. The adaptability of the side walls to two different mirror-image configurations allows both flexibility of orientation and visual variety. When the units are placed back to back, they form a through-block slot facing out to two different streets.

In the single-family unit pictured on these two pages, the introduction of the diagonal vector in plan provides the elongated rectangular space with a dynamic internal spatiality that belies its compactness and counters the monotony of serial repetition on the larger scale. The partially inscribed circle at the entry acts similarly to open up the "box," and the rounded corner created on one side of the front elevation, depending on the configuration, serves volumetrically to separate the house from the one next to it. The theme of the rotated circle within the rectilinear box also suggests the larger concept of the units' spatial rotation to produce the various serial arrangements.

The purpose of the project is to suggest an alternative to the ubiquitous suburban "ranch" house. This compact prototype, for a typical half-acre tract, offers the suburban resident both a sense of community and privacy from his neighbors. While the yard is shared in the party-wall configurations, the elevating of the garden to roof level provides each family with its own piece of nature and an overview of the surrounding landscape. The vertical organization not only gives each interior space greater amplitude, but at the scale of the neighborhood, the three-story double and quadruple modules afford a density and character lacking in the usual suburban development.

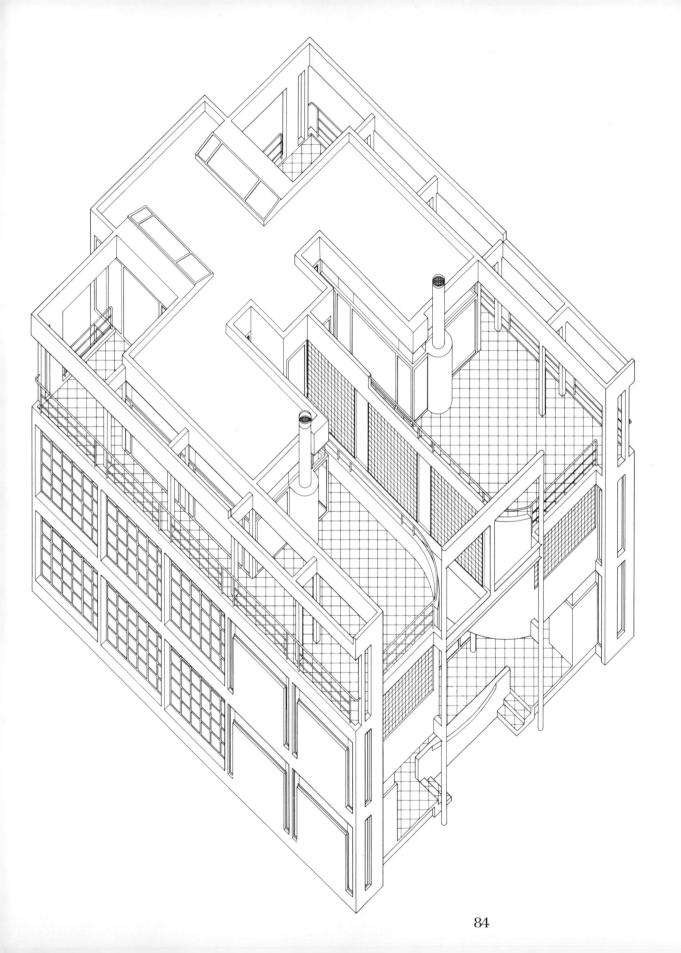

Axonometric view of double unit

Axonometric view of single unit
Axonometric view of back-to-back
double unit
Axonometric view of quadruple unit

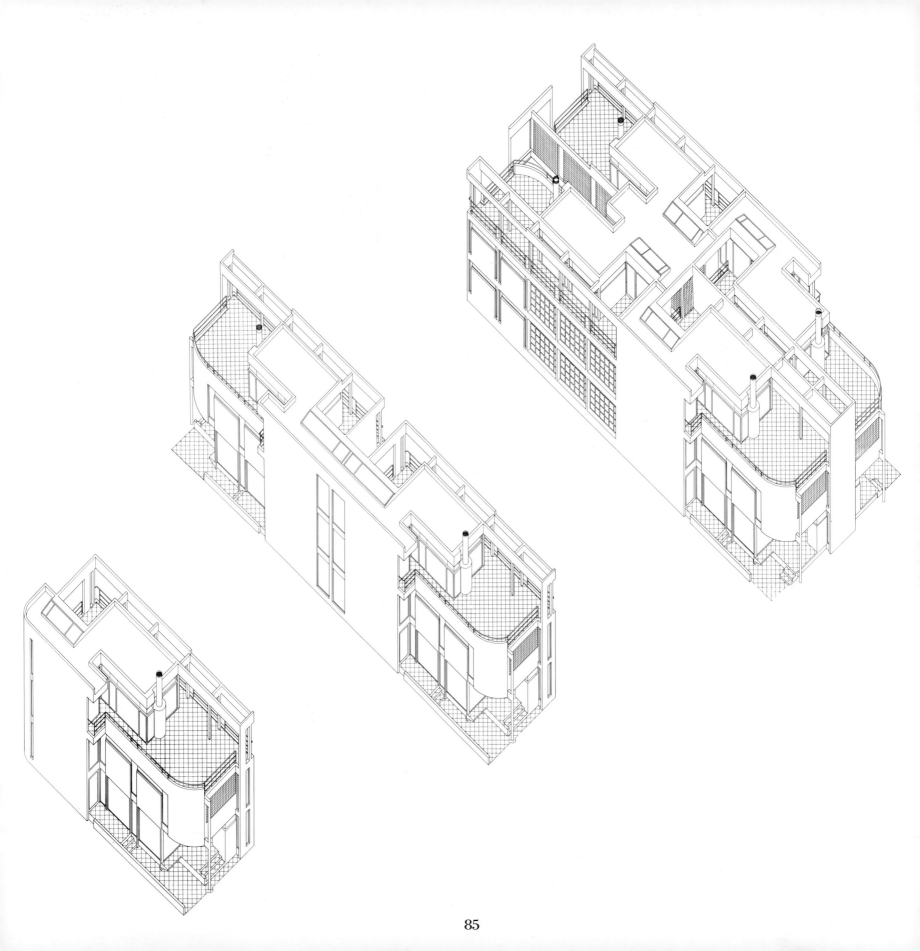

Maidman House

Sands Point, Long Island
1971–1976

Ground level plan

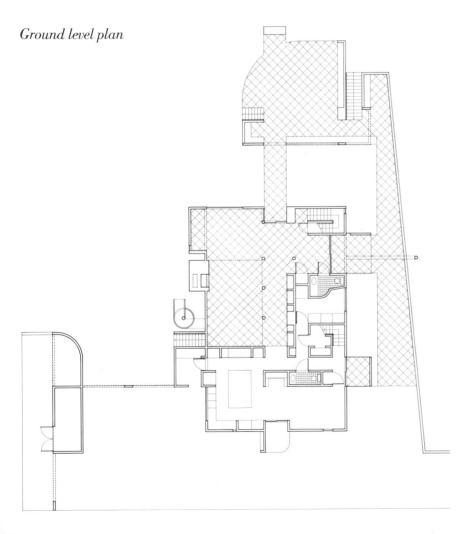

The Maidman House is a renovation of an existing house on a property overlooking Long Island Sound not far from New York City. The house had an outmoded organization and was in poor condition, lacking both amenity and any identifiable style. What it did have was a magnificent setting, including hundred-year-old maple and oak trees and a parklike surround sloping gently down to a sandy beach. The transformation involved gutting all of the interior except the main stair, while retaining the foundations, basement, exterior bearing walls, and roof.

The plan has been reorganized in a simple and traditional way: the more public family-use spaces on the first floor, the master bedrooms on the middle floor, and the children's bedrooms on top. The double-height living room culminates in a skylit shaft that passes through the children's playroom, piercing the roof, and connecting the house's horizontal layers. On the rear elevation other vertical elements—including a corkscrew slide for the children (or fire escape), the old brick chimney, and a slit window on axis with the entry—counterpoint the more pronounced horizontals of the front elevation—an open cornice line and an elongated entry terrace that mediates the slope of the site. The planar expression given to the front facade by the open cornice rigged out from the old roof and to the two side elevations by treating them like high bookends provides a foil to the somewhat squat volumetric mass of the house, and is an architectural clue to the fact that the house had a former identity.

As always, the filtration of light throughout the house and the celebration of the landscape through carefully framed views and openings are primary themes. While the natural color of the wood siding on the exterior maintains the kind of dialogue with the landscape typical of the previous houses, the use of expanses of bright color on interior surfaces as a contrast to the predominant white gives the space inside a special warmth and vivacity.

5| 10| 15| 30|

Axonometric view

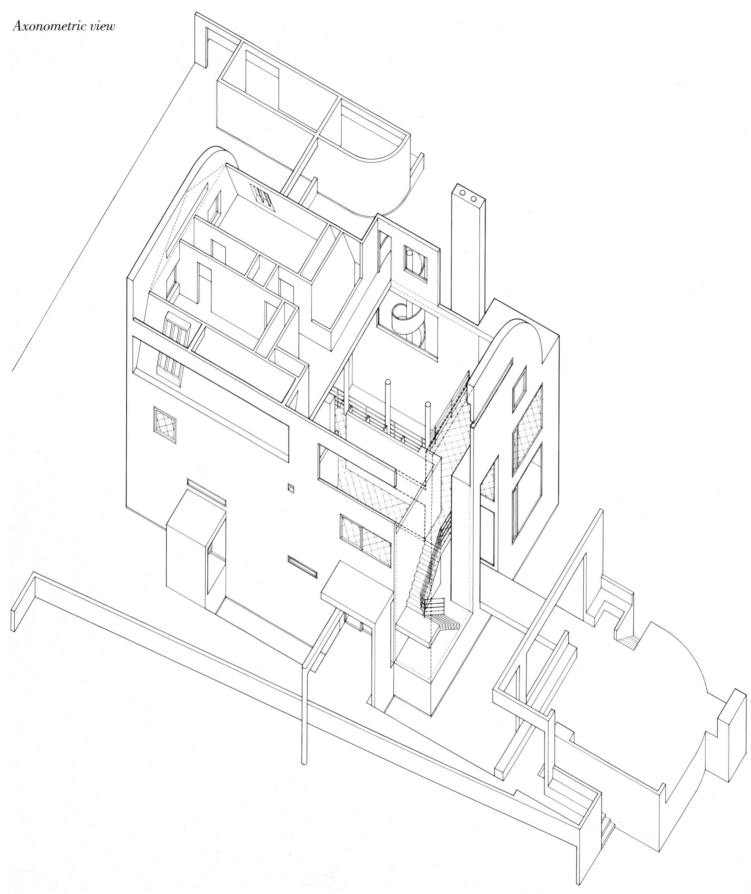

88

The deck on the north side of the house was originally intended to be made into a glazed pavilion, a kind of summer living room to contrast with the indoor living room used during the rest of the year.

90

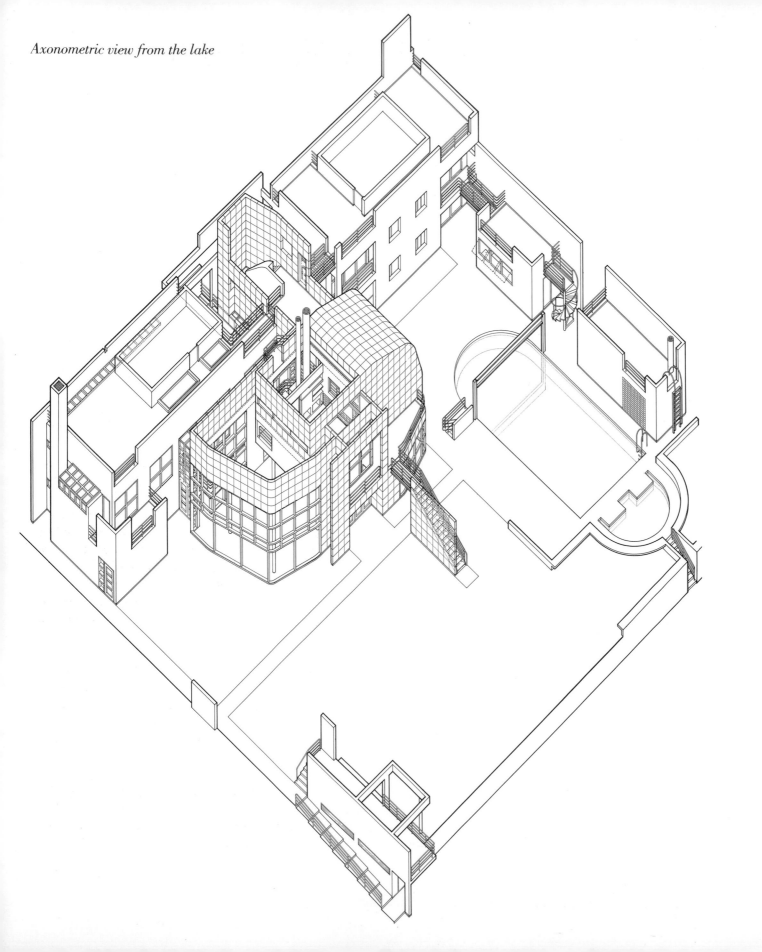

Axonometric view from the lake

House in Palm Beach

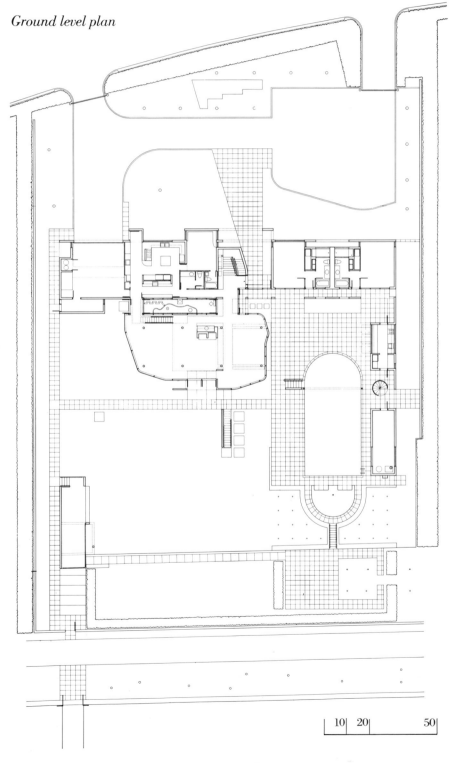

Ground level plan

Palm Beach, Florida
1977–1979

Located on a narrow, side-walled, flat site, this private residence has an open view of Lake Worth to the west. The parti is clearly organized to take advantage of its orientation. Within the front block to the right and left of the entry are the private spaces: to the right, the master bedroom suite above the ground-floor service areas; to the left, a guest wing with two bedrooms and baths on each floor. Behind this, facing the water, are the public areas, a pavilion for entertaining with a library above. As in the Douglas and Shamberg houses, the plan is an inversion of the expected sequence of spaces; one must penetrate the private zones on the street side in order to reach the public areas facing the view. This inversion serves to heighten the dramatic impact of the latter. Here, though, the diagram of public and private is pulled apart more decisively than in the earlier houses, so that there is a very strong separation of the elements in both plan and section. Thus, the private spaces are rectilinear; the public spaces, curvilinear. The separation is also clearly articulated in terms of materials. The private spaces are covered with an opaque material, stucco; the public spaces with a reflective one, enameled metal panels.

The rectilinear front block is set back from the street by an automobile forecourt. The minimally fenestrated front wall, with its compressed layers of cut-away planes, its extension from one side of the site to the other, and its recessed central entry, further affords privacy, serving as a massive horizontal gate, and at the same time unifying formally the two private wings, the master and guest portions of the house. The master suite, entered through a solid, canopied doorway in the central recess, can be shut off from the guest wing if desired, while the guest wing is treated like a small motel, with separate entries to each of the four units in the back, off the ground-level terrace and off an upper breezeway reached from the central stair.

10 20 50

The thickened "wall" front of the master and guest wings acts as a backdrop to the elaborate, extruded form behind it, which when viewed from the lake appears as a monumental volume. Separated from the master suite by a compressed courtyard space, this volume has a complex curvature: the plan of the dining room on one side echoes the section of the living room on the other. On the elevation facing the lake, the volume is eroded on the second level to become a balconied observation deck giving onto a staircase descending toward the water, and a planar brise-soleil allowing a framed and more sheltered view from the library. The first level of this volume is largely glazed, while the upper level, containing the library, is metal-paneled; this reverse materiality relieves the massiveness of the form at ground level, buoying it while also cupping the light along its curved surfaces in a controlled way.

The imposing headlike volume with its brise-soleil oculus looking out to the lake sits in an open gardenscape full of many inviting elements: a swimming pool, a pool house reached by an open-grid bridge from the "motel" wing, a "moon pavilion" at the northwest corner of the site, a manicured lawn like the putting green of a golf course. The contrast between white metal panels giving a thin-wall expression to the public spaces and the Floridian-tropical white stucco making a thick-wall enclosure for the private spaces is punctuated by extensive glazing, flying bridges, and flamboyant open gridwork.

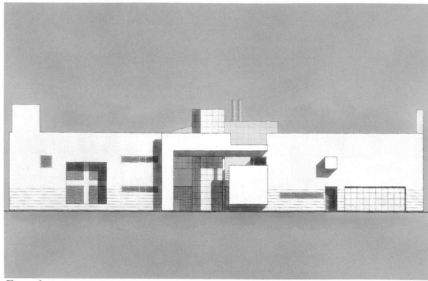

East elevation

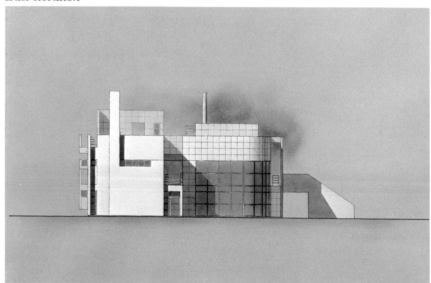

North elevation

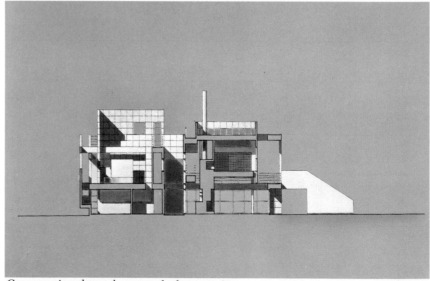

Cross section through master bedroom suite

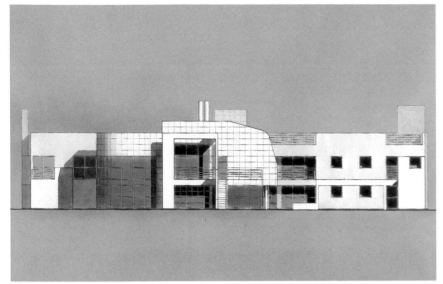

West elevation

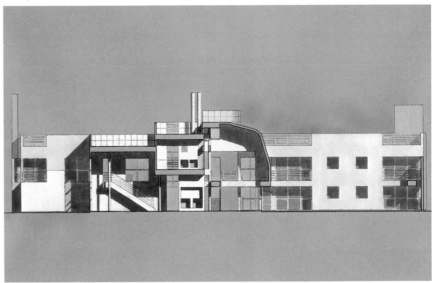

Longitudinal section

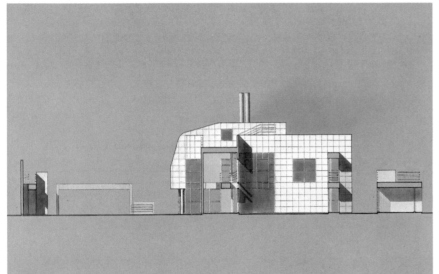

South elevation

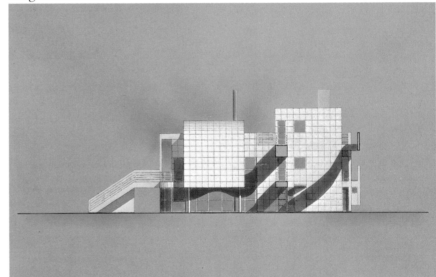

Early study for front elevation

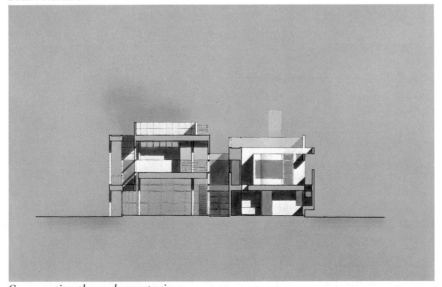

Cross section through guest wing

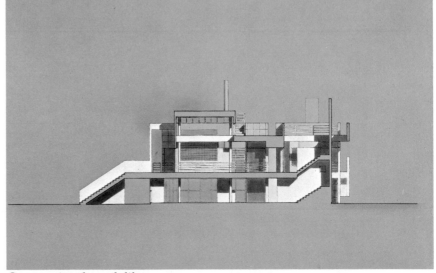

Cross section through library

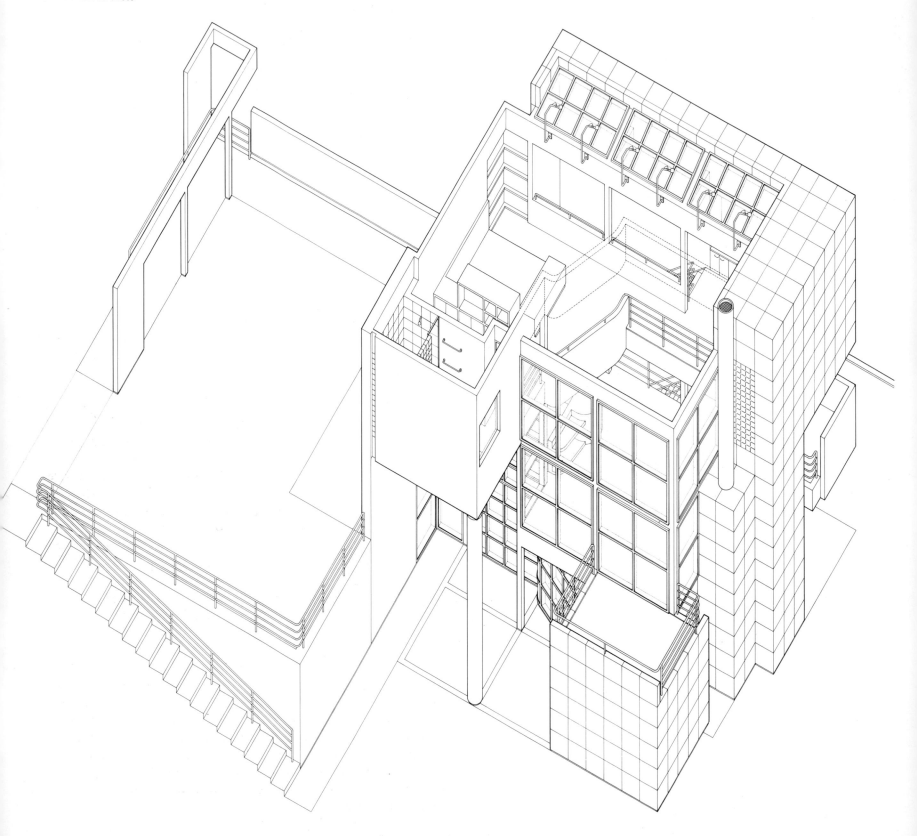

Giovannitti House

Pittsburgh, Pennsylvania
1979–1983

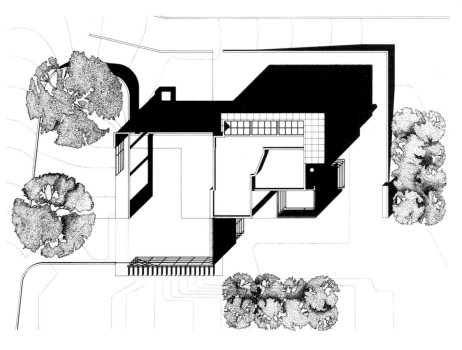

The small, sloped surburban site for this 2,200-square-foot house for two people is surrounded by other residences, so the need for privacy was an important consideration, as was the desire to create views and a sense of space beyond the immediate confines of the site. The design and organization of both the exterior and interior spaces developed from these concerns.

The overall plan consists of an eroded double square, with one square elevated into a three-story cubic volume and containing most of the program, and the other square devoted to the service functions of garage and kitchen on the ground level and an open terrace above. The three-story volume is carved away on the ground level to provide a second terrace, this one shielded from view and partly roofed by the projecting volume of the third floor. Inside, the program is organized vertically, giving all the spaces of this small house an unexpected amplitude. The dining room and guest room, located on the first level, are accessible from the garage and kitchen. The living room and the formal entry to the house, on the second level, are contiguous to the parapeted terrace over the garage. The library and master bedroom are on the third level. A wood stair adjacent to the entry area connects all three floors.

On the facades, porcelain-enameled steel panels and stucco protect the private spaces from view, while a delicate, steel-framed glass skin allows light to penetrate the public spaces. The openness of this skin permits views to the outside which are balanced and framed by more massive solid forms, as well as by the large existing trees on the property, which have been left intact. Throughout this small house there is a subtle dialogue between open and closed spaces, private and public realms, with each element enhanced by the play of contrasts and transitions.

North elevation

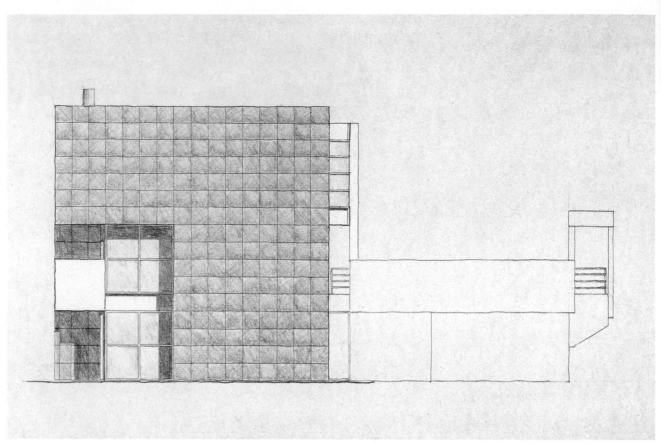

West elevation

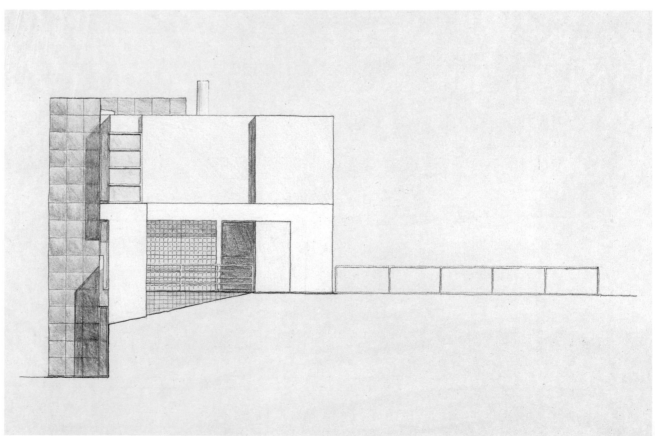

| 2| 5| 10| 20 |

East elevation

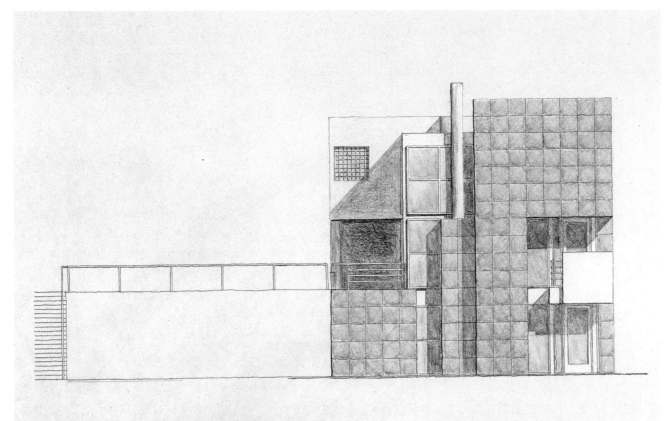

South elevation

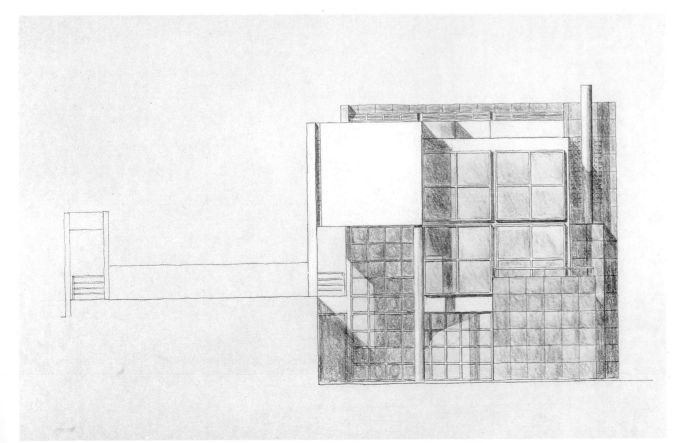

99

Ground level plan

Entry level plan

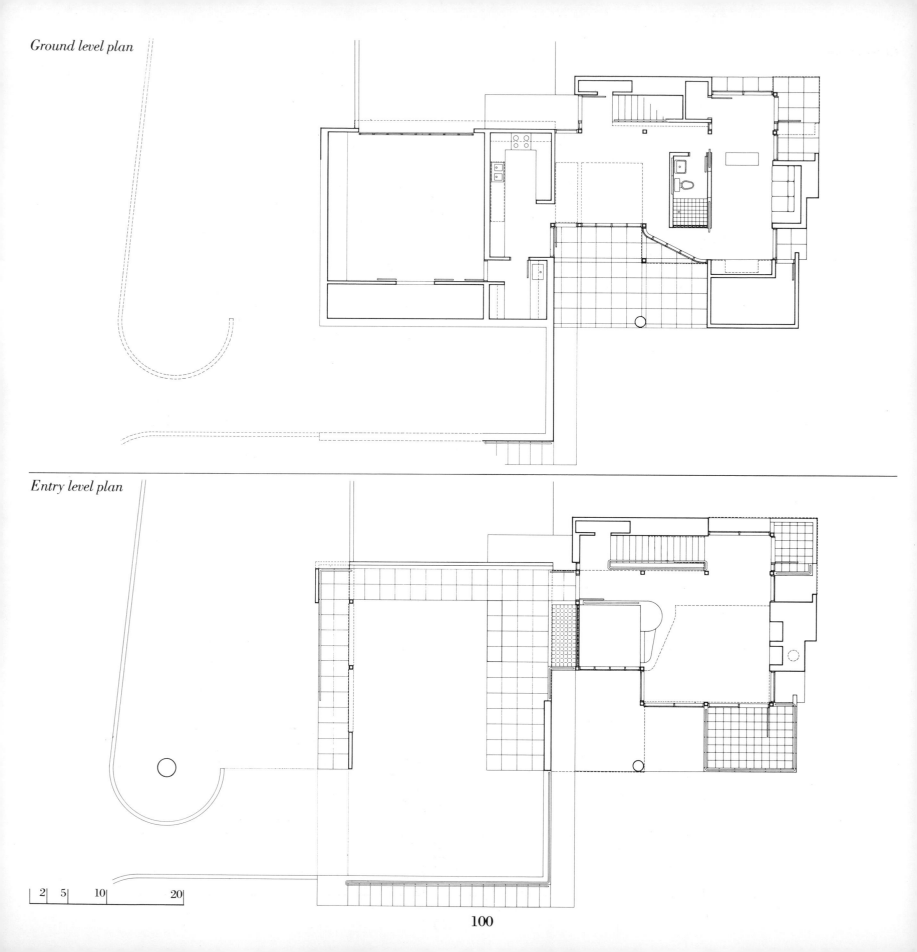

2 5   10   20

Cross section

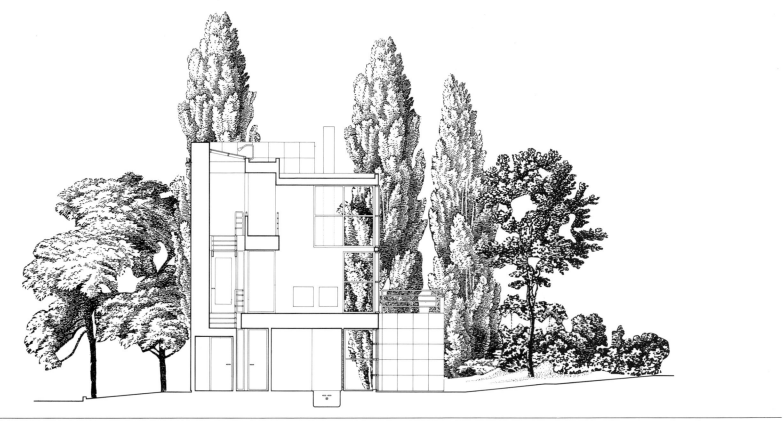

Longitudinal section

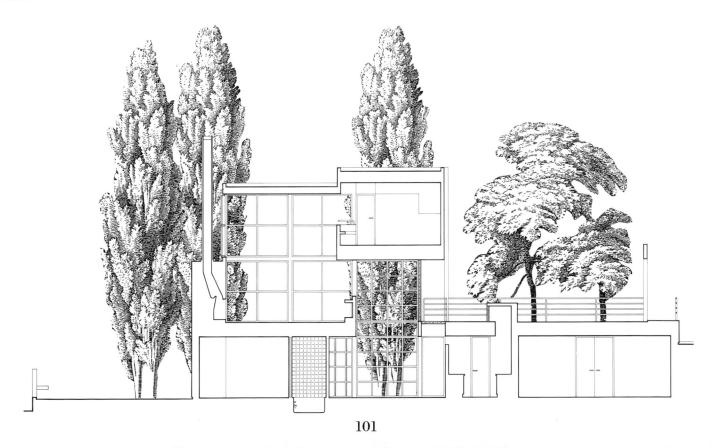

The tightness of the site and the compactness of this small house are relieved by the asymmetrical relation of the house to the site, which makes possible longer views and perspectives of the garden to the southeast. The interconnection of levels and the extension of the social spaces out to several different terraces allow further interpenetration of inside and outside.

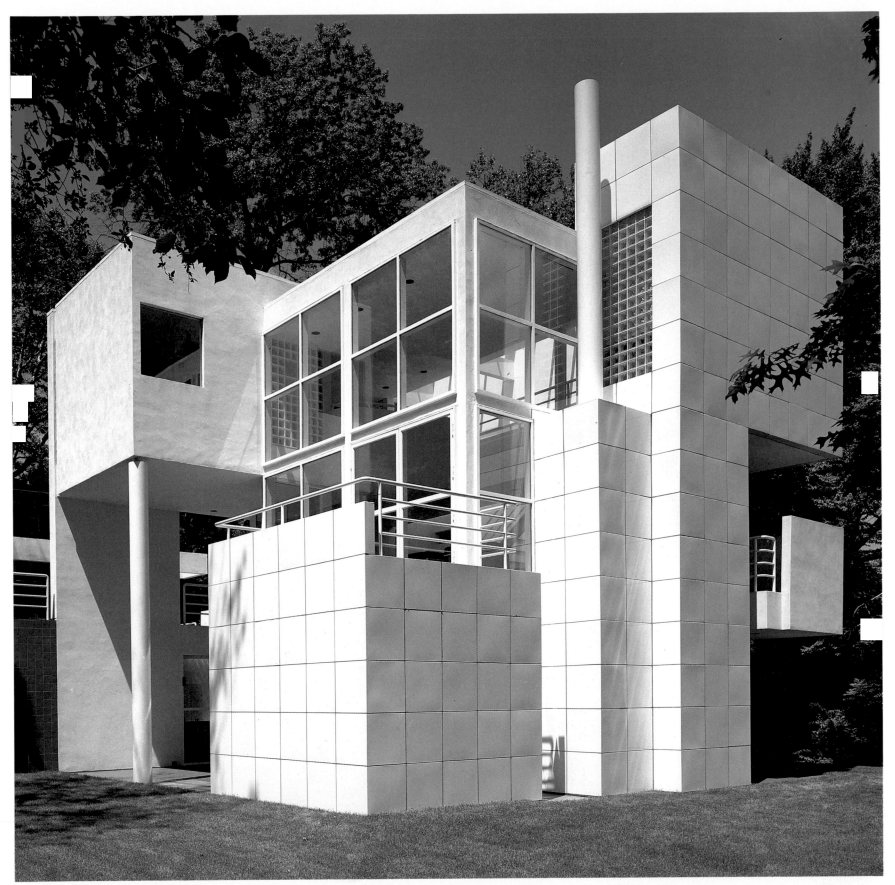

Westbeth Artists' Housing

New York, New York
1967–1970

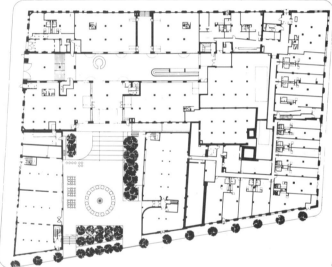

Street level plan

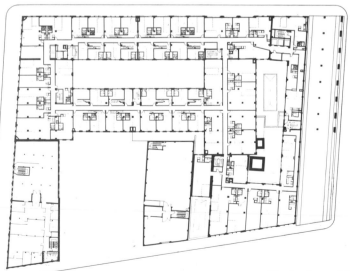

Typical corridor floor plan

Westbeth is a former commercial structure converted into housing for artists. It was conceived as an integrated, self-sufficient community that would provide the residents not only with loft space in which to live and work, but also with gallery space, theatrical facilities, and film, photography, and dance studios: in short, with a total environment in which to pursue their work, from conception to performance or display. The whole enterprise would have been impossible without the sponsorship of the J. M. Kaplan Fund as well as the National Council on the Arts, which initiated the project and also provided the seed money for purchase of the buildings, originally the Bell Telephone Laboratories.

Occupying a city block at the west edge of Greenwich Village a few blocks south of Fourteenth Street, the Bell Laboratories are an aggregate of thirteen massive steel-and-concrete structures, whose utilitarian form resembles that of many other such buildings in large cities throughout the United States. These buildings continue to be an excellent resource for low-cost family dwellings—quality structures that today would be too costly to build. The fireproof structure, built between 1898 and 1920, rises thirteen floors and affords over 600,000 square feet of floor space with high ceilings, large windows, and thick masonry walls. The building commands views on three sides: west to the Hudson River and north and south to upper and lower Manhattan.

Because the physical structure of Bell Laboratories was left essentially unchanged, the apartments, studios, and duplexes take a variety of forms. However, the transformation of the program made it possible to eliminate through-corridors on all but three of the ten floors, thereby increasing living area at the expense only of circulation space.

A narrow existing courtyard is the organizational focus for the whole complex. By removal of a roof and two floors, this courtyard was opened to the sky. Semicircular steel balconies project from the apartments surrounding it to provide additional egress from the duplex units and to engage the courtyard space. The main entrance to the building is located at one end of the courtyard. This entrance controls the public access to the structure. The courtyard also provides an outdoor area for the Westbeth community, serving as a buffer from the street and as a place where private and public spheres meet. Several secondary entrances on the surrounding streets, providing access to the courtyard, have also been retained from the previous organization. The old truck entrance allows pedestrian access on West Street, while arcades on Bethune Street and through a small community park off Bank Street allow access from north and south.

The participation of the residents in the design of their own living units brought into being an idea long contemplated by architects and others. Needless to say, Federal Housing Authority officials had to be convinced that their customary standards for the partitioning of space in middle-income housing were inappropriate to the domestic requirements of the working artist. One hopes that an easing of regulations such as that which allowed Westbeth to escape the rigid mold usually determining the form of our residential structures will serve as a precedent for the design of more conventional housing. So far, unfortunately, the model of Westbeth has not been adopted, despite the more liberal attitudes that now prevail in public housing.

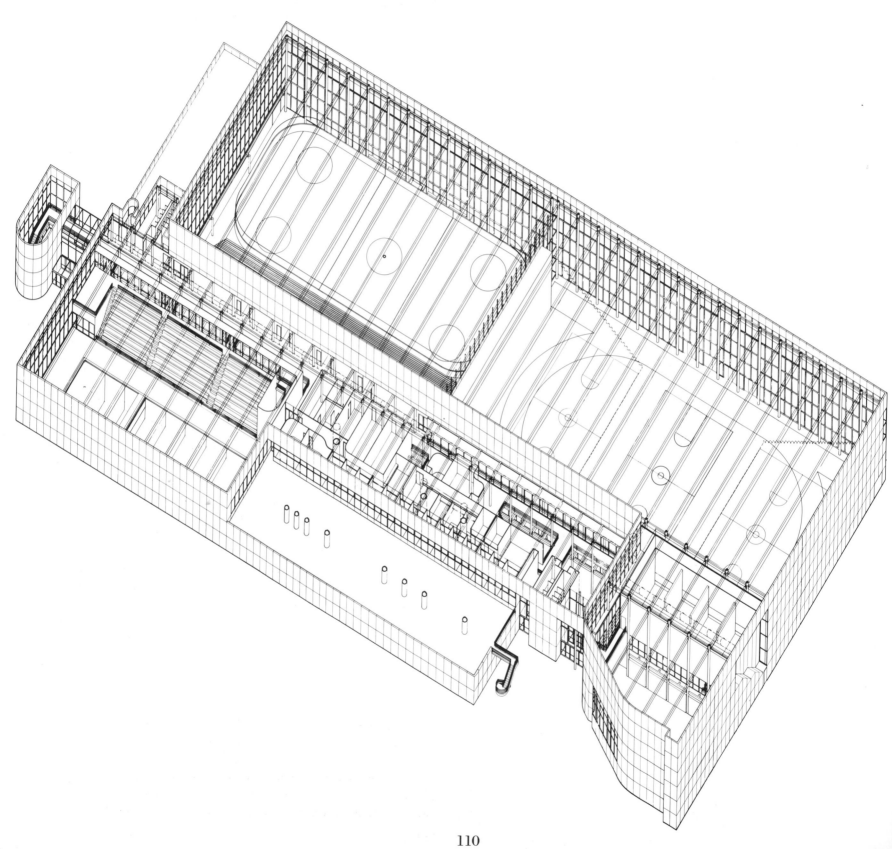

Fredonia Health and Physical Education Building

State University, Fredonia, New York
1968

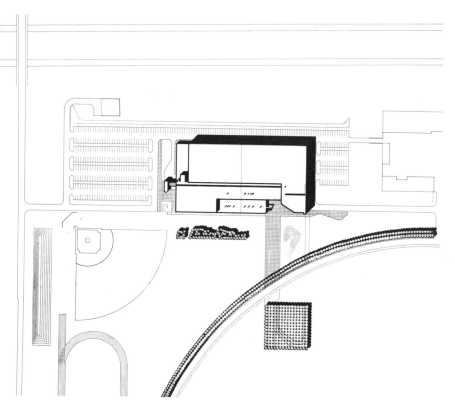

The Fredonia campus is situated on relatively flat land on the outskirts of town. The master plan for the campus, designed by Henry Cobb of I. M. Pei & Partners, uses a ring road to control access to the various facilities. The site for the Health and Physical Education Building is at the northwest corner of the campus, outside the ring road and along a north-south arterial road leading to a throughway at the northern boundary of the campus. The chief site considerations were to provide students with pedestrian access across the ring road and to allow the public direct access and parking off the arterial road. As the trees around the outer edge of the ring road prevented bridging the road physically, a large mass of trees is planted inside the ring road on axis with the main entry to signal the presence of the building. A broad path leads from the ring road to the recessed entry. From the north-south artery, an access road leads to public parking.

The building is devoted to a variety of athletic activities. The programmatic elements are arranged along both sides of a two-level, glass-enclosed circulation spine running most of the length of the 535-foot building. The spine deflects at the main entry to allow access off a square, two-story vestibule. At the other end, it concludes in a free-standing stairway linking the upper and lower levels and giving access from the parking lot. The continuous tube of glazing allows natural light to filter into both levels, mitigating the tunnel effect of the corridors. These corridors are the only uninterrupted horizontal planes in the building. The athletic spaces consist of volumes of different heights, related only through the spine and the common system of enclosure. The latter, a thin skin of metal panels, is designed so that its bracing and girt system is entirely exposed on the interior. The separation of the structural grid from the enveloping wall and window system creates a rhythmic, repetitive articulation of spatial elements, serving to unify the diverse components formally. The whole assembly functions like a machine, an arrangement of parts pragmatically combined in an integrated relationship.

111

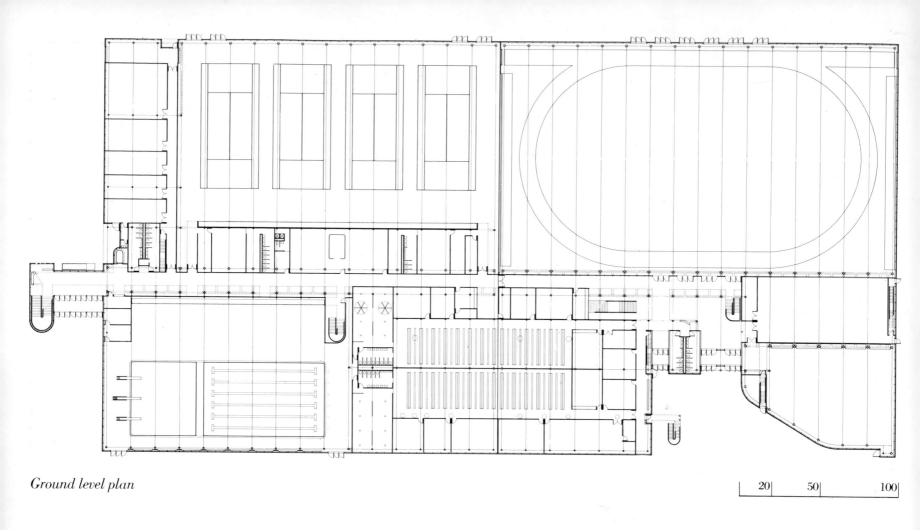

Ground level plan

20 50 100

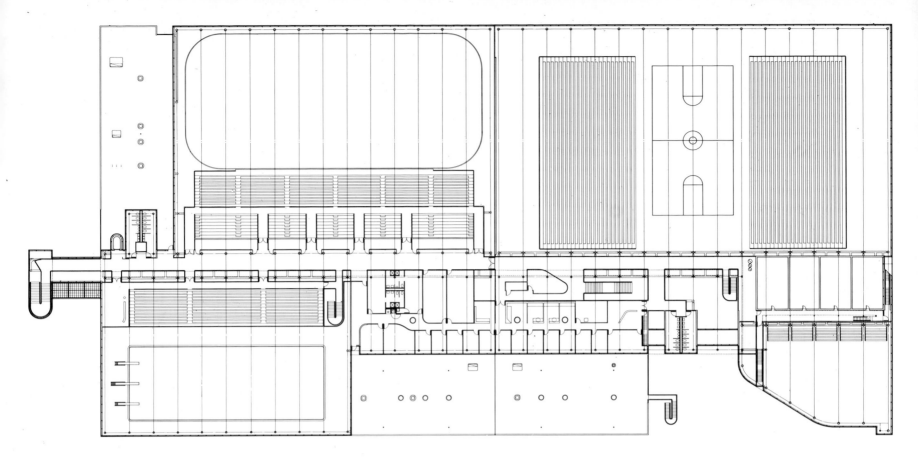

Upper level plan

Program

Structure

Entry

Circulation

Enclosure

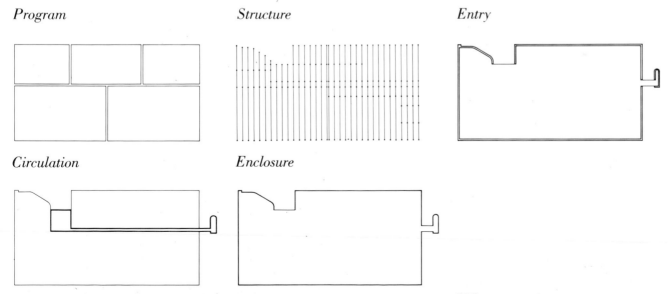

Section through circulation spine facing south

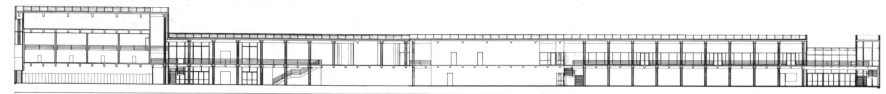

Section through squash courts and entry facing north

Section through arena and hockey rink facing south

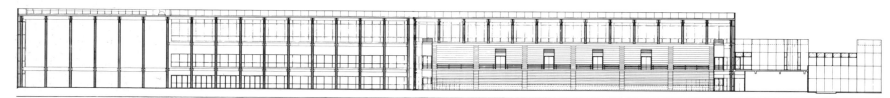

Section through swimming pool and gymnasium facing north

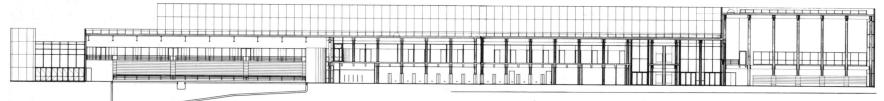

Section through lockers and hockey rink facing west

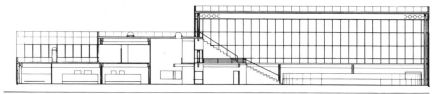

Section through hockey rink and swimming pool facing east

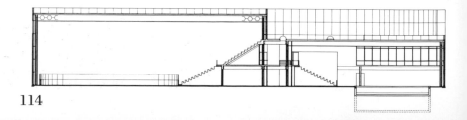

20| 50| 100|

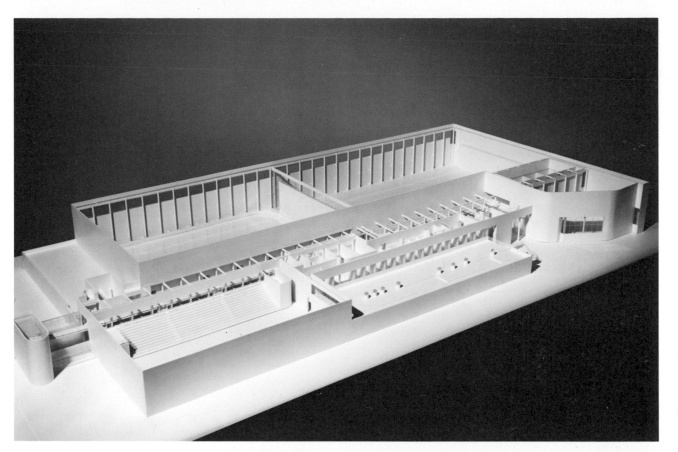

Twin Parks Northeast Housing

The Bronx, New York
1969–1974

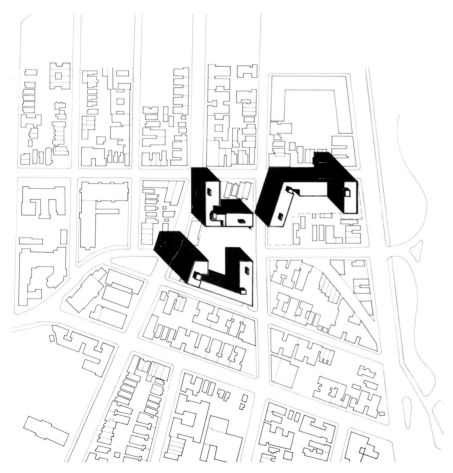

The East Tremont section of the Bronx, the site of Twin Parks Northeast Housing, is an old Italian neighborhood that has recently become racially mixed. The area exhibits the classic symptoms of urban decay: vacant lots, boarded-up storefronts, traditional row-housing now fallen into tenement use, and a landscape of broken glass, strewn garbage, and crumbling brick. In a 1967 study, the Urban Design Group of the New York City Planning Commission identified certain pockets of land that were not large enough for conventional development. On these sites, the Twin Parks Association, a non-profit, community-based company, was empowered by the city to sponsor moderate-income housing. The concept was to integrate the new buildings into the existing urban context in such a way as to revitalize that context and to provide a maximum of usable private and public space for the needs of both the residents and the community at large.

The site of Twin Parks Northeast occupies parts of three adjacent city blocks. The slabs are wedged in between the existing tenements on the blocks and scaled and oriented to fit with them, thereby reinforcing the existing street "walls." The irregular street grid gives the buildings their two different axes of orientation, and provides a device for relating them across the blocks. Their dark brown color and masonry texture further relate them to the existing buildings, while their elevational treatment and massing give definition to the center and edge of the blocks, and differentiate between public and private spaces.

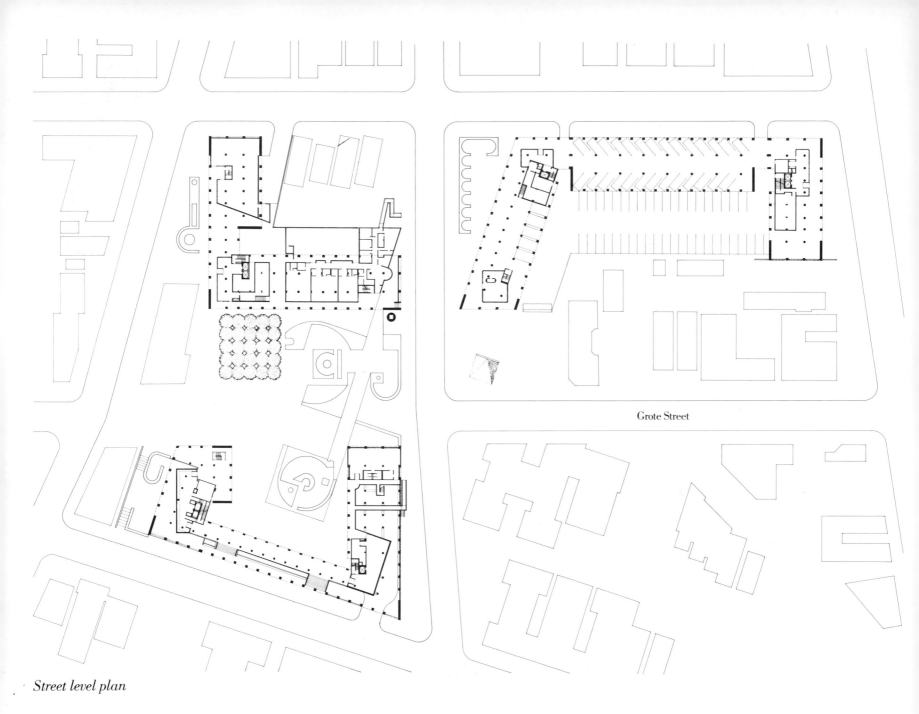

Street level plan

Grote Street

| 10 | 25 | | 50 | |

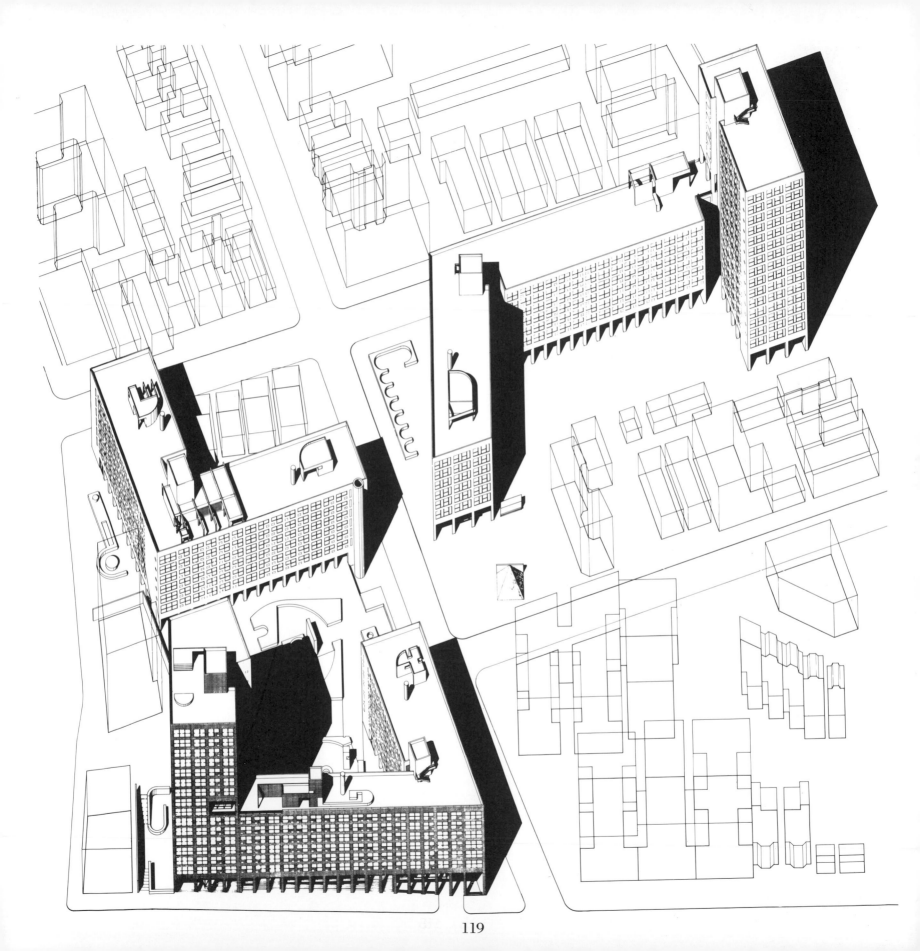

An earlier plan called for closing one of the two interior streets, Grote, by bridging it with one of the slabs, so as to bring the blocks together and give physical continuity to a plaza below. Subsequently it proved impossible to create such a bridge. Grote was ultimately closed, but only after construction was well along. The design, as realized, consists of three separate buildings that are unified primarily by their plan relations.

The major outdoor space provided by the project now is located in the closed portion of Grote Street. This semiprotected plaza is designed to serve both the project's residents and the surrounding community. Like the courtyard at Westbeth, it provides a meeting and play space, and serves as a focus for pedestrian circulation through the neighborhood.

All three building blocks are lifted above the ground on *pilotis* so that the public spaces can be entered from all directions at ground level. The arcades created by the *pilotis* give onto entry foyers. The two tower-slabs, each sixteen stories high and rising at diagonally opposite ends of the site, overlook a small park on Crotona Avenue at one end and the Bronx Zoo on the other, anchoring the composition and establishing a central axis.

Twin Parks Northeast is intended not as an architecture of isolated and free-standing buildings in space, but rather as a place of urban continuity. It emphasizes the adaptive capability of the existing city grid to new structuring, and incorporates some of the quality and texture of traditional building within a humane, modern vocabulary. In both its form and its organization, it expresses the attitude that one of the principal roles of a building in an urban milieu is to make a larger urban statement, to be the generator of social and communal values.

Twin Parks, along with the Fredonia Health and Physical Education Building, Monroe Developmental Center, and Bronx Developmental Center, was commissioned by a state agency. Unfortunately, public projects of this type and on this scale are no longer a reality today. Because of changes in the political and economic climate, there is no government creation of public housing and other public institutions in the way there was in the late 1960s and early 1970s. It is not because the need for such projects is no longer present.

Axonometric view of corner site prototype

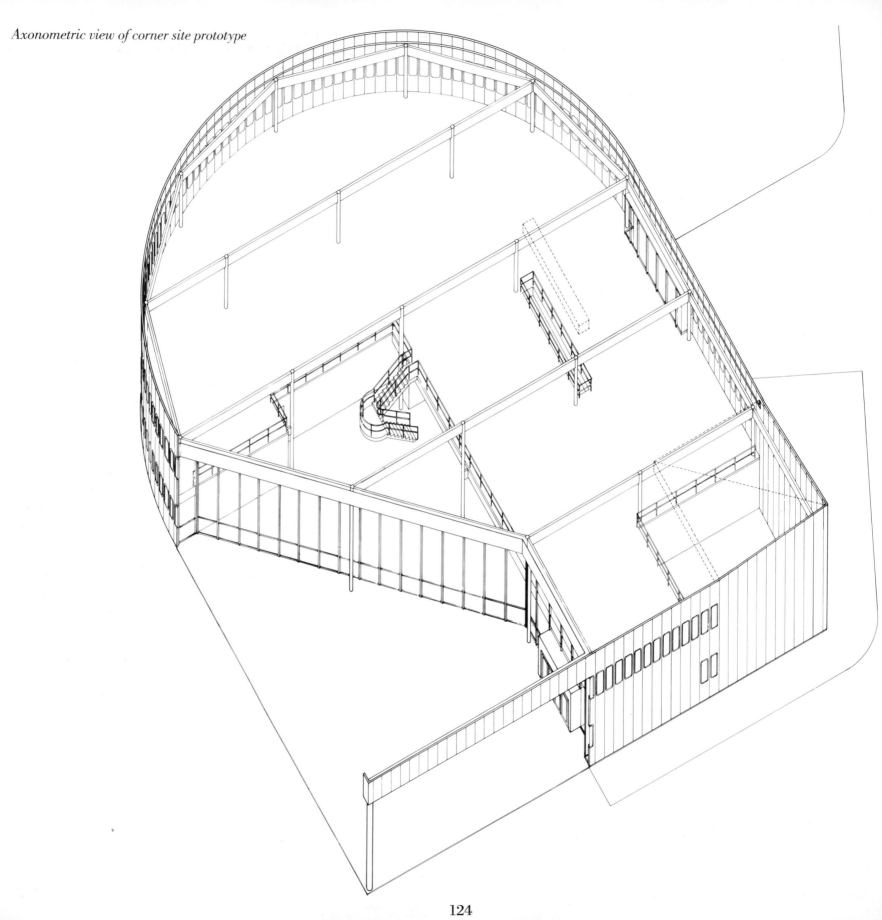

Charles Evans Industrial Buildings

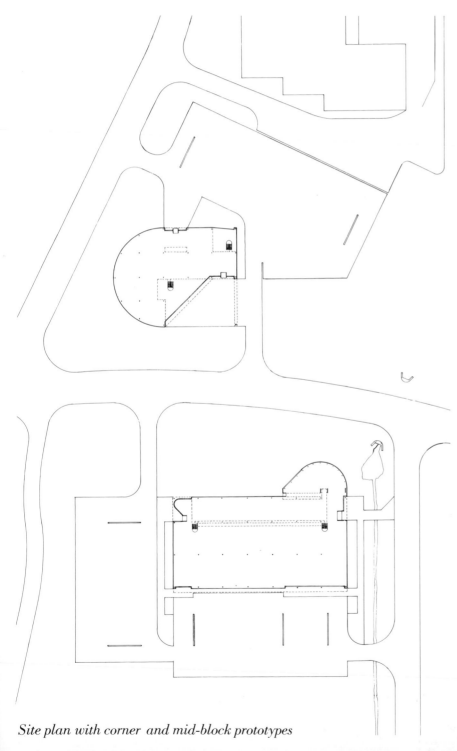

Fairfield, New Jersey, and Piscataway, New Jersey
1969

This combination of warehouse and office space is intended to offer a flexible and inexpensive alternative to the architecture of the suburban "strip." The exterior envelope of lightweight metal panels suggests its adaptability to a variety of sites and scales. The simple structural grid would allow future tenants to organize their space to suit their own needs.

Two basic building types were designed for the Charles Evans Company. The first, linear in form, places office and display space along the highway frontage. Behind this space, which may be organized on one or two levels, is a two-story warehouse area, which can be expanded to accommodate increased storage or manufacturing needs.

The second building, a variation of the first, is designed to respond to the particular requirements of a corner site at an intersection. The emphasis here is on office and display space rather than on a warehousing facility.

Both buildings offer the possibility of occupancy by more than one tenant. Unspecific as to function and site, these prototypes maintain a recognizable formal identity through their consistent surface treatment, structural principle of organization, and spatial clarity.

Site plan with corner and mid-block prototypes

125

Monroe Developmental Center

Rochester, New York
1969–1974

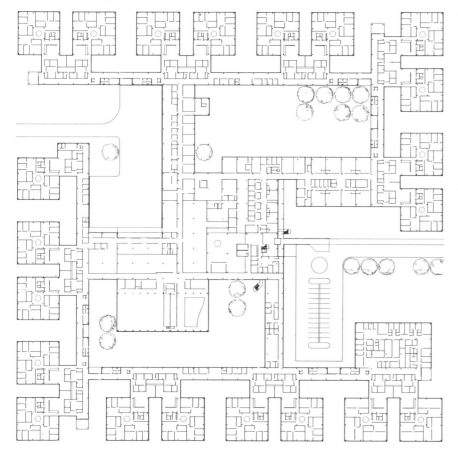

Ground level plan

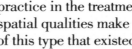

The Monroe Developmental Center, commissioned by the Facilities Development Corporation for the New York State Department of Mental Hygiene, is located on forty acres on the periphery of Rochester's increasing urban sprawl and adjoins the Rochester State Hospital campus. Almost treeless and flat, the open site fronts a public road. The center houses five hundred retarded persons, ranging from infants to young adults. Designed to shelter, feed, and provide for the educational needs of these residents, it is modeled on a small urban community.

The plan of the complex is a large eroded square, with the residential units creating its outer edge and connected by stems to the main circulation corridor. These units, facing outward, are designed to give residents a feeling of connection with the outside world. Each unit accommodates twenty-four occupants in a single-story building, thus allowing easy access to the gardens and maximizing the independent movement of invalids. The communal facilities are located in the interior of the plan, providing an inward focus for the center's social activities. These facilities include a gymnasium, swimming pool, cafeteria, classrooms, offices, a domestic training center, a physical therapy unit, and a community diagnostic clinic. Throughout, cloistered courtyards of various sizes, sheltered by low vegetation, trees, and sculpted berms, serve as outdoor extensions of the adjacent interior spaces. The educational cloister provides sun-screened outdoor classrooms and an outdoor theater; a second large courtyard adjoining the gymnasium and pool offers more active play spaces. The smaller courtyards between the residential units resemble suburban backyards.

The center is designed to be flexible enough to respond to changing practice in the treatment of the mentally retarded. Its organization and spatial qualities make it significantly different from other institutions of this type that existed when the project was conceived.

Designing for the physically and mentally disabled is not such a "special" problem after all. The architecture is still basically concerned with creating spaces that uplift the spirit and provide an environment of quality for all users—patients, nurses and doctors, visitors.

Bronx Developmental Center

Bronx, New York
1970–1977

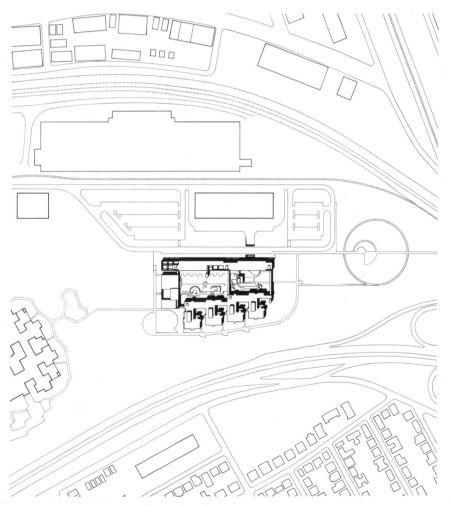

The Bronx Developmental Center, like the Monroe Developmental Center, was commissioned by the Facilities Development Corporation for the New York State Department of Mental Hygiene. It was originally planned as a total-care residential facility for 750 physically disabled and mentally retarded children. As built, the project houses 380 and also serves as an out-patient facility. While the program's complex technical requirements demanded particular attention, the design is above all an attempt to create a sense of place that responds to the special feelings and needs of the residents.

The triangular site occupies part of an industrial no-man's-land, a traffic island bounded by the Hutchinson River Parkway on the east and a network of railroad tracks on the west. Isolated on an elongated rise within an otherwise flat and amorphously defined hospital campus, it lacks any distinguishing features from which to derive a set of design concepts. It was apparent that the new building could not be related to its context in a conventional way. The strategy was therefore to allow it to create its own context—to turn its back on the negative surrounds by providing a positive internal one, to open the complex inward to an inviting reality where the residents would be shielded from the hostile landscape.

The two major programmatic elements divide around the lateral axis of the composition: the support services wing in the rectangular block on the west, and the residential units and services in the stepped volumes on the east. The gymnasium and physical therapy building on the south, and the two large courtyards, each with a corridor at its northern edge, stitch the composition together.

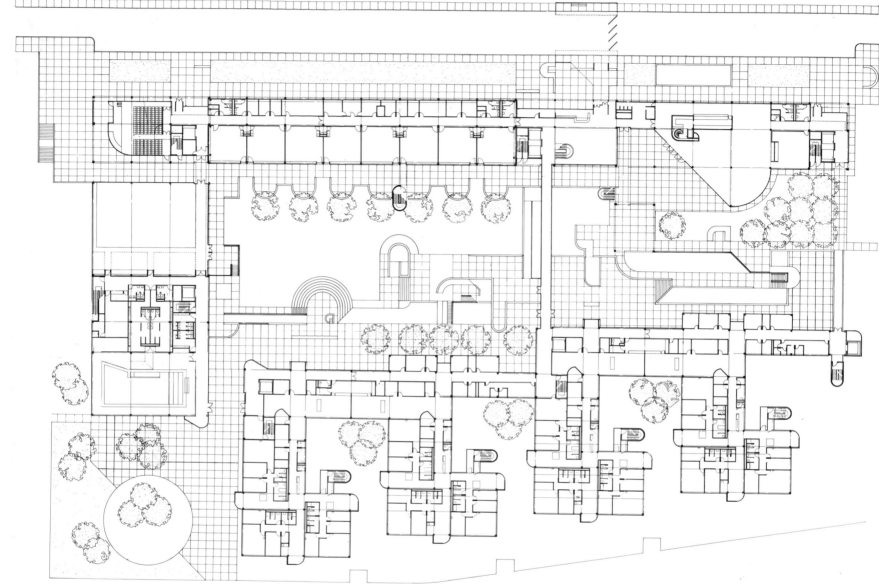

Entry level plan

20| 50| 100|

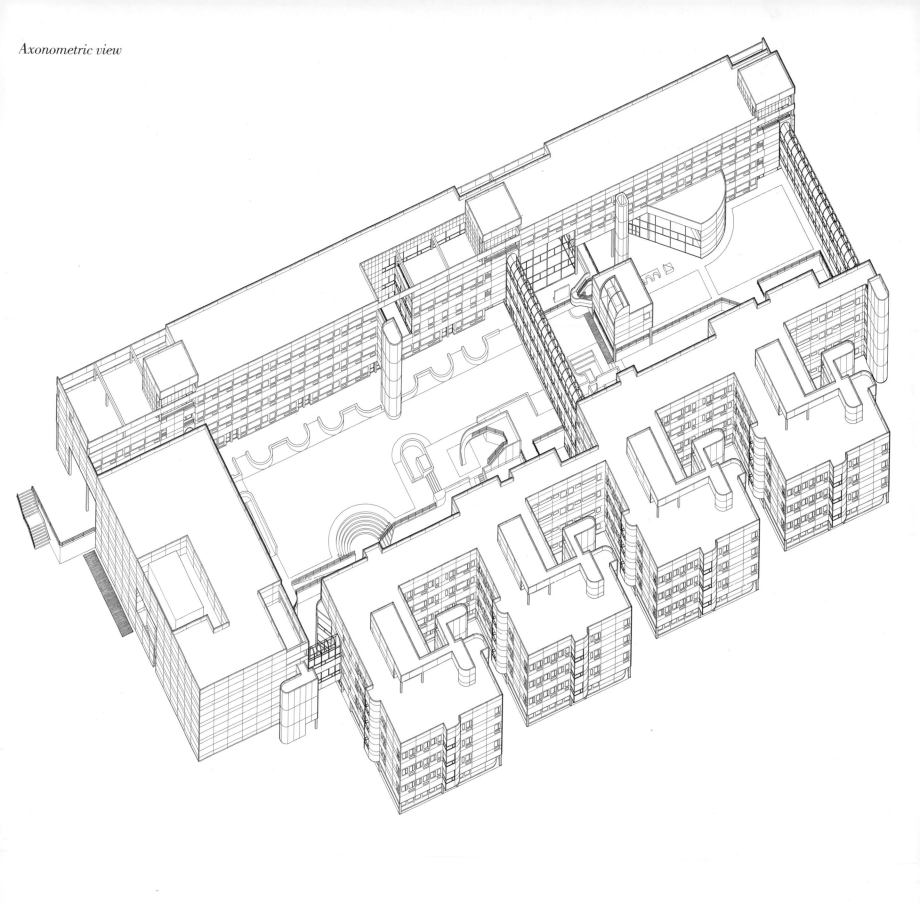

Axonometric view

Northwest elevation of support services building

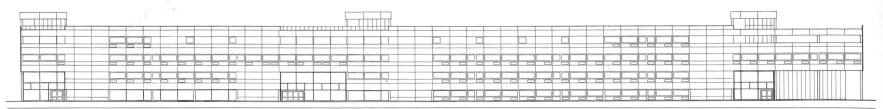

Southeast elevation of support services building

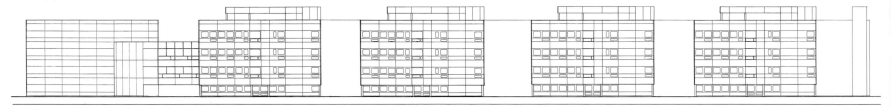

Northwest elevation of residential buildings

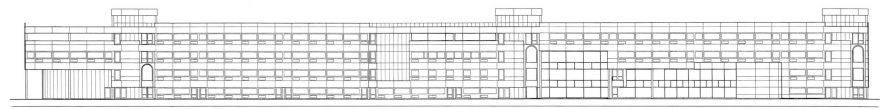

Southeast elevation of residential buildings

Northeast elevation of building complex

20| 50| 100|

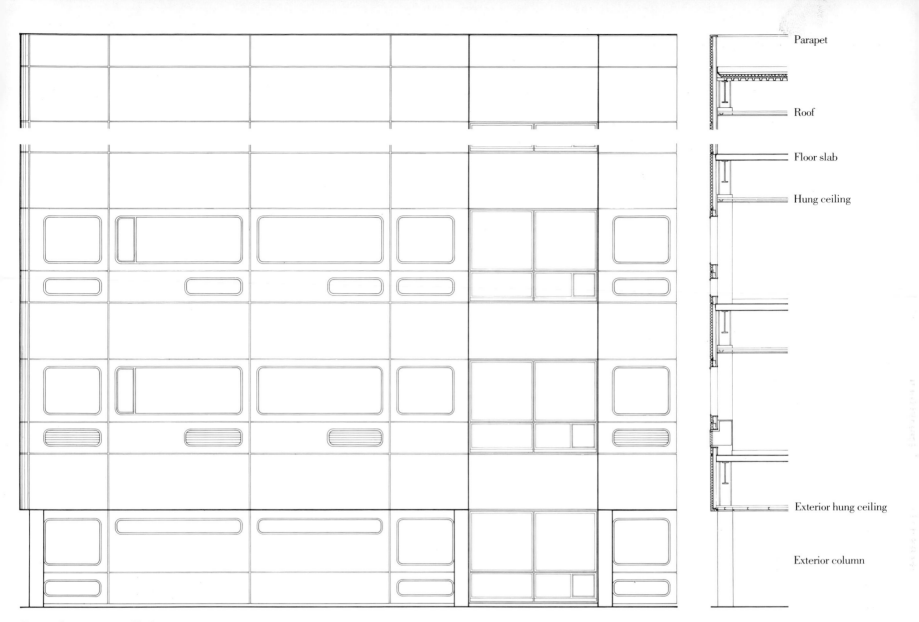

Partial exterior wall elevation and section

Parapet

Roof

Floor slab

Hung ceiling

Exterior hung ceiling

Exterior column

2 5 10

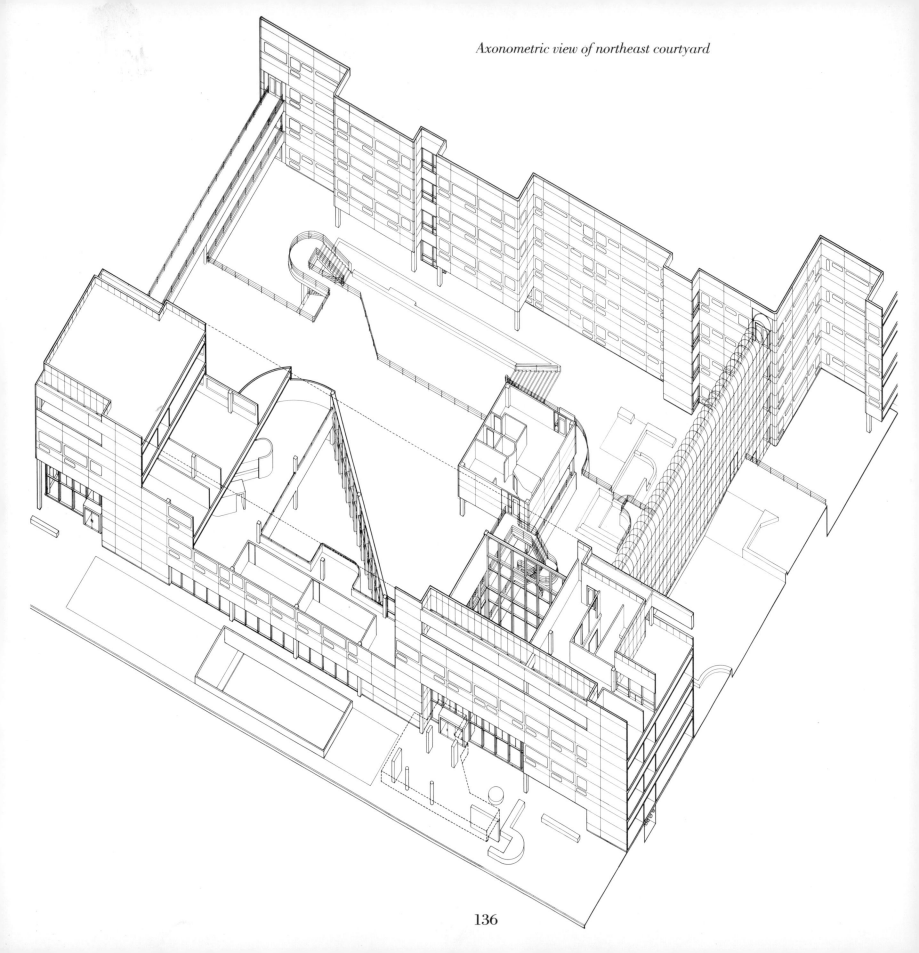

The support services wing houses the administrative, therapeutic, and educational functions and provides the public access to the complex. The continuous front facade of this long, four-story spine presents a massive wall, a protective filter through which the outside world must pass to reach the realms behind. The recessed portions of the smooth exterior wall serve to distinguish the ground-floor spaces from those on the upper floors, clearly articulating base, middle, and upper levels. Further elevational modulation occurs in the panelization at the points where double-height spaces occur: at the building entrances the panels give way to glazing, and at the south end a columned recess locates a semicircular auditorium underneath upper-level administrative facilities.

The views into the courtyards from the support services building reveal a complex and diverse facility behind. An enclosed stair tower and other volumetric forms projecting into the courtyards situate themselves within the landscaped terrain and mediate between the scale of the support services block and that of the residential zone on the other side of the courtyard.

On the inside edge of the residential zone and interconnecting the four units behind is a second spinal system containing services intended to be more decentralized than those in the main building. This pulled-away and sheared spine is the mediator in a progressively more differentiated sequence of volumetric layering, from the frontal monolithic block back to the individual residential units, expressing the public-to-private organization of the complex. The offices for physicians, nurses, and social workers located along the secondary spine are indicated on the exterior by a series of volumetric projections, giving the facade an undulating quality, and countering the screenlike tautness of the support services wing.

The residential units themselves are L-shaped and stepped back progressively toward the north. These buildings are of a more domestic scale, much like adjacent houses. Each incorporates three suites for eight residents, an arrangement that creates a family-like environment of comparative privacy. The organization of the individual suite allows for a further elaboration of the separation between public and privates spaces. Each suite may be used as a "family-care apartment" simulating a normal domestic environment, as a training suite in conjunction with the staffing space, or alternatively as a special, independent apartment with its own private entrance. This flexibility was planned to allow the residential spaces to function for out-patient as well as day-patient programs, for parents wishing to stay with their child, and for special overnight intensive care.

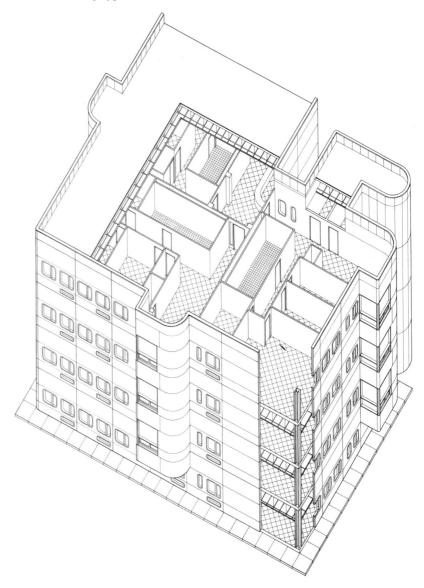

Axonometric view of typical residential unit

Discussion of the Metal-Panel Wall System

The history of the development of the exterior metal-panel wall system at the Bronx Developmental Center, and of the issues posed by a metal skin, begins with the design of the Health and Physical Education Building at Fredonia in 1968. The particular program of that facility led to the use of a simple metal-panel curtain-wall enclosure for the building. Research was undertaken to determine what systems were commercially available and how they might be implemented. Most of the available metal-panel wall systems were geared to industrial warehouse buildings and, though simple in concept, were quite rigid and crude in their application and detailing. The sophistication demanded by a more refined architecture was lacking. At Fredonia (illustrated at left) an existing wall system based upon a box-type porcelain-enameled steel panel was manipulated to fit, and supported by an exposed grid system of girts. This led in 1969, in the projects for the Charles Evans Industrial Buildings, to the use of a laminated sandwich-panel spanning between floors, and in 1971, in the fifteen buildings for the Olivetti Corporation, to the use of box-type panels.

The three basic types of exterior metal-panel systems may be summarized as follows:
1. Laminated panel
Layers of material are glued together under pressure to produce a non-load-bearing but strong panel capable of spanning between floors without girts. Sandwich panels, also laminated, are composed of rigid board insulation compressed between two metal faces. The outer face of the panel can be manufactured with a flange and set within an extruded aluminum or pressed steel frame.
2. Box-type panel
This panel is fabricated from two metal pans with insulation in between. The box is supported on a girt system, and both faces of the box serve as finished surfaces, exterior and interior.
3. Rolled-sheet panel
This panel consists of a metal pan on the exterior, with an insulation backing behind that is structurally supported on a girt system. The inside face is finished with either another metal sheet or a conventional interior finish material such as gypsum wallboard.

Because all three systems are used primarily in industrial warehouse buildings, most manufacturers limit their products to sections with a vertical dimension of 12″ to 36″, designed to be attached directly to the face of the building.

By the time the Bronx Developmental Center was designed in 1970, the potentials and limitations of metal panels as an exterior

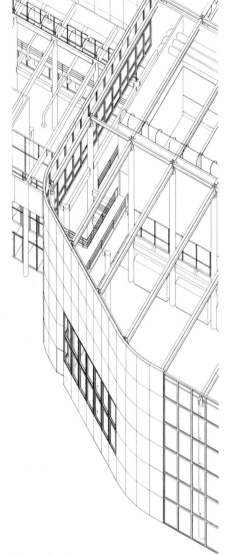

Detail of Fredonia metal-panel wall system

cladding system had become apparent. Early designs for the Developmental Center were based upon a specific type of aluminum, laminated sandwich-panel system that offered several advantages: 1) the possibility of using the panel as a total wall in which the two faces of the panel could serve as the finished surfaces of interior and exterior, 2) gasketed joints and large flat panels, 3) a reflective "natural" aluminum finish, and 4) an integration of the window into the panel wall as part of the total system. Because of the horizontal orientation of the panels, a girt system was employed which supported the panel ends lengthwise. Also, because of the unusual typical dimensions of the individual panel—5′9″ high by 11′6″ wide—and because the panel had to be able to take a large window, the thickness of the total exterior wall system was increased to 7½″. The panel was assembled in the factory, with windows stamped out and girts attached, so that the three-part, 12′0″ high by 11′6″ wide section could be shipped to the site as a unit and then installed directly onto the building frame. Subsequently, for reasons of economy it was necessary to change to a more conventional type of rolled-sheet metal-pan panel, and an extensive vocabulary of sizes and window openings was then elaborated to articulate the building wall.

The basic 12′0″ by 11′6″ floor-to-floor panel is subdivided into three sections (fig. 1). The lower section, 2′6″ high, corresponds to the height of parapets in the building. This panel is intended to take narrow horizontal cut-outs, which are used primarily for louvers that vent the mechanical units behind them. The middle section, 5′0″ high, allows for the major window openings. The upper section, 4′6″ high, serves as a spandrel panel for the ceiling and the main structure. The overall typical panel width, 11′6″, is determined by the basic module of the structural grid and by the building layout.

The thickness of the total exterior wall is 7½″. For the typical corner condition, a curved section of 7½″ radius is employed (fig. 2). Other outside and inside corner conditions are obtained by extending or shortening the panel size; the radial corner is also varied with a square one according to particular requirements (fig. 3).

When a recessed condition is required, the panel is sheared flush with the column (fig. 4). The column is concealed with a column cover, and the exposing of the panel end reveals the 7½″ exterior wall dimension. All panels which do not occur on the outermost plane of the building are reduced in width to 2′10½″, thereby expressing the layer of planes on the elevational surface (fig. 5). This

2′10½″ dimension is further reduced to 2′3″ at an inside corner panel, and increased to 3′6″ when the panel butts a perimeter panel. The vertical circulation elements are similarly articulated, by panels reduced in width to 2′10½″ (fig. 6).

Figure 7 shows the types of window which occur in the 12′0″ by 11′6″ panel: at sill height, the full-panel window (type A) and the half-panel window (type C); below, the half-panel strip window (type H). The first two, illustrated in place in the panel shown in figure 8, may be modified to operate as sash windows (types B and D). The strip-window cut-out below accommodates either a ventilating louver for a unit ventilator (type I), or glass (type H). Types E, F, G, and J are used for special conditions.

The window wall has an aluminum frame that fits into the girt system in the same way as do the panels (fig. 9). The mullions have a depth equal to the panel thickness (7½″), and the glass is recessed from the frame, this setback contrasting with the flatness of the panel skin. The window walls are divided into 11′6″, 5′9″, and 2′10½″ vertical sections, and 7′6″ and 4′6″ horizontal sections, thus emphasizing the grids of the plan and the facade as well as articulating their contrast with the panel skin. The system includes two basic units: type A expresses the floor-to-ceiling height, and type B, the spandrel unit. Type A is used either alone or in conjunction with type B, where double-height and triple-height spaces occur. These units of the window-wall system are designed to coordinate flexibly with those of the metal-panel wall.

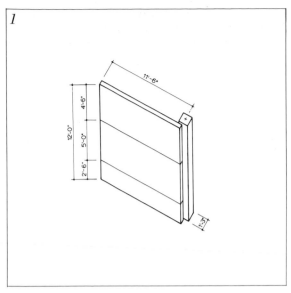

1

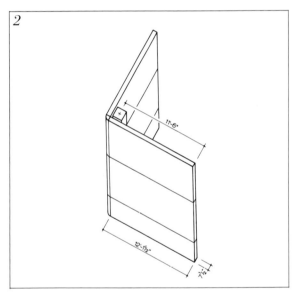

2

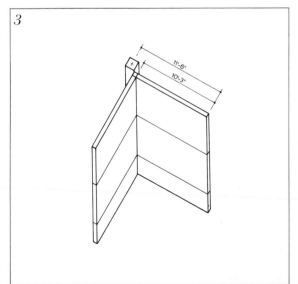

3

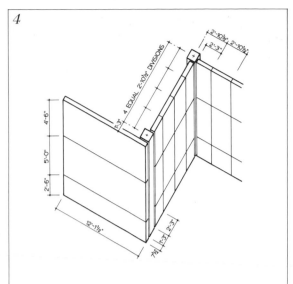

4

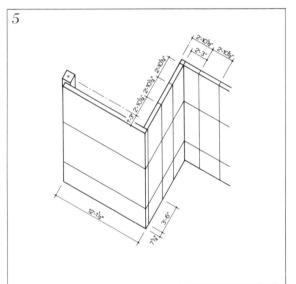

5

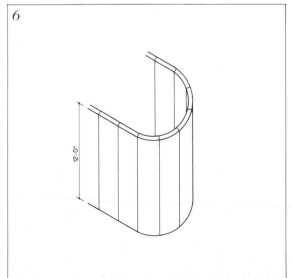

6

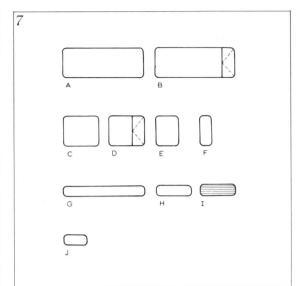

7

8

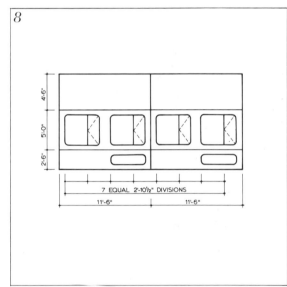

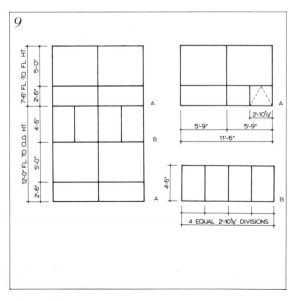

9

The original program called for a facility nearly twice this size. In 1970 one of the current architectural notions was expandability and flexibility; every component was supposed to have within it the potential for future expansion. As fate would have it—and quite fortunately—the opposite happened here, and the program continued to shrink during the stages of design. The original concept, however, remained intact.

Once when this building was nearing completion, a carload of people drove up and asked whether they could live here. When told it was a facility for the mentally disabled, they said they would like to apply for a job. To the architect this seemed a great compliment in terms of the intention to create a livable and appealing environment.

144

The two courtyards linking the east and west sides of the complex are closed off by corridors, one glazed and one open. The gymnasium and physical therapy building plugging the axis on the south faces onto the larger of the two courtyards and, since much of the rehabilitation program involves physical activity, is set up to take advantage of indoor-outdoor training areas. The courtyards are seen as an integral part of the rehabilitative and educational program as well as a focus for the surrounding buildings. They are carved and sculpted into a kind of enchanted terrain and treated as large exterior rooms, three-dimensional playgrounds offering alternative aspects: quiet and active, hard and soft, natural and constructed. The southern courtyard has an amphitheater and an elaborate system of ramped circulation. The dominant feature of the northern courtyard, besides the radial cafeteria for staff members projecting into it from the main block, is a small house, a training space simulating domestic conditions and designed to help residents make the transition from full to out-patient care.

The cladding used on all exterior surfaces of the building is a system of clear anodized aluminum panels, with windows and vent openings punched out at the factory. The horizontal placement of the panels allows for greater window-size flexibility than would be possible if standard-width panels were used in the conventional vertical position. The panel skin is modified to accommodate the specific light and enclosure requirements of the different parts of the program, as well as to express the layering of public and private spaces and the unity of the whole. The coordinated vocabulary of dimensions and openings gives a consistent, sensible expression to the building's organization and structure. At once abstract and hierarchical, the panels reflect the interrelated purposes of the center and propose a new order within the negative external environment. (For a more detailed history and description of the panel system, see the discussion on pages 138–139.)

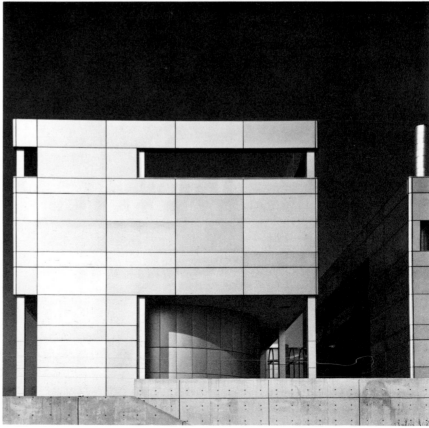

The design of the Bronx Developmental Center involved the translation of a complex program into an architecture based on significant relationships of built form. Despite the technological sophistication of its finish, the building is not an attempt to address certain theories of systems analysis current at the date of its design and their possible application to the needs of specialized communities of this type. Rather, it embodies the idea that the making of a place has most of all to do with a positive notion of community.

This is a small sampling of the interior spaces that exist within this diverse complex. The residential apartments, the medical and clinical facilities, the dental suite, the cafeteria, the auditorium, and the gymnasium all have their own character and quality, and are distinguished by the coded use of nearly four dozen colors throughout.

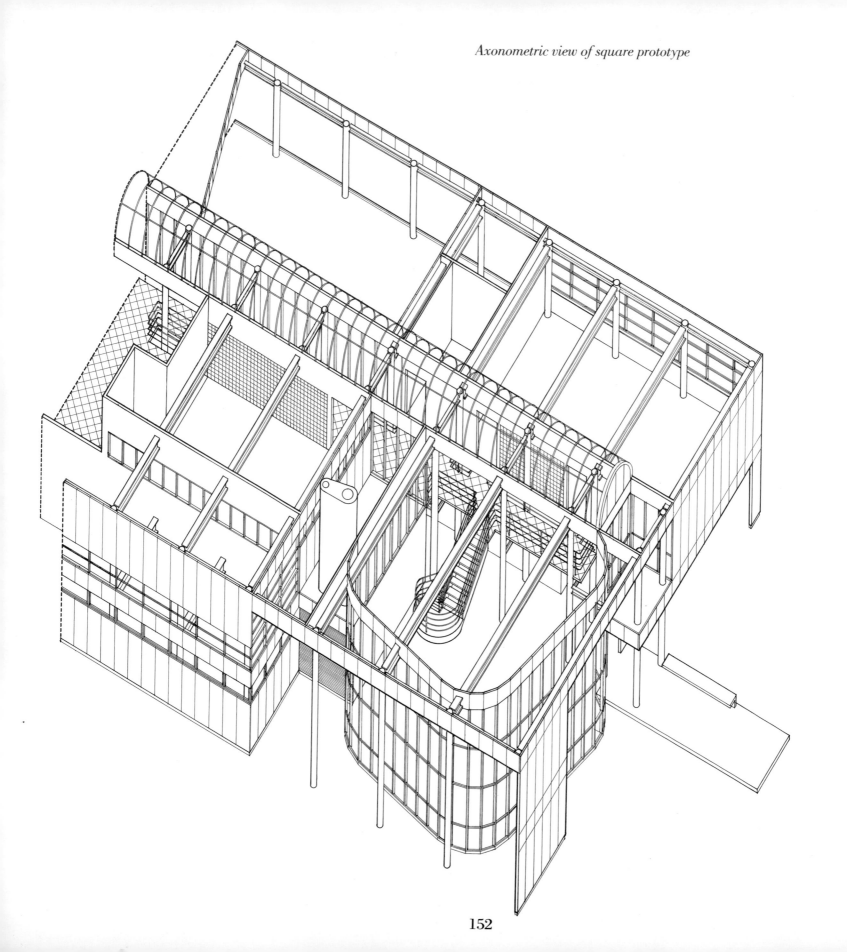

Branch Office Prototype for Olivetti

Irvine, California; Brooklyn, New York; Minneapolis, Minnesota; Boston, Massachusetts; Kansas City, Missouri; Paterson, New Jersey 1971

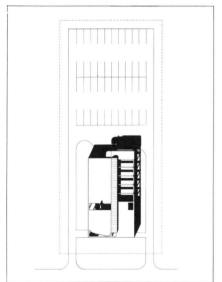

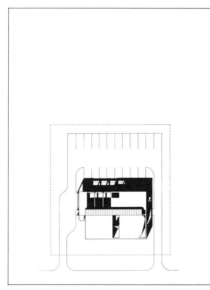

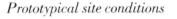

Prototypical site conditions

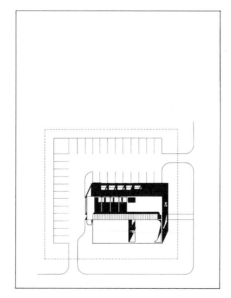

The Olivetti Corporation commissioned a sales-and-service building prototype that could be built on any site and still have an identifiable image. The design had to function either on a commercial strip or in an industrial park, and to have flexibility in size, a capacity for expansion, and a sense of self-containment.

In its pure form, the proposed prototype evokes an image of the industrial process, of prefabricated lightweight parts mass-produced in the factory and assembled on the site. Its appearance is that of a rationally ordered yet flexible space within a structure of interdependent elements. In a sense, it is an architectural expression of the client's own aesthetic of business machines, combining sophisticated technology with a refined formal order.

The building depicted on the following pages represents a basic variant of the prototype, for a square site. The entrance facades are located at opposite ends of a central spine. The main entry facade is recessed and fixed; the rear facade expresses the growth potential of the building, as the lightweight steel spiral stair need only be removed to extend the structure by the required number of modules. The building consists of three superimposed grids: a ten-foot structural grid, a two-foot grid of metal panels, and a four-foot grid of windows. These grids, flexible but with a precise formal relationship in plan and elevation, are articulated as separate, thereby imparting to each system (structure, enclosure, fenestration) an identity that is both individual and part of the larger order. As at Fredonia, a top-lit circulation strip connects all parts of the building and constitutes a major formal feature. The public or display area is distinguished by its frontal, highly glazed, free-form shape. Because a display area need not expand in the way office, service, and storage spaces do, this space can be developed as the most recognizable aspect of the building and thus lend it a strong identity.

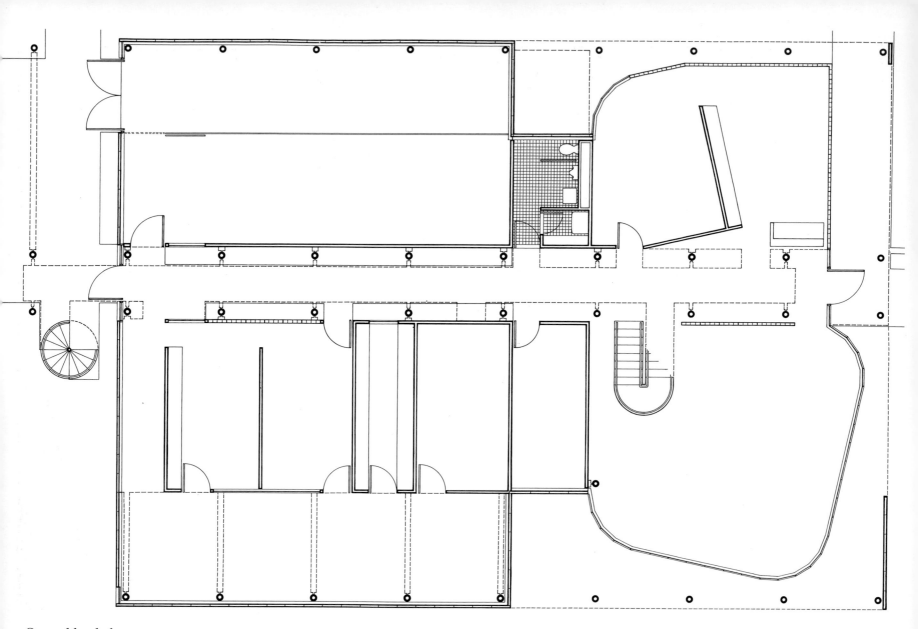

Ground level plan

| 2 | 5 | 10 | 20 |

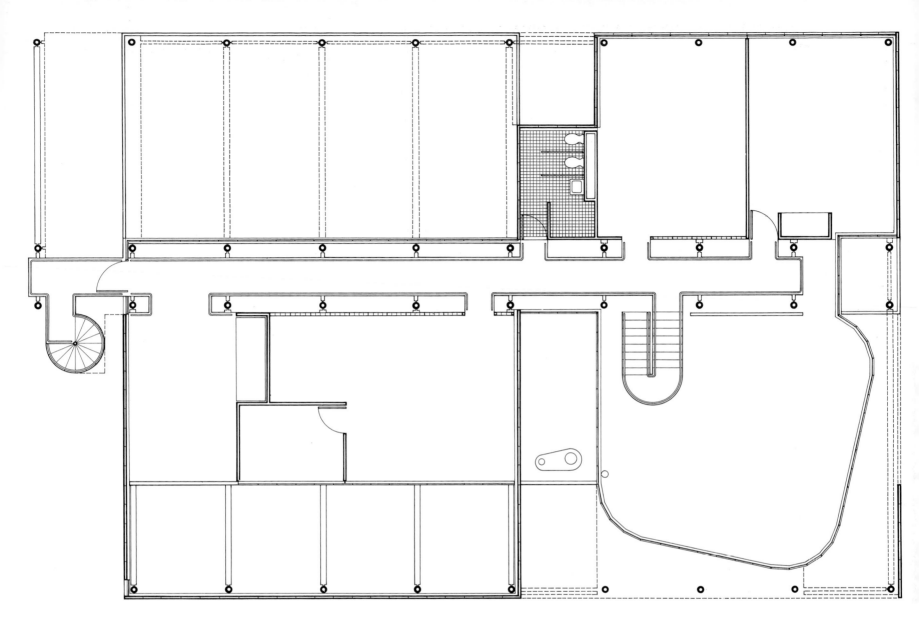

Upper level plan

Program

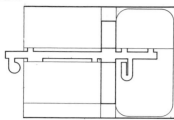

Structure

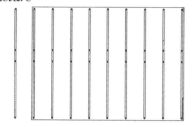

Entry

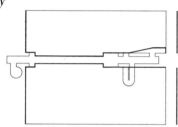

Circulation

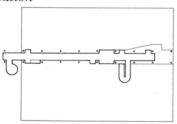

Enclosure

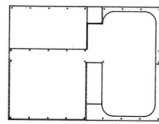

Entry elevation

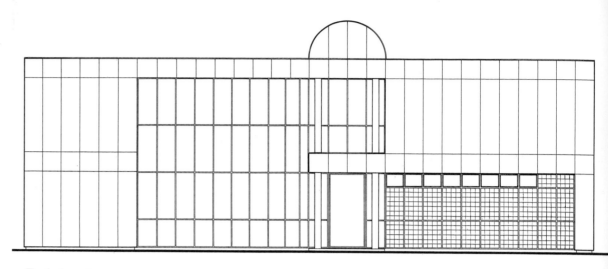

End elevation

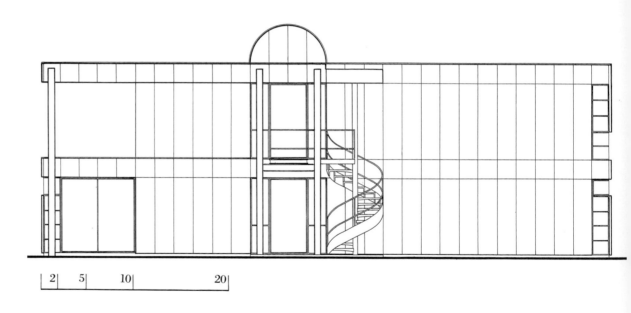

| 2| 5| 10| 20|

Front elevation

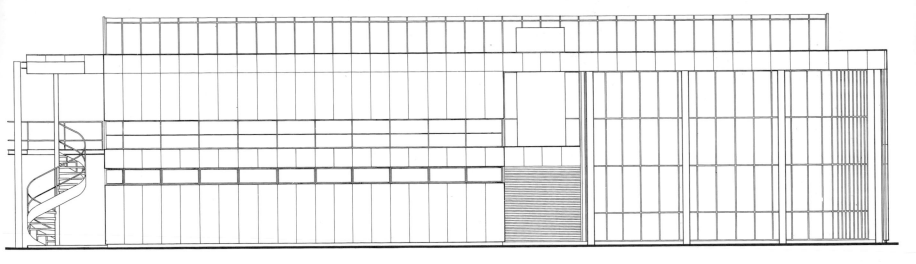

Rear elevation

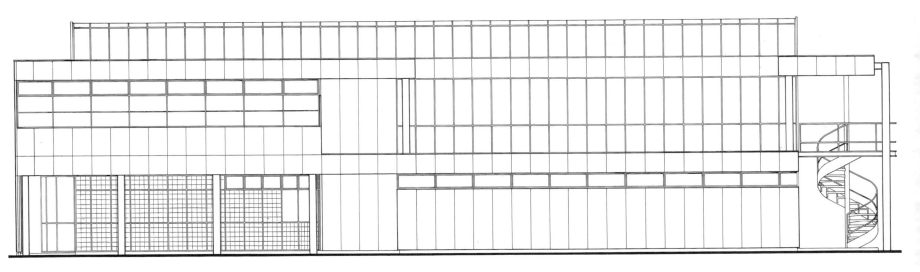

A dialogue is set up between Italian rationalist design and an American vision of technology.

Modification of the Olivetti Branch Office Prototype

Riverside, California; Albuquerque, New Mexico; Tucson, Arizona; Fort Worth, Texas; Portland, Maine; Memphis, Tennessee; Roanoke, Virginia
1971

Several of the Olivetti facilities required much less space than those for which the original prototype was proposed. A modification was designed that retains the basic organizational structure and disposition of the elements. Because of its smaller size and its location in areas where the building codes are less restrictive, the building is framed in wood, and the exterior is finished in fiberboard panels.

The original intent of the prototype, to fabricate the components of all the buildings at one time and in one place, shipping the unassembled parts directly to the sites or storing them until needed, proved to be unfeasible given the realities of labor, materials, storage, and shipping costs. The modified prototype reflects the fact that the use of mass-produced components is not in all cases a certain means of saving money.

Olivetti's pioneering intention to build quality commercial buildings in Europe and North and South America was unique in the corporate world in the 1960s and 1970s, and set a standard which other corporations later came to emulate. Unfortunately, owing to the financial situation at the time, the buildings pictured on these pages, as well as other Olivetti projects by such architects as Le Corbusier, James Stirling, and Hans Hollein, were never realized.

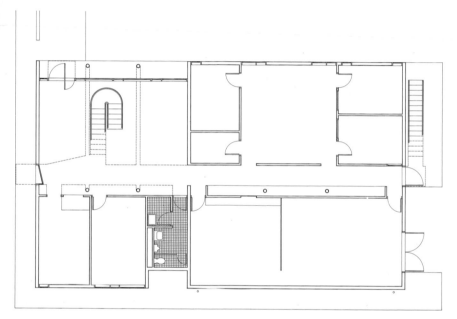

Ground level plan

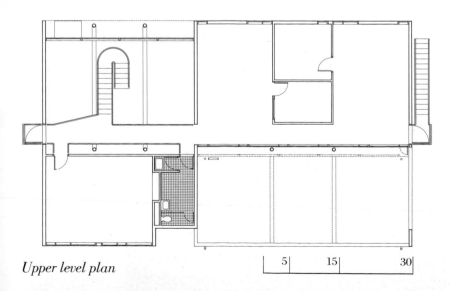

Upper level plan

5   15   30

161

Cut-away axonometric view

Dormitory for the Olivetti Training Center

Tarrytown, New York
1971

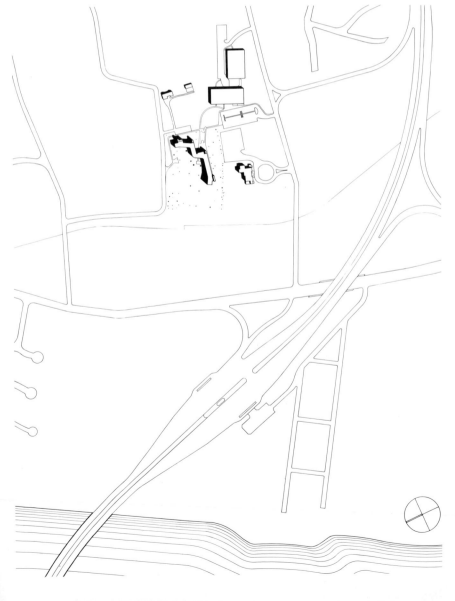

A dormitory facility for an adjacent Olivetti Training Center, this building is designed to house two hundred Olivetti trainees for periods of four to six weeks. It is one of two Olivetti buildings planned for a specific site, the other being the corporate headquarters for Washington, D.C. The four-story dormitory follows the contours of a sloping site, winding its way through century-old trees. The curving W-configuration of the ground plan reflects three major site considerations: the location of the trees, the inclination of the slope to the Hudson River below, and zoning laws and side-lot restrictions which force the building to turn down the slope while maintaining a north-south orientation.

The building accommodates the trainees in double rooms and contains a number of communal and recreational spaces. A continuous circulation spine follows the outside edge of the W-configuration on four similar floors. The two-person units lining this single-loaded corridor face the river. Where the building turns down the slope, two floors are gained below, and these house services and social spaces. At the elbows of the curves, the corridors meet in small open areas, gathering places for the trainees. The main entrance is at the center of the building, and opens into a four-story public space which resolves the converging horizontal and vertical vectors of the scheme. Balconies projecting from the upper-level corridors into the central space unify the floors. The elevator and stair towers pulled out from the main structure serve as counterpoints to this centralized focus.

The articulation of the aluminum panels on the front elevation relates rhythmically and thematically to that on the more open rear elevation. At the inflection points of the curved surface, the panels give way to glass: on the rear, a balconied, eroded section of glazing responds to the axis of entry, while on the front, the panels are replaced by curving runs of windows.

163

Axonometric view
of typical bedrooms

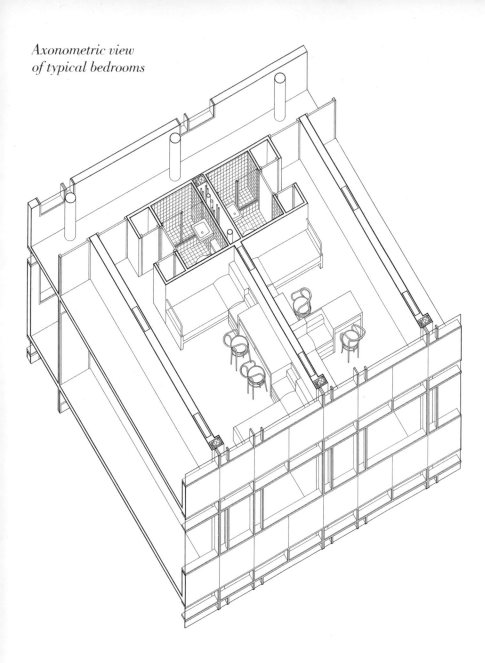

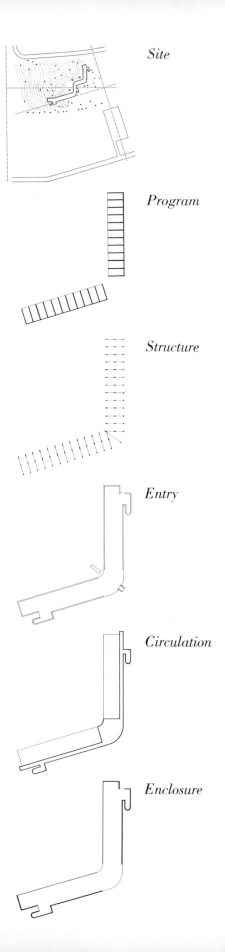

Site

Program

Structure

Entry

Circulation

Enclosure

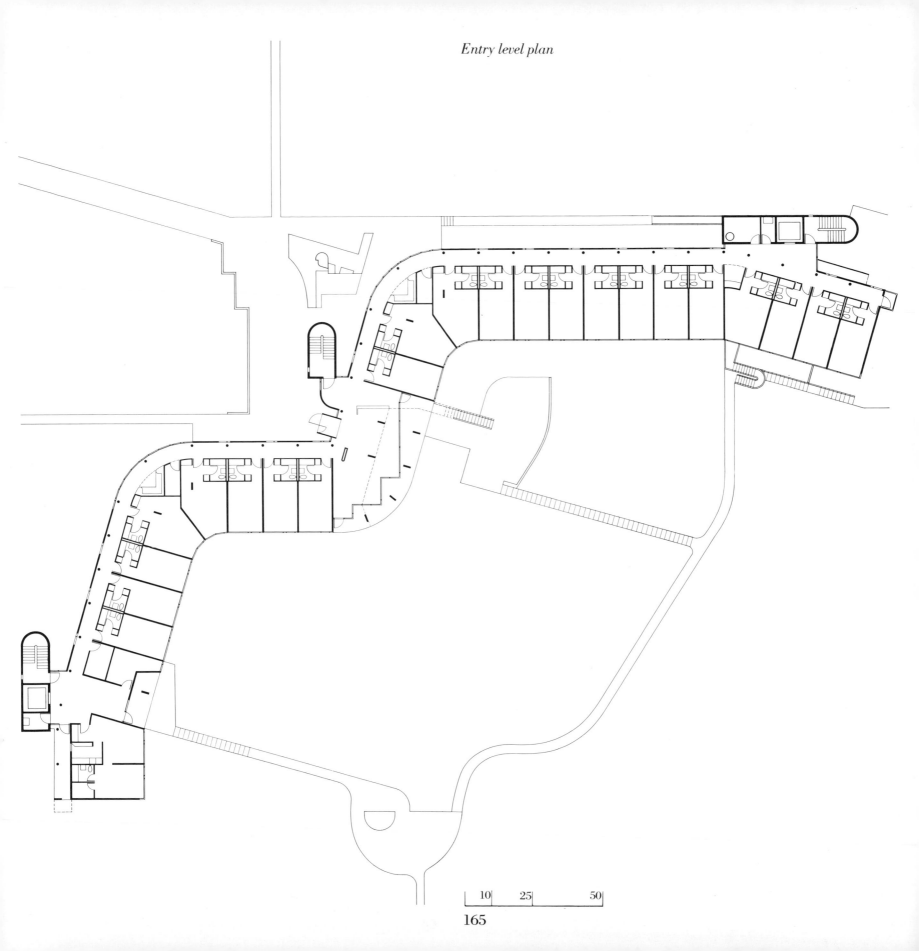

Entry level plan

North elevation

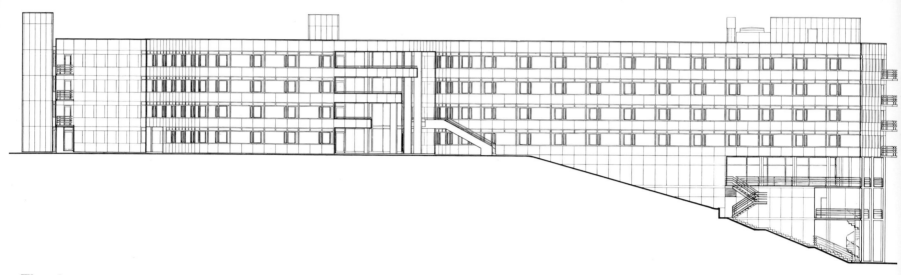

West elevation

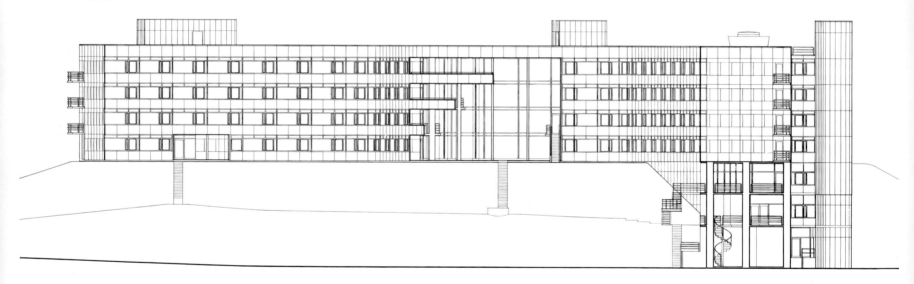

| 10 | 25 | 50 |

South elevation

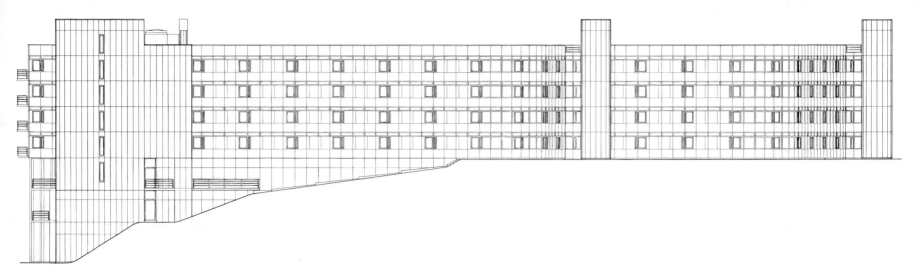

East elevation

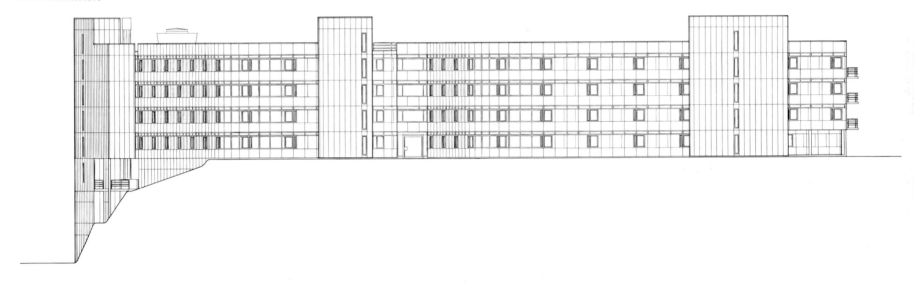

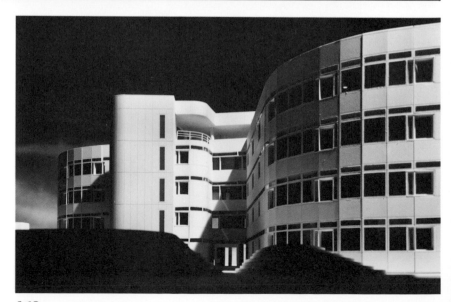

This is the first building to break
from the exigencies of the right
angle in order to respond more
organically to the topography of its
site. The section preserves the
geometry of planar layering.

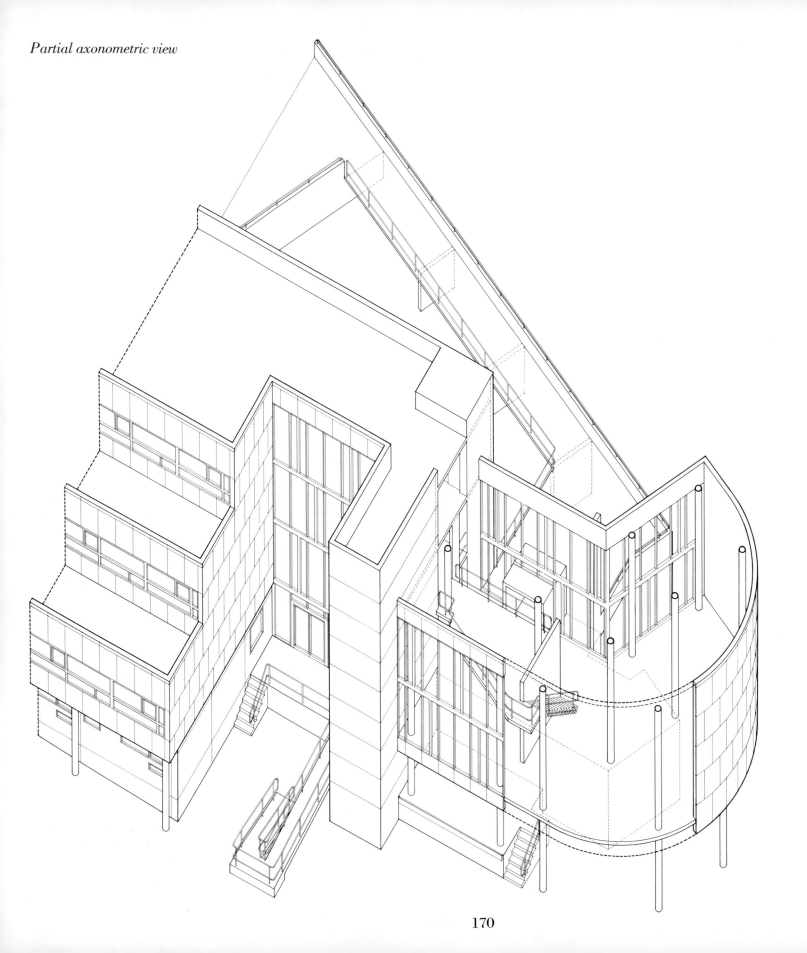

Olivetti Headquarters Building

Fairfax, Virginia
1971

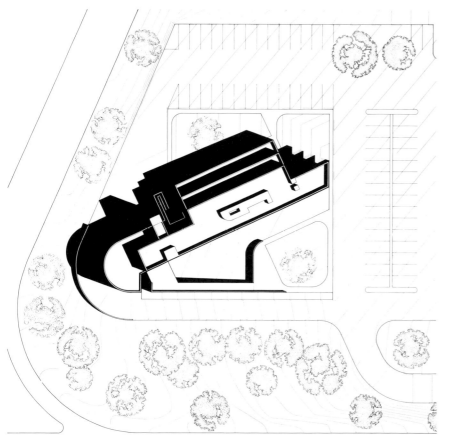

This proposed office headquarters for Olivetti is on the outskirts of Washington, D.C., near U.S. 50, in a semi-urban industrial development strip offering little visual amenity. The diagonal slope of the site and its corner location determined the building's siting and orientation.

Three separate sales operations—local, regional, and national—are housed in the building, along with a service and spare parts division. Each operation is located on a separate level; the stepped levels are intended to express formally the hierarchical organization of the sales structure. A double-loaded corridor on each floor separates the zones of private and public space, dividing the fixed office spaces on one side from the free-planned spaces for administrative and clerical personnel on the other. The vertical circulation is pulled to one end of the spine, and the separation is articulated by glazing in elevation.

On the other side of the vertical circulation and at the corner of the site, the office building format is modified to accommodate a large, open display space for computers and office machinery. At the joint where this curved display area meets the circulation elements are the two entries to the building. The main entry, to the sales and administrative area, is reached by way of a ramped exterior bridge on the south elevation, parallel to the road. The secondary entry, to the service area, is reached by a driveway that takes advantage of the slope of the site; it is located on the north elevation at the lower ground level.

Although all the buildings for Olivetti were conceived as independent structures, they reflect common themes and employ similar materials. Like Olivetti's products, they share an aesthetic and provide the company with a recognizable architectural identity.

171

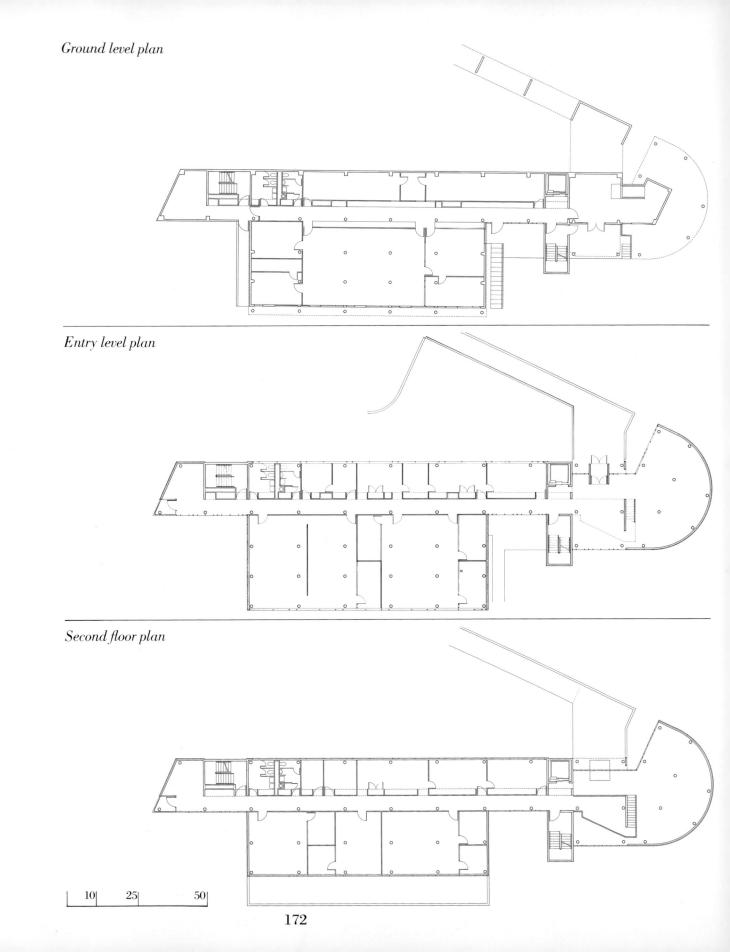

Ground level plan

Entry level plan

Second floor plan

10 25 50

Third floor plan

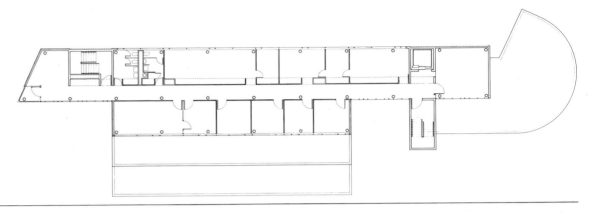

North elevation

South elevation

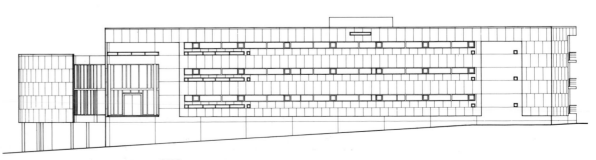

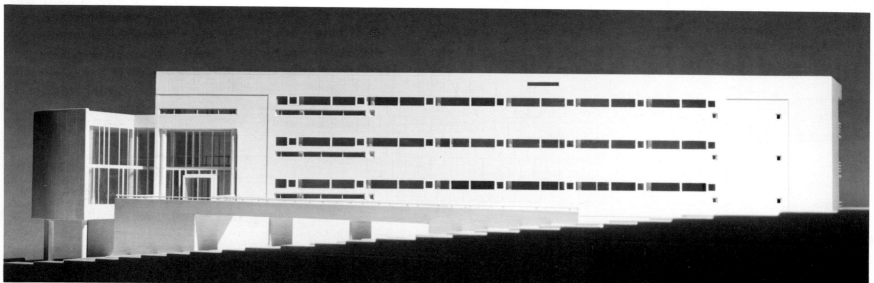

Designs are inevitably changed by the realities of construction. Frozen in the "cardboard" state of abstract models, the Olivetti buildings retain some of the purity of an International Style image. They need to be transformed by a real context.

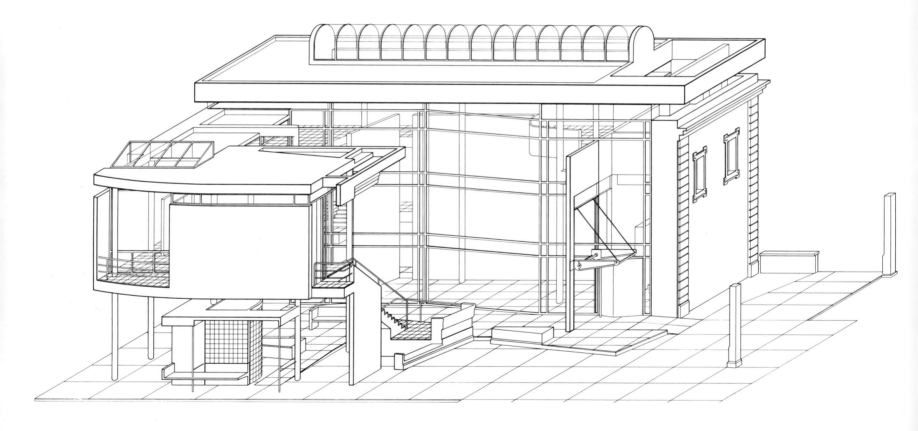

176

Museum of Modern Art at the Villa Strozzi

Florence, Italy
1973

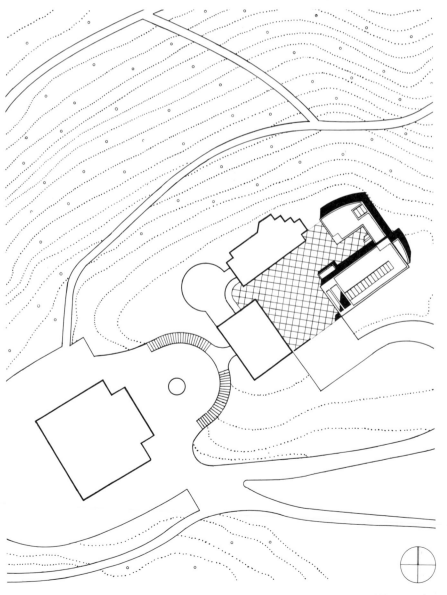

This project involves one part of an existing four-building complex on eight hectares of land in Florence, to be restored by the city of Florence for use as a municipal museum of modern art. The four buildings—a villa, an orangery, and two stables enclosing a courtyard—were designed in the second half of the nineteeth century by the Florentine architect Giuseppe Poggi. They are set in a landscape of Tuscan orchards and cypress trees on the south bank of the Arno River, overlooking the city from an elevation of about forty meters. The project illustrated here is for a conversion of the stable on the east side of the courtyard to an exhibition building for sculpture and painting.

Originally, an interior renovation was envisioned, but the dilapidated condition and undistinguished architectural quality of most parts of the building convinced the Superintendent of Monuments that only the two principal exterior walls, visible from the approach and enclosing the courtyard, were worth preserving. Under the present proposal, these walls are to be restored to their original character, while most of the remainder of the building will be gutted. The new construction, contained by the old walls, will open to north light and to views over the city.

The new roof plane is to be raised above the existing cornice, extending beyond the old masonry walls. Especially from inside the courtyard where one will see them strongly contrasted to the light steel-and-glass frame of the new construction, the old walls will appear mainly as screening facades, the new structure rising independently above and inside them.

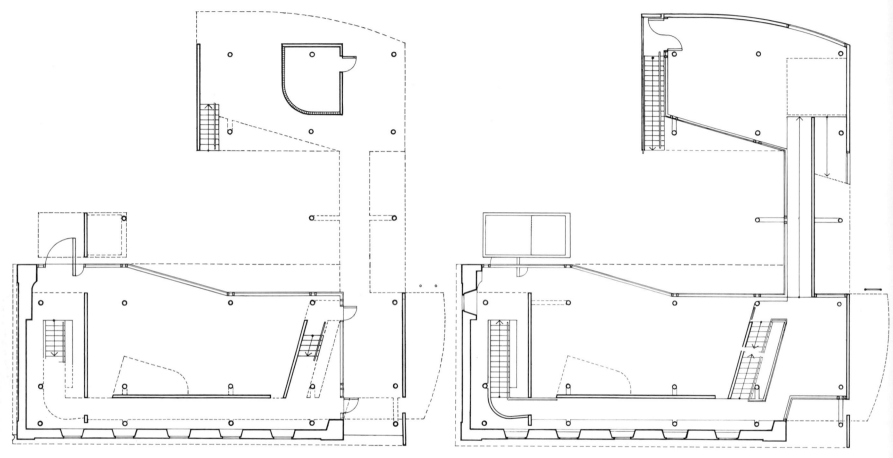

Middle level plan

The concept for relating the old to the new here was that of a building within a building—a flexible, contemporary public space within an old masonry shell. The lightweight steel-and-glass structure open to the courtyard serves to fill the old walls with light and air, integrating a new form of architecture with an older one.

On the courtyard side, the ramped circulation and the exhibition pavilion at ground level define a new courtyard space, onto which the upper-level galleries open. This courtyard, for the display of sculpture, is conceived as a stage set against the backdrop of the buildings. Within, the exhibition space is organized around an interior circulation ramp allowing continuous, controlled movement and bridging the two main gallery spaces. These two skylit galleries will accommodate changing art exhibitions, while the impressive views of Florence framed by large windows will provide a permanent exhibition of the city.

5 | 15 | 30 |

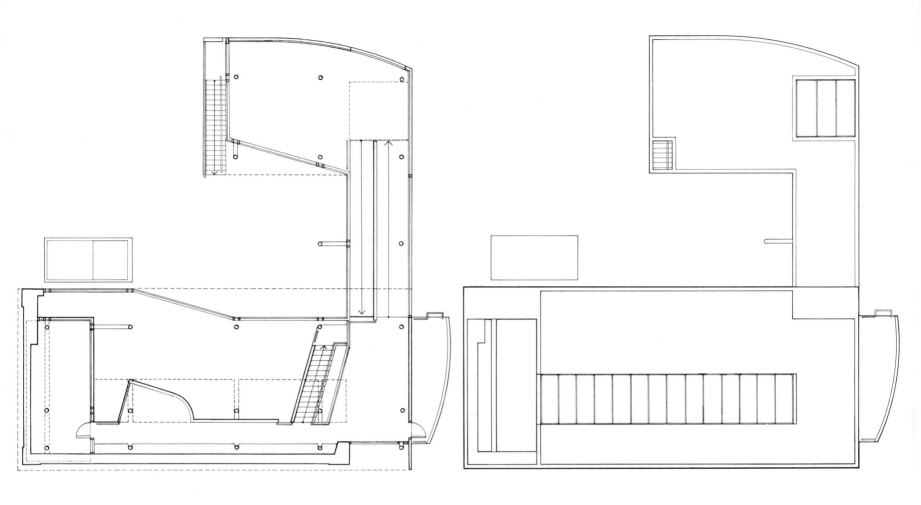

Southeast elevation

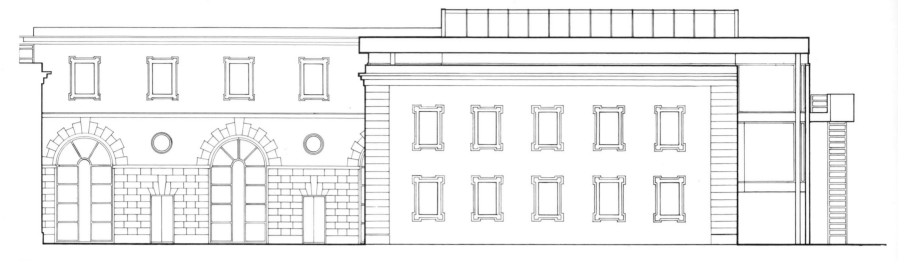

Northwest elevation

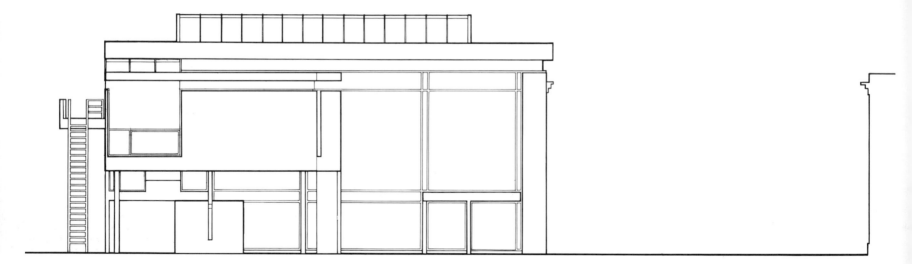

Southwest elevation

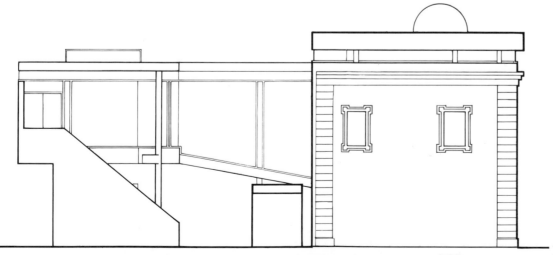

5   15   30

180

Longitudinal section through large exhibition space

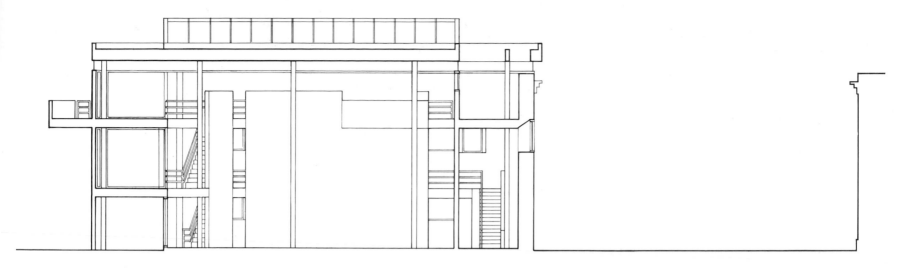

Cross section through large exhibition space

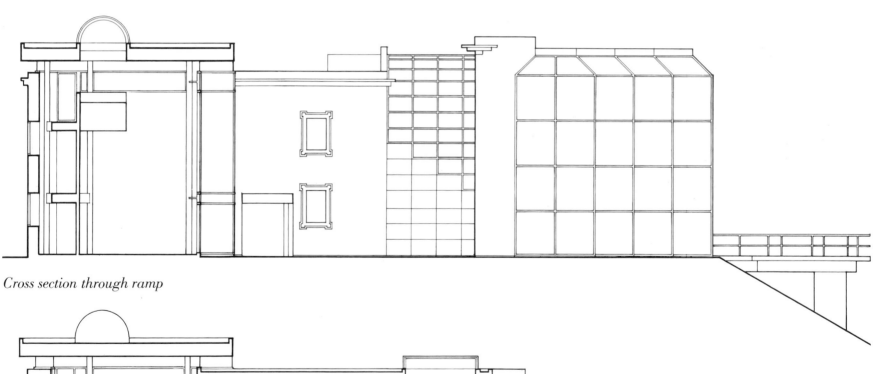

Cross section through ramp

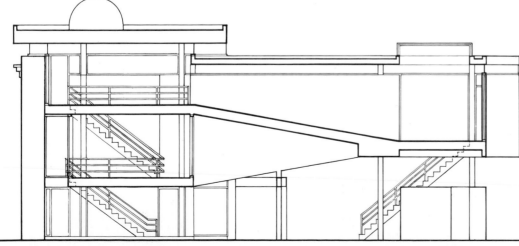

181

The model and the stables in their present condition are seen from the same view.

Cornell University Undergraduate Housing

Ithaca, New York
1974

Cornell University overlooks both the town of Ithaca and Cayuga Lake from its position between two deep gorges that descend to the lake below. The site designated for these two dormitory buildings is in Cayuga Heights on the edge of the campus, flanked by private homes and the North Campus dormitories. A section of the site has already been developed by the university as open playing fields and a large parking area. At present the site contains undulating golf fairways, with clusters of large oaks, beeches, and pines.

Traditionally the university has built two types of housing for its students, dormitories and married-student housing, but never undergraduate coeducational apartments similar to those available off campus. The opportunity to do so arose because students requested a wider range of housing alternatives than was available in traditional dormitory facilities. This facility for five hundred students, made up of units accommodating from four to six people, departs from the traditional collegiate cloister as well as from the dormitory cell. In acknowledging the trend toward informal living, the apartment layouts are designed to handle different kinds of mixed occupancy. All units consist of kitchen, bathroom, living-dining space, and individual bedrooms.

The serpentine form of the projected four-story buildings evolved as a response to the rolling terrain and trees. The two dormitories follow the contours of the site, bridging the open space of the fairways, and interrupting the natural flow of the landscape as little as possible. Because of the grade, the ground story of one building is on level with the second story of the other, and both structures are low in comparison with the surrounding trees. The lower two floors contain three-bedroom (four-person) duplex apartments. At the bends of the undulating structures, as well as on the upper two floors, are single-story apartments. These are designed to accommodate four and six people.

185

Ground and upper level floor plans

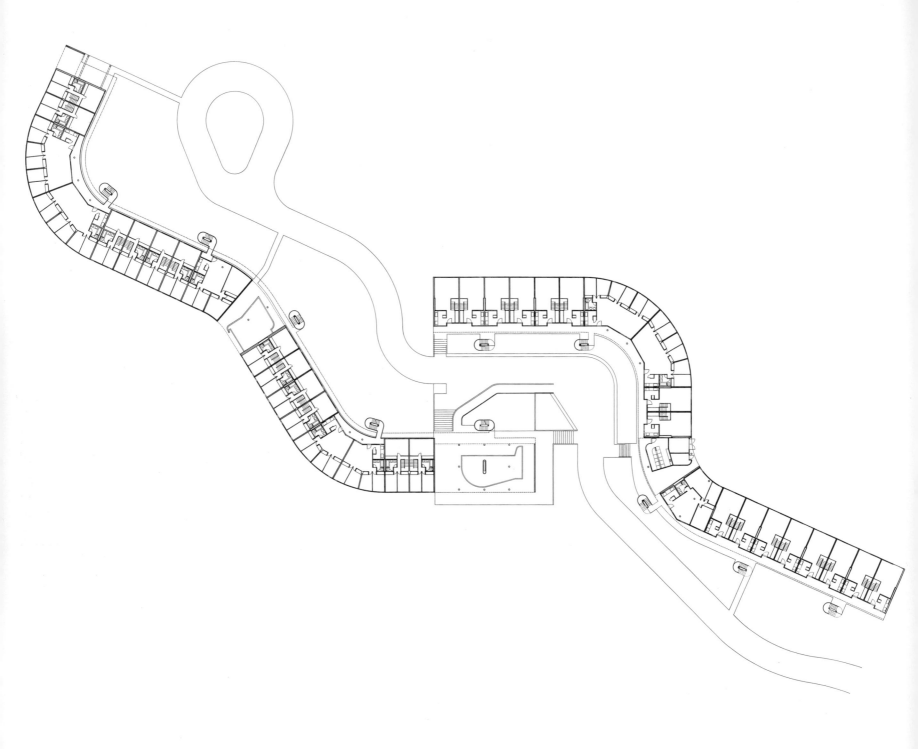

20| 50| 100|

Partial south elevation

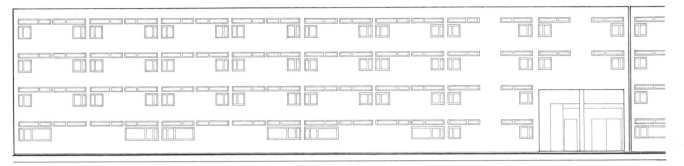

Partial north elevation

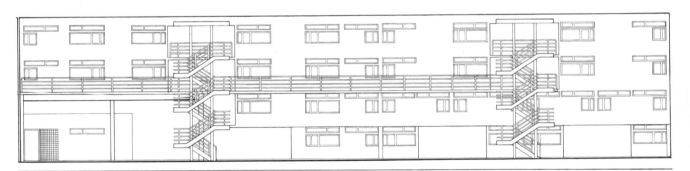

Cross section through courtyard

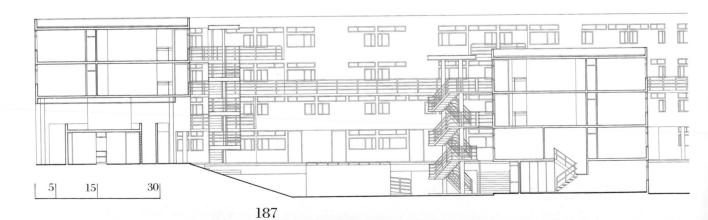

| 5 | 15 | 30 |

The two entry elevations—the public facades—are diagonally offset from each other across a court and a looping path. In deference to the landscape, there is no formalized system of movement through the terrain, and entrance and circulation are decentralized. The exterior access to the individual units is either from ground level or, at the third level, from an exterior balcony that runs the entire length of the building and permits circulation through the upper levels without returning to the ground. Erosions at ground level, balconies, and stair towers along the taut, curving facade planes mark the circulation points. On the rear facades, the bedroom spaces look outward to the landscape from an uninterrupted plane, thereby maintaining the distinction between the public and private sides of the dormitories.

The fireproof structure consists of poured-in-place concrete slabs and concrete-block bearing walls spaced at seventeen-foot intervals. Columns are introduced only where the bearing walls recede, to articulate the change from duplex to single-story units, and where the exterior wall is cut back at ground level.

Since the Dormitory for the Olivetti Training Center was never brought to fruition, this project for Cornell, for a similar program, intentionally continued an investigation of that earlier plan-form. Here, the shape and interrelationship of the two building volumes make for a large-scale sculptural ensemble. Rather than blocks imposed on a landscape, the two bypassing serpentine forms appear to be walls meandering across a hillside.

The Atheneum

New Harmony, Indiana
1975–1979

The Atheneum, located on a rolling plain near the banks of the Wabash River at the edge of New Harmony, is the starting point for the tour of the historic town, and is intended to serve as a center for visitor orientation and community cultural events. The town's physical and symbolic link with the water and the outside world, the building is a place of arrival and initiation. Its architecture is conceived in terms of the linked ideas of architectural promenade and historical journey.

Historically New Harmony was one of the most significant utopian communities in America. Founded in 1815 by George Rapp's Harmony Society and then reestablished in 1825 by the British social reformer Robert Owen, it constituted itself on a socialist model of cooperative society. Architecture, like the phalanstery which was to be built in New Harmony by the architect Stedman Whitwell, assumed the role of agent of social and economic change; in the words of Owen's French counterpart Charles Fourier, the problem was "to find the architectural conditions most appropriate to the needs of individual and social life, and to construct according to these conditions the type of habitation which would constitute the social beehive of the rural commune." This utopian vision of the relation between habitation and social life may still be felt in the now-restored Harmonist architecture extant in the town.

The Wabash floods to varying heights every year, and building on a flood plain is not without problems. It is for this reason that the Atheneum is elevated on a podium of earth. Like Rapp's "boatload of knowledge" which arrived in New Harmony with its cargo of settlers, the building seems to float above the water, a porcelain-paneled object from another time and context.

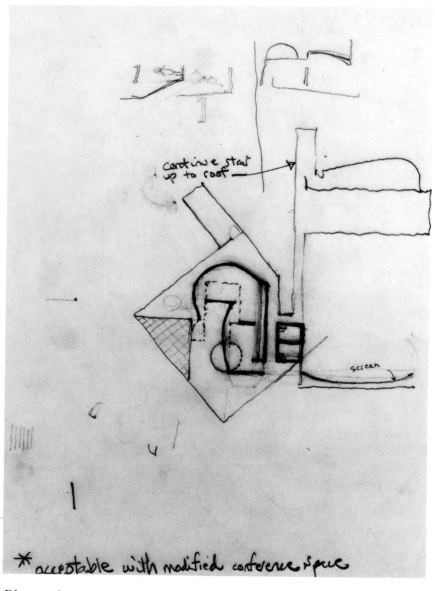

continue stair
up to roof

screen

* acceptable with modified conference space

Plan studies

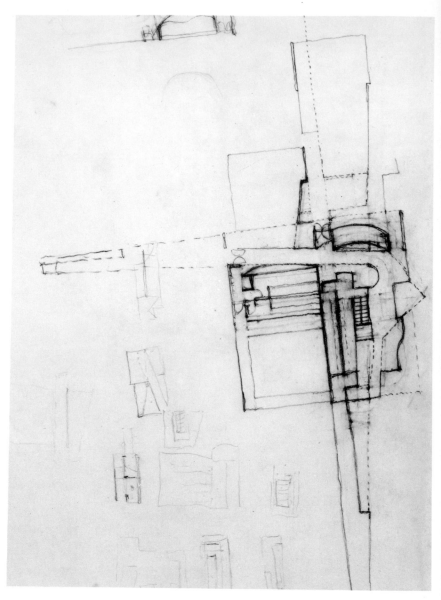

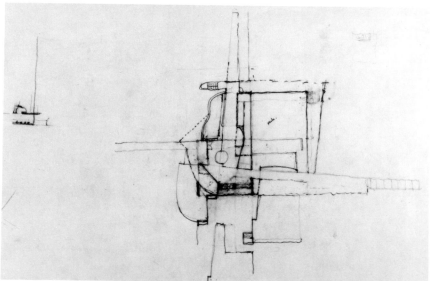

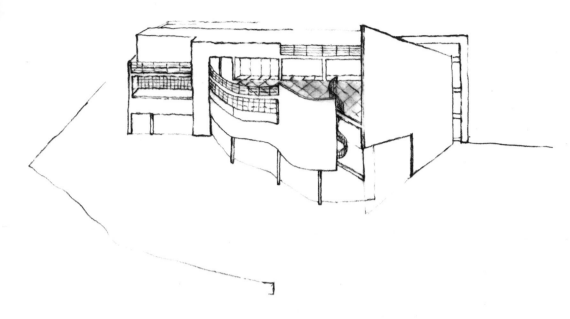

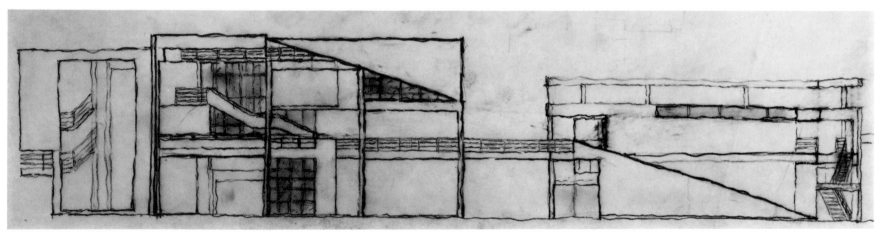

Elevation studies

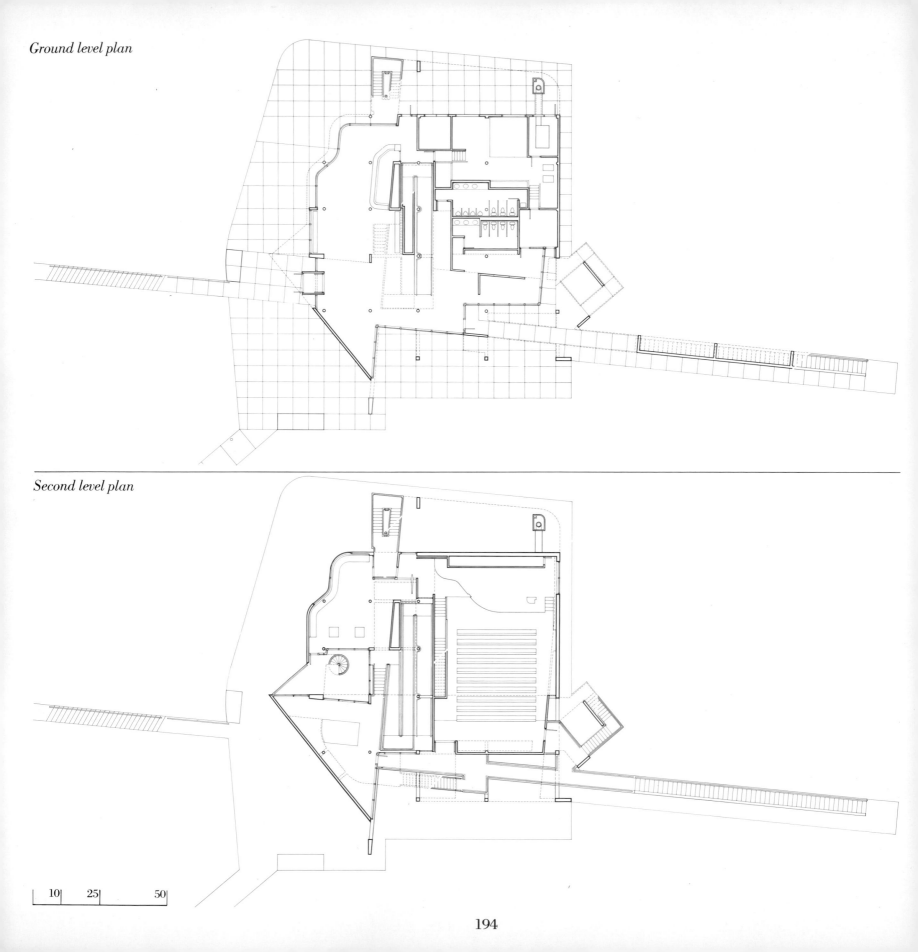

Ground level plan

Second level plan

| 10 | 25| | 50| |

Third level plan

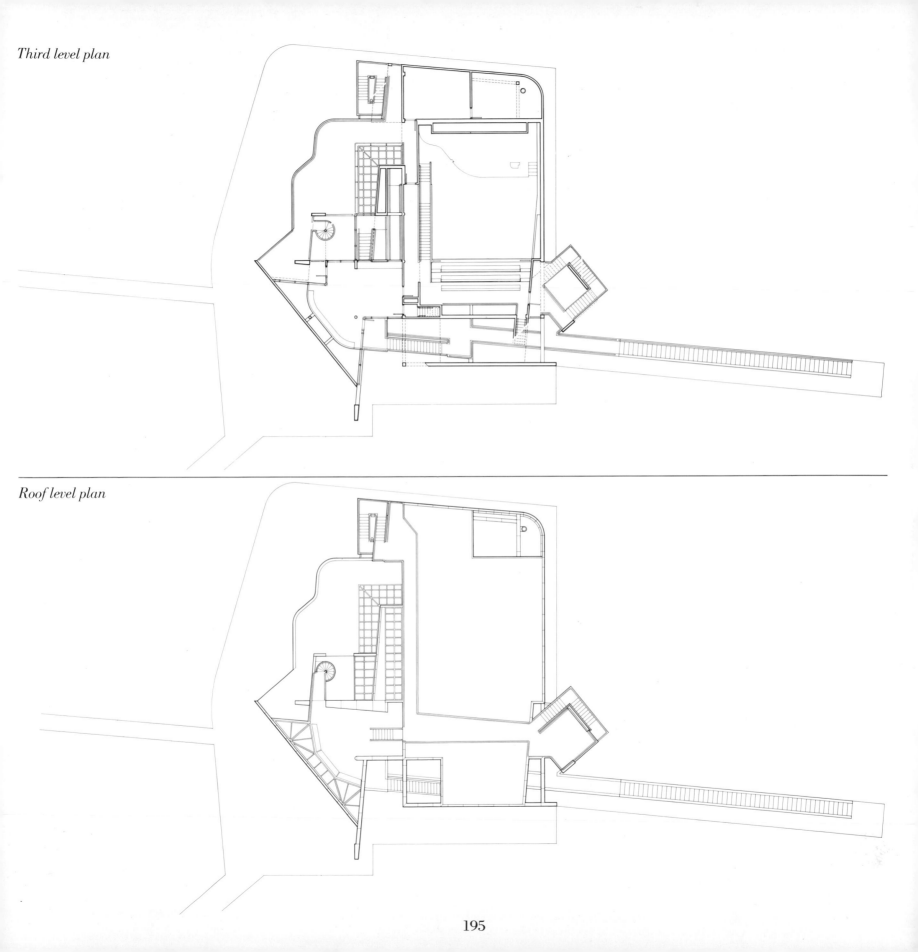

Roof level plan

*Longitudinal section
through entry foyer facing east*

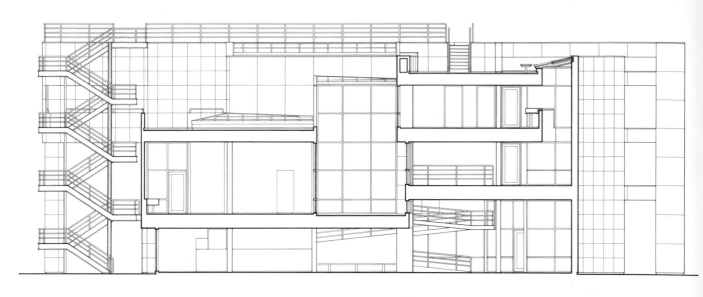

*Longitudinal section
through auditorium facing west*

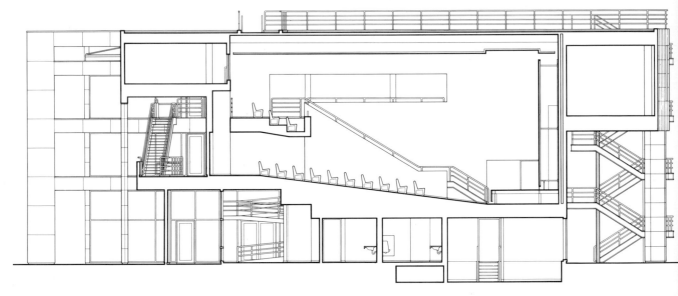

Cross section facing north

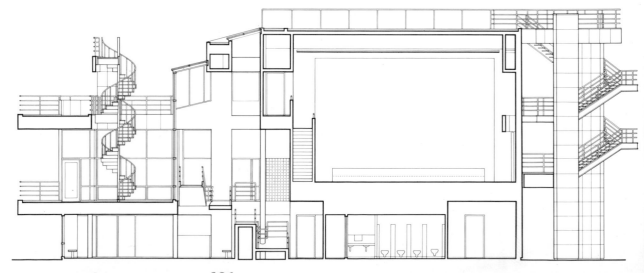

| 2 | 5 | 10 | 20 |

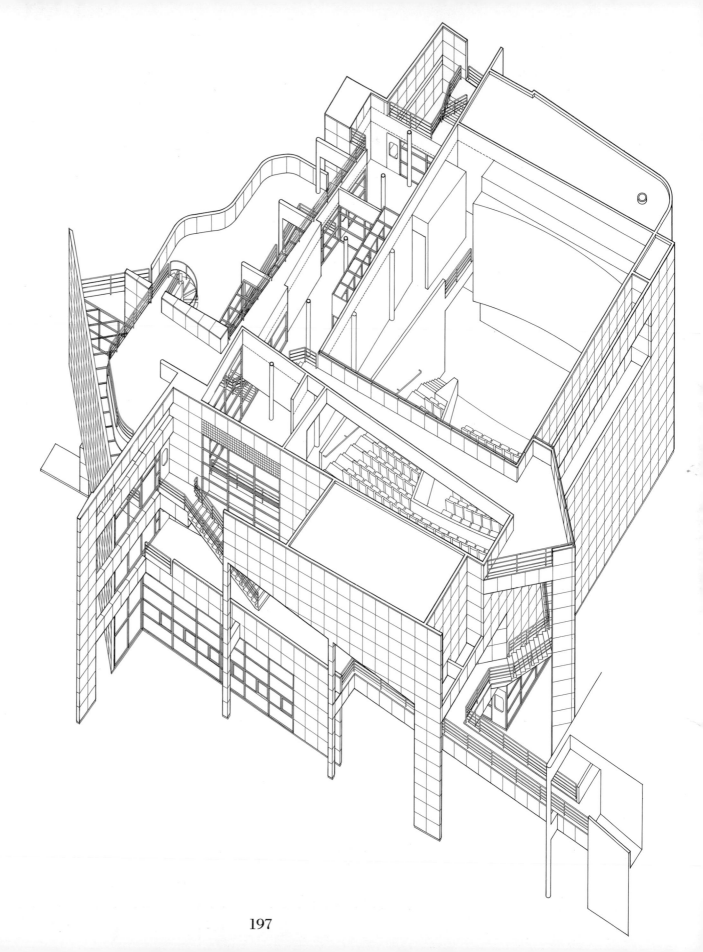

A visitor arriving by boat is deposited on a path that leads up through the field to the building. On reaching the podium, the water route is joined by a path from the parking lot. A three-story plane set at a forty-degree angle to the podium acknowledges the point of arrival. This plane conveys the visitor to the actual portal, a doorway shifted five degrees in orientation to announce the primary grid of the building. The building has two dispositions: the primary orthogonal grid, a response to the existing street grid of the town, and a secondary grid shifted five degrees. The latter takes its cue from the skew edge of the town and the river bank.

Once the visitor has crossed the threshold, the entry box, like a small compression chamber, propels him past adjacent pockets of space to the foot of the internal circulation ramp. From here, the entire movement system through the building is a continuous experience, of which the interior ramp is chief mediator and armature. This ramped circulation spine, as it leads from the entry-orientation level to the exhibition and lounge spaces to the film theater, progressively unfolds the content of the building.

As the ramp winds upward from the orthogonal grid and regains the five-degree offset orientation of the path from the river, the entire building is set in motion, the geometry of overlaid grids inducing a sense of spatial compression at certain points, tension at others; as one circulation path inflects toward another, one feels spaces narrowing, then opening up—of grids almost colliding. This collision resonates throughout the complex interior as the ramp, illuminated by a flood of light from above, resolves the two grids in plan and section. The ramp arrives on the second level at an exhibition space which contains a model of old New Harmony lit by a canted skylight. The light penetrating from skylights throughout the building serves to dematerialize the shifting wall planes and throws the changing ceiling and floor heights into relief. Upon reaching the exhibition space on the third level, the visitor can look back on the internal route he has traveled, through staggered interior slots and windows framing the essential spaces, as well as forward to what is to come. Framed views to the exterior allow controlled glimpses and anticipations of the town and the landscape. Finally the visitor moves to the rooftop and upper-level terraces where the route of egress takes him through punctured planes that continually refer to and refract the scene outside.

At the uppermost roof terrace, the visitor finds himself confronted with the town. On axis with the major monuments of New Harmony— the restored log cabins of the Harmonists, the Pottery Studio, the Roofless Church designed by Philip Johnson, and the commemorative gardens built in honor of Paul Tillich—this small space affords a panoramic vista like that from the prow of a ship. From here the visitor descends by way of a second ramp—this one elongated and stepped, an uncoiled version of the interior one—leading out of the building to the adjacent restaurant and amphitheater, and into the town itself.

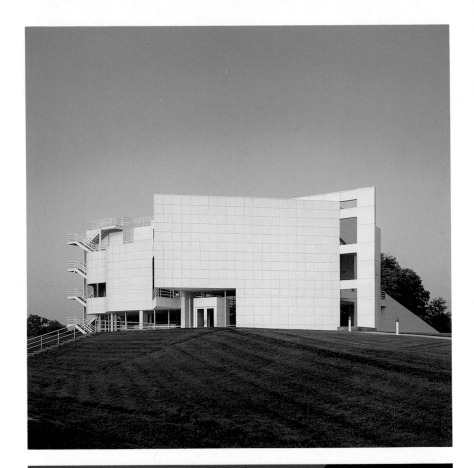

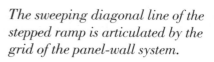

The sweeping diagonal line of the stepped ramp is articulated by the grid of the panel-wall system.

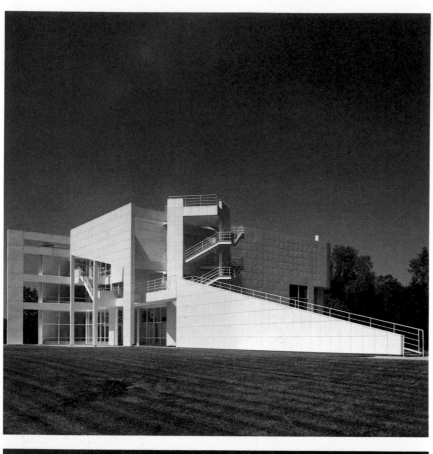

The elevated walkway at the third level is the final link in the circulation system ending with the stepped ramp leading out to the historic area.

The 15,000 square foot building of steel frame construction is faced with prefabricated 2'6" square porcelain-enameled panels.

A recurrent criticism of this building seems to be that it has too much architecture. Think of the "extravagances" of Baroque architecture.

The white interior and gray carpeted floors and seating enhance the stark simplicity of the theater.

All four levels can be seen through the south window wall. At night, dramatic lighting reveals the building's architectural complexity.

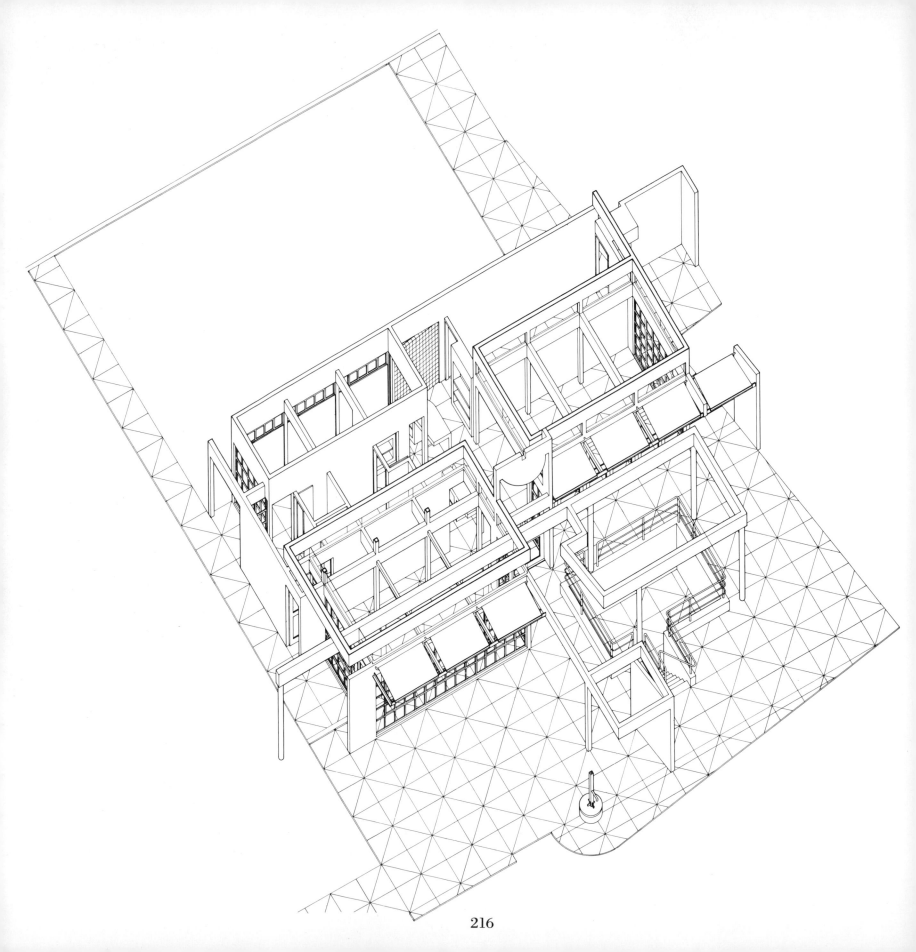

216

Sarah Campbell Blaffer
Pottery Studio

New Harmony, Indiana
1975–1978

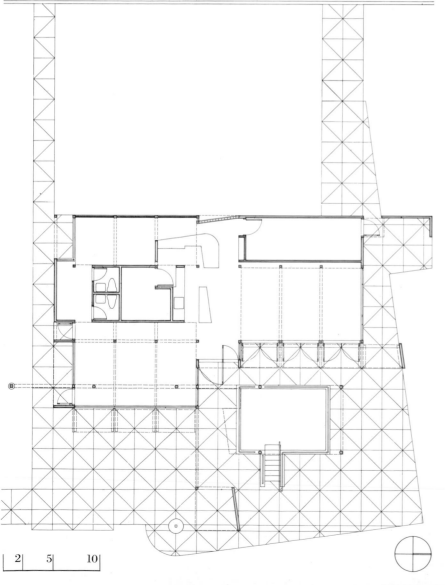

This pavilionlike structure, commemorating Sarah Campbell Blaffer's dedication to the creative crafts, contains a pottery workshop as well as an office and small exhibition area. Used primarily in summer, it is designed to foster the free rein of creative energies and social interchange.

The building sits on a flat site on axis with Philip Johnson's Roofless Church just to the east and the Atheneum to the west. This axis, slightly inflected by the angle of the adjacent fields, determines the primary orientation, and is reflected in the building as a central circulation spine. The series of planar partitions along the axis becomes progressively more solid, until a rear plane with minimal fenestration ends the movement, serving as a back wall. While this orthogonal geometry is in large part intended as a foil to the rounded hexagonal volume of the Roofless Church, it is the church's height that determines the horizontal datum of the roof line. The cornices, canopies, and planes slipping over, under, and past each other create a complex interplay of horizontal and vertical relationships and a dynamic between roofed and roofless spaces.

The materials are chosen to convey a sense of openness, transparency, and pavilionlike delicacy: wood, glass, glass block, steel, canvas awnings. The large existing trees provide a natural contrast to the white structure. The railed pit with a stairway leading down into it, underneath an open-frame canopy, is an excavation site containing the foundations of an original Harmonist house which stood on this spot until it was destroyed by a fire. This archaeological indentation in the earth adds another conceptual layer to the architecture erected over it: in its literal and symbolic depth, it enriches the meanings of solid and void, past and present culture.

217

The Pottery Studio, with its front lawn and walkway, relates to the domestic scale of the houses of New Harmony, as well as to the public scale of the Atheneum and the Roofless Church, with which it is on axis. At the foot of the free-standing gate element seen in the photograph at left is a memorial stone.

Manchester Civic Center

Manchester, New Hampshire
1977

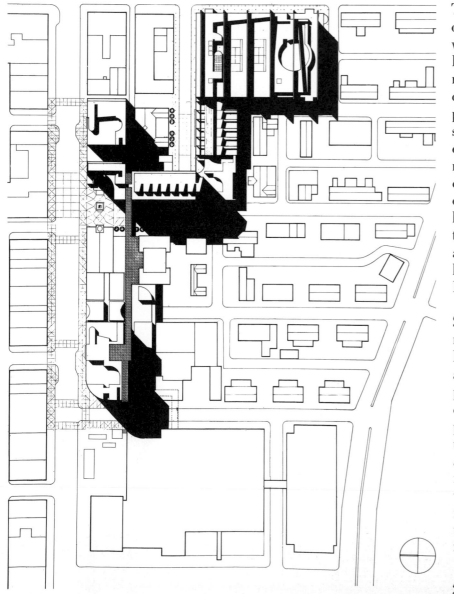

The decline of downtown Manchester, once a flourishing urban center on the Merrimack River, began, as in many other American cities, with the end of World War II and the acceleration of suburbanization. By the 1970s a comprehensive plan of revitalization had become necessary. The proposed scheme shown here focuses on an area of the city just west of Elm Street, a major traffic artery with an emerging pattern of commercial growth. As the site is not directly on Elm, a special kind of relationship had to be created with the street. An effective device was borrowed from the typical developer shopping mall: the use of a major element of attraction at either end of the complex. In this case, the two magnets on Elm Street are a double office-tower building on the north and a 250-room hotel on the south, both twelve stories high. In between them, the plan consists of a two-story glass-enclosed mall that parallels the main street and serves as a kind of life-line activating the intermediate zone of older buildings. The arcaded mall also functions as an artery of support for Elm Street, attracting and rechanneling pedestrian use.

South and west of this first line of development are two other major new buildings: a two-story exhibition hall and a large civic arena. The large-span exposed trusses of the arena, major elements at roof level, are scaled down at the sidewalk, alternating with stairs and entry points to provide a lively street wall. All-weather access to the exhibition hall and arena may also be gained from the spine paralleling Elm Street. Careful attention has been paid to integrating the project into the old urban fabric. The scheme includes both high and low buildings, providing a sense of scale that mediates the imposition of a modern, high-rise image of downtown in a historic and vernacular context. The organization of the new complex is also intended to imply its extendability in many directions. However, as the basic urban grid would be left intact, the intervention is as respectful as it is assertive.

New York School Exhibition

State Museum, Albany, New York
1977

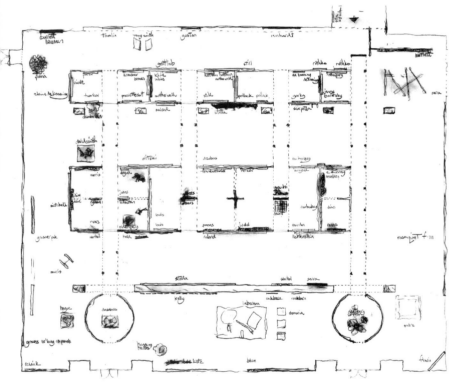

Plan of installation

For an exhibition of the work of New York School painters and sculptors, a vast 42,000-square-foot space had to be designed, constructed, and installed in just eight weeks. The volume of the hall turned out to be a boon, as many of the works were very large—a couple of them over eighty feet long—and the scale of partitions and appropriate viewing conditions accordingly became the major issues. To accommodate the variety of works, an abstract interior "cityscape" was conceived as the working metaphor for the space. Wood-framed gypsum-board partitions were arranged to create two broad "thoroughfares" for the large compositions and sculpture. These were cut perpendicularly by four narrower columnar "alleyways"— traversable either actually or visually—and separated by a three-dimensional grid of smaller-scale enclosures. Two cylindrical enclosures at the back of the hall provided special in-the-round viewing space for two pieces of sculpture, and served compositionally as the "receptors" of the orthogonal energies.

The construction was roofless except for the cross-alleys, which were sliced horizontally by overhead canopies painted black on the underside; these defined the parallel circulation routes accessible from the outer corridor on the entrance side. The compositional play of symmetry and asymmetry was set off by the asymmetrical position of the main entry in the otherwise symmetrical space, as well as by the requirements of the artwork itself.

The whole scheme was predicated on providing a variety of aspects from which to engage the works. Having a sense of being both inside and outside, the viewer was able to rediscover previously seen works from new perspectives, and to take advantage of long axial views, glimpses through windowed planes, and layered spatial relationships. Experientially the installation became an abstract microcosm of the city itself, an appropriate backdrop to the urbanity of the art on display.

223

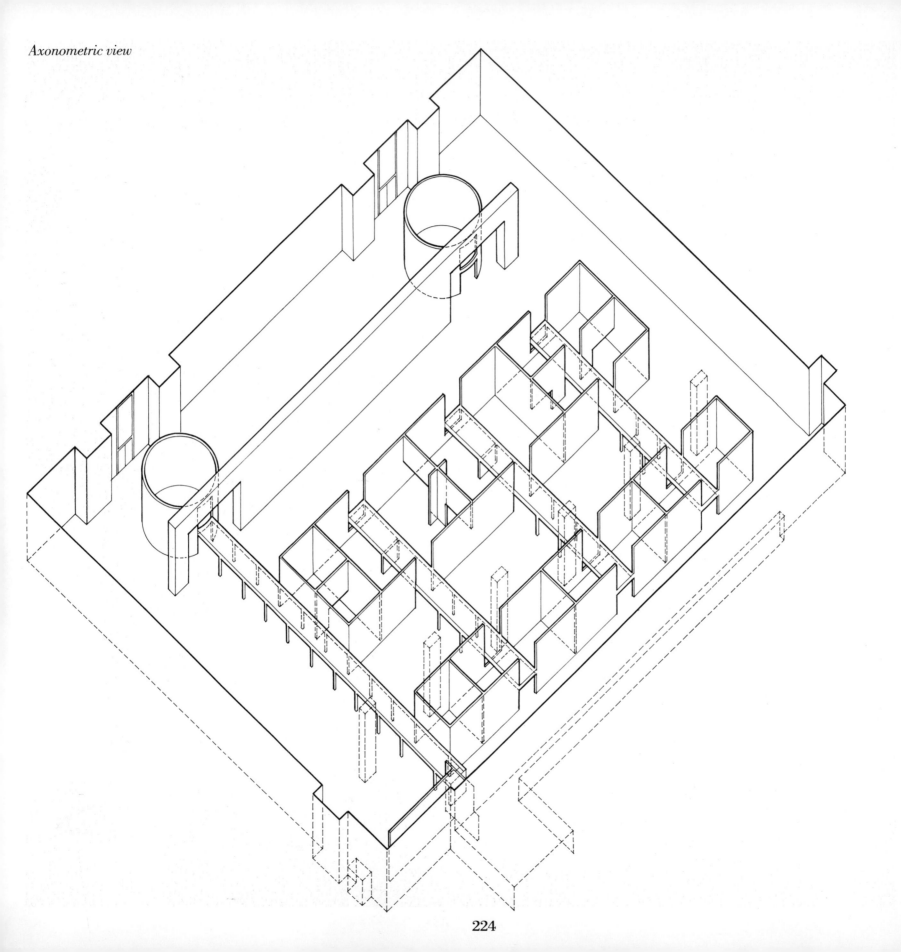

 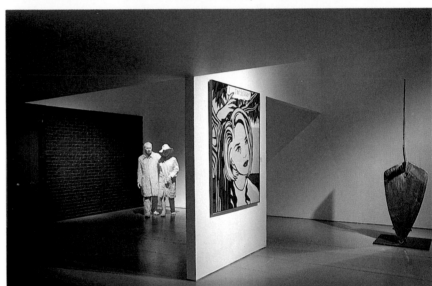

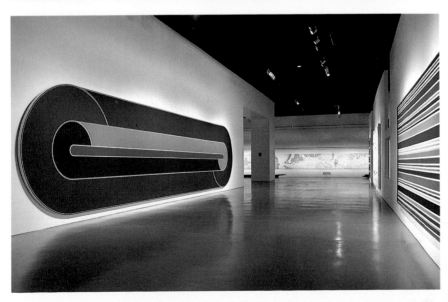 

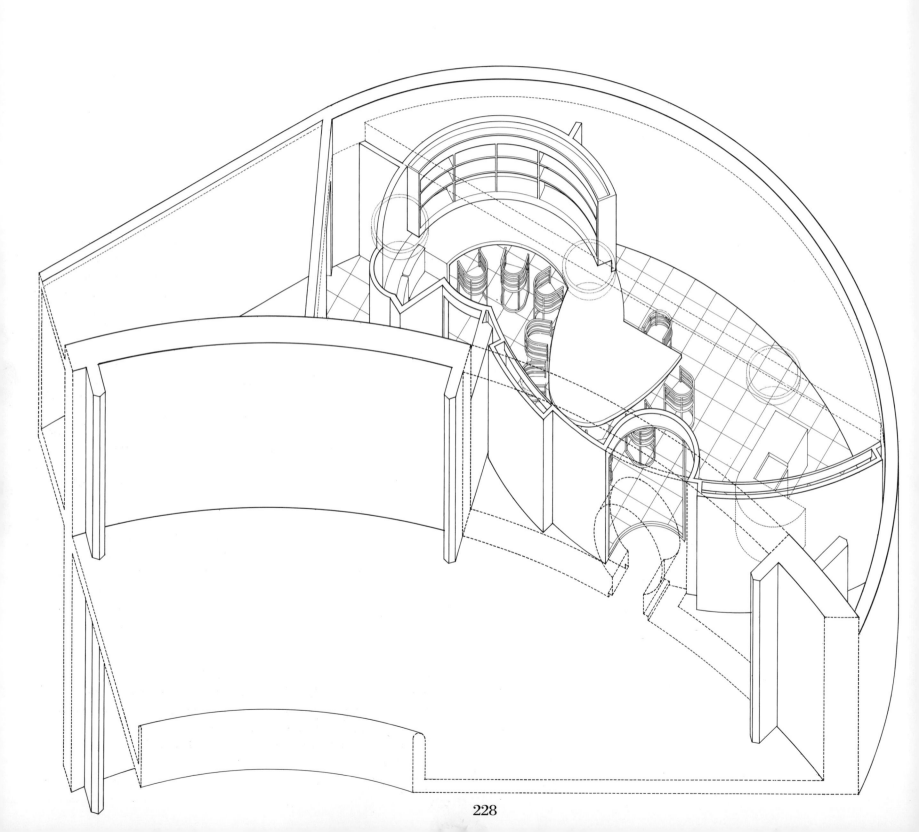

Aye Simon Reading Room

The Solomon R. Guggenheim Museum, New York, New York
1977–1978

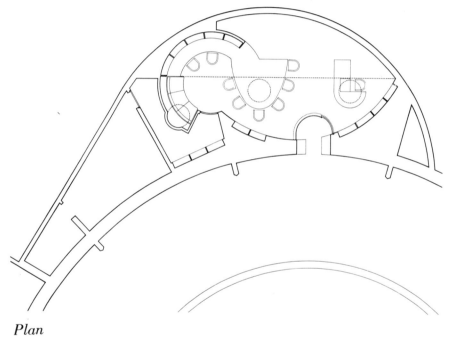

Plan

| 10| | 25| | 50|

Frank Lloyd Wright had originally designated a small, curved room on the second floor of the Guggenheim Museum, along the windowless Fifth Avenue edge of the building underneath the spiraling rotunda, as a repository for his drawings and models of the museum, but over the years it was used as an employee lunch room and a storage area. In 1978 the museum decided to have the space converted into a reading room.

In effecting the transformation, three original round skylights were taken as the primary organizational cues. Each of the skylights focuses on a major activity area: reception, reading table, and built-in banquette. All of the furniture—including the banquette, bookshelves, tables, chairs—is of curvilinear, light-finished oak, and was especially designed for the space.

The portal to the almond-shaped room, which is entered from the second level of the spiral ramp, is in the shape of a giant keyhole or moon gate. This round shape helps to mask the transition from sloping to flat floor plane and to minimize the distortion that the canted wall surface would have accentuated in a more rectilinear form. It also echoes the shape of the elevator, which is directly opposite it across the ramp. Beyond this thick-walled, ceremonial doorway, a semicircular vestibule restates Wright's theme of the circle and further mediates the change in floor levels, modulating and deflecting one's entry into the room.

The room is a homage to the master who designed the museum. Without reproducing the Wrightian style verbatim, its square-spindled wood furniture, Eastern-inspired portal, arcing geometries, and air of intimacy are an attempt to evoke Wright's spirit and to coexist harmoniously within the unique context of this twentieth-century monument.

As an architect, one can never understand a building so well as when one actually works on it. Once the design of the reading room began, the Guggenheim took on a whole other dimension of meaning than it had for the visitor or student of drawings. The opening in the wall had to be round.

Furniture for Knoll International

1978–1982

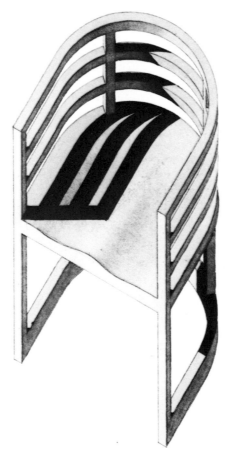

Furniture is an integral part of virtually any spatial conception. Whether built-in or movable, it is yet another means by which interior space can be manipulated and shaped. It serves to give scale, to define volume, to distinguish areas of movement from those of stasis, to punctuate, to populate and provide variety, and, of course, to accommodate functional needs. While a smaller and less complex order of design than architecture, it is nonetheless a spatial composition with laws of structure, function, and aesthetics.

The refurbishing of the Aye Simon Reading Room in the Guggenheim Museum was the occasion for the first design of a chair in curved wood. The chair was intended to relate to the oak-paneled interior of the room and to harmonize with Frank Lloyd Wright's architecture and furniture. From this chair designed for a specific space came the idea for an entire collection of wood furniture that could have more universal application. Knoll International undertook the manufacturing of such a collection, which to date includes the chair, conference/dining tables, coffee table, stools, and a chaise longue.

The chair developed in much the same way as a work of architecture. The basic geometry of a double cube, one half above the seat, the other below, was carved into to produce the curved frame. Then the proportions of the frame, the wood members, the spaces in between them, and the height and width relative to table, desk, and elbows were tested and refined. The goal was to produce a taut, elegant object, sensuous but highly controlled. The initial version in wood was subsequently "dematerialized" by the application of a black or white lacquer finish; this glossy and homogeneous surface works to articulate the spare lines and tight voids of the frame and to clarify the contrast of curves and right angles, without sacrificing the inherent grace and tensile properties of the wood. (The collection actually includes both versions: the natural-finish chairs are made of white oak, the lacquered chairs of beech.)

233

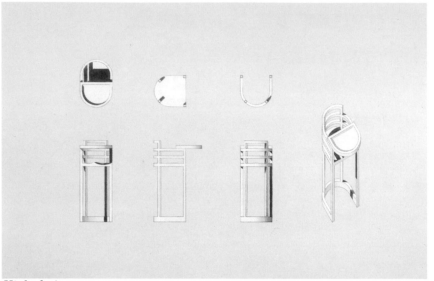

High chair

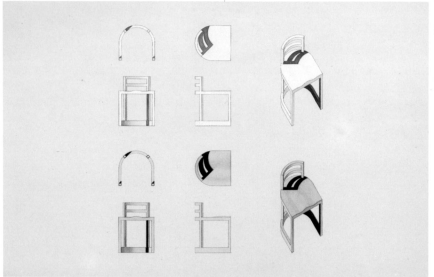

Armless chair

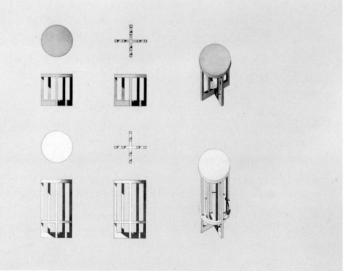

High and low stools

Armchair

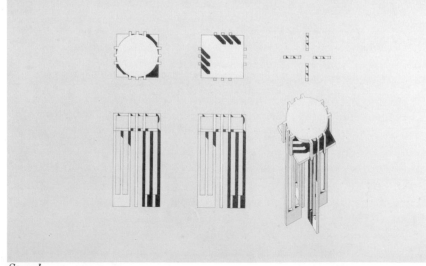

Stand

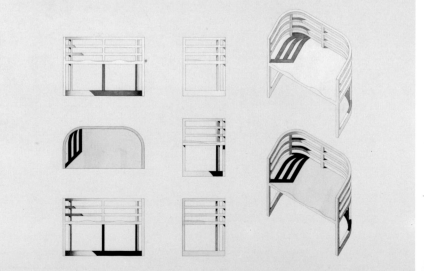

Settee

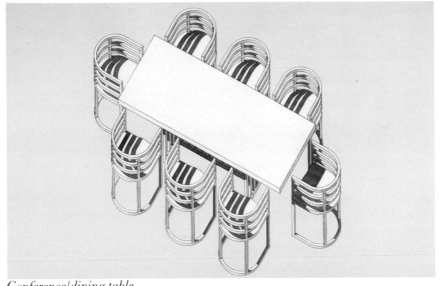

Conference/dining table

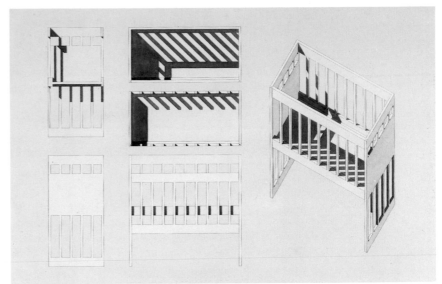

Crib

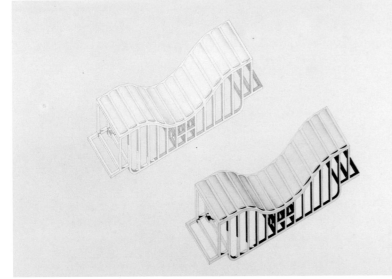

Chaise longue

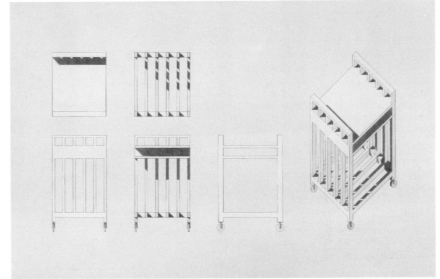

Trolley

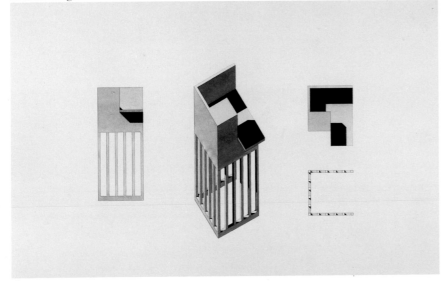

Lectern

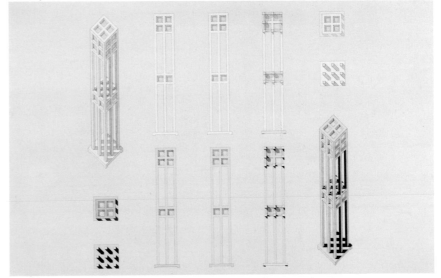

Lamp

The goal was to produce a taut, elegant object, sensuous but highly controlled. The initial version in wood was subsequently "dematerialized" by the application of a black or white lacquer finish; this glossy and homogeneous surface works to articulate the spare lines and tight voids of the frame and to clarify the contrast of curves and right angles, without sacrificing the inherent grace and tensile properties of the wood.

The system of proportions established for the chair was then applied, with necessary modifications, to the entire collection, making for a strong formal and functional interrelationship among the different pieces. The height of the chair arm, 27½ inches, is the same as that of the table and the high stool, for example. Similarly, the same structural principle is maintained throughout: every wood connection is a mortise and tenon, one of the most precise ways of joining wood furniture. Still, while the formal vocabulary, the abstract interplay of verticals and horizontals, and the overall conception and structure are consistent, each piece is a discrete object, usable in many different contexts. The chaise longue, for example, is symmetrical, and, with no differentiation between head and foot, may be used in any orientation or angle in space. The wide proportions permit two people to recline at once, and also afford stability for rocking. The deep curve of the upholstered seat—leather, suede, or velvet—plays against the shallow curve of the wood rocker and the abstract lattice it creates with the vertical spindles.

No work of art is conceived in a historical vacuum, and beyond the inspiration of Wright, the influence of other twentieth-century masters of furniture design must be acknowledged: Rietveld, Mackintosh, Le Corbusier, and Breuer, as well as the Viennese—Wagner, Loos, Hoffmann, and the Wiener Werkstätte. Le Corbusier's influence, which may not be as apparent as that of some others, is in the dimensions; they are roughly based on his Modulor.

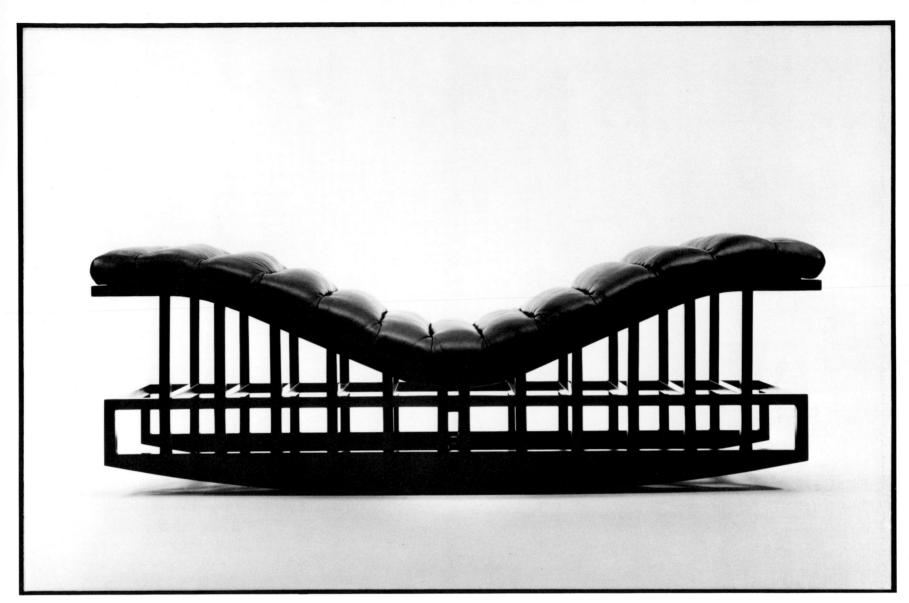

237

Hartford Seminary

Hartford, Connecticut
1978–1981

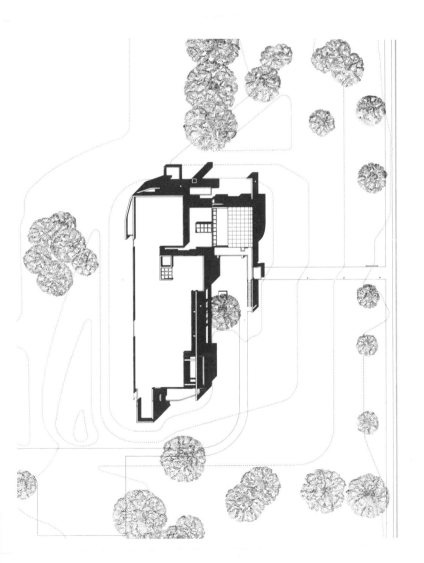

In 1972 the Hartford Seminary gave up its role as a traditional residential divinity school for the Protestant ministry and established itself as an interdenominational theological center. It now offers advanced degrees to both clergy and laypersons, as well as research and consulting services and public policy programs. To accommodate its changed needs, the seminary decided to sell its campus and build a single structure that would house all of its activities and at the same time project a new image of scholarship and service.

The new building takes in a total area of 27,000 square feet, including a large meeting room, a chapel, a library, a bookstore (all open to the public), classrooms and areas for part-time and full-time faculty, as well as workrooms and offices. The corner site is flat, and the context is that of a residential suburban campus. Loosely knit blocks of Gothic Revival stone buildings that formerly housed the seminary face the site from across the street, and a mixture of neo-Tudor and neo-Colonial houses fills out the surrounding neighborhood.

Because of the seminary's dual role as an introverted institution devoted to contemplation and scholarship, and an extroverted one engaged in fostering religious understanding in the world at large, the building has been conceived of in two ways. It consists of a partially cloistered, inward-directed organization of spaces, a place for peaceful gathering and quiet study. At the same time, it is intended to be the center of a larger domain that reaches out to the public, informs it, and invites it to take part. As such, the building's only organizational hierarchy is the architectural distinction made between public and private areas of activity: public spaces dominate private ones.

Site

Program

Structure

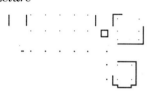

Entry

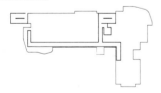

Circulation

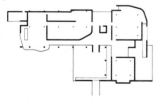

Enclosure

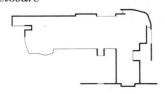

Ground level plan

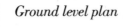
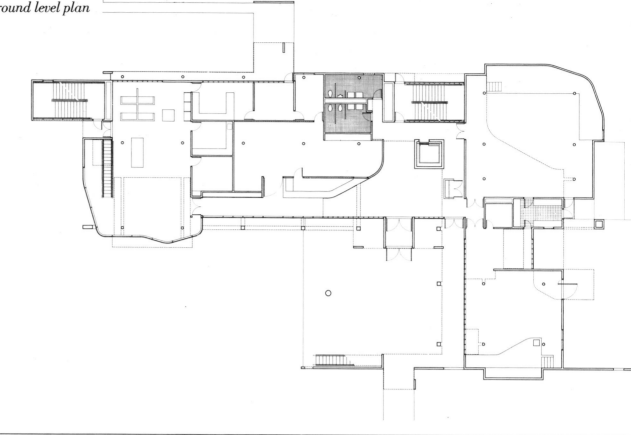

Second level plan

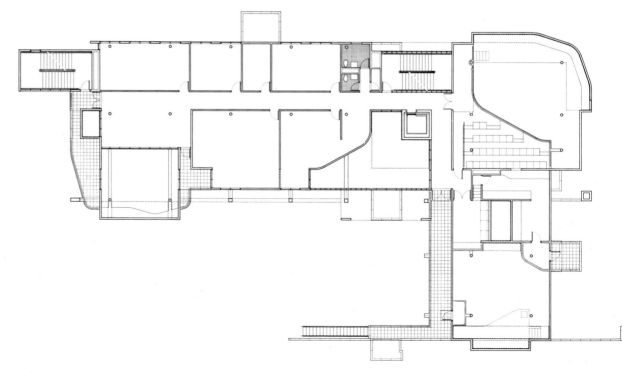

| 10| | 25| | | 50|

Axonometric view

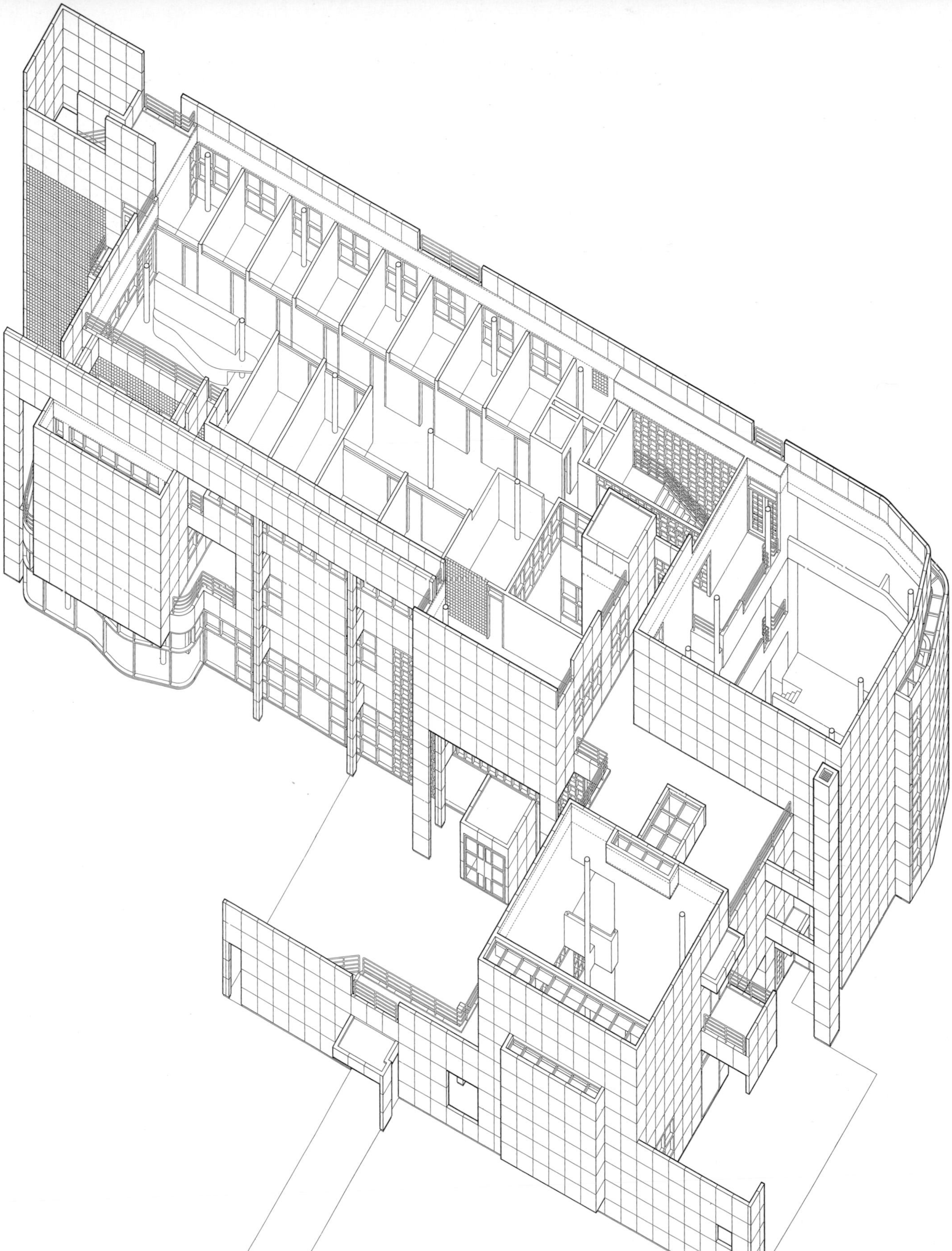

East elevation

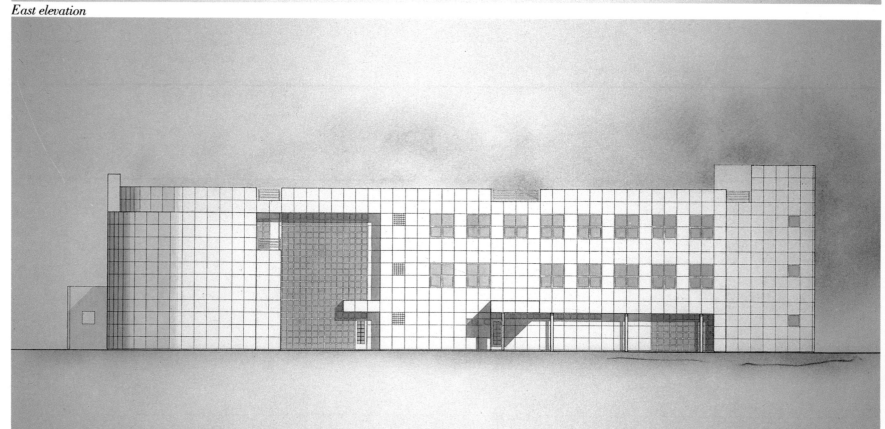

West elevation

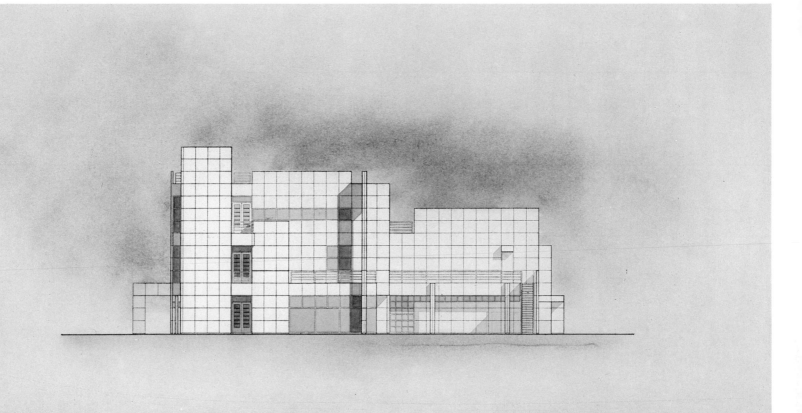

North elevation

South elevation

Longitudinal section through elevator

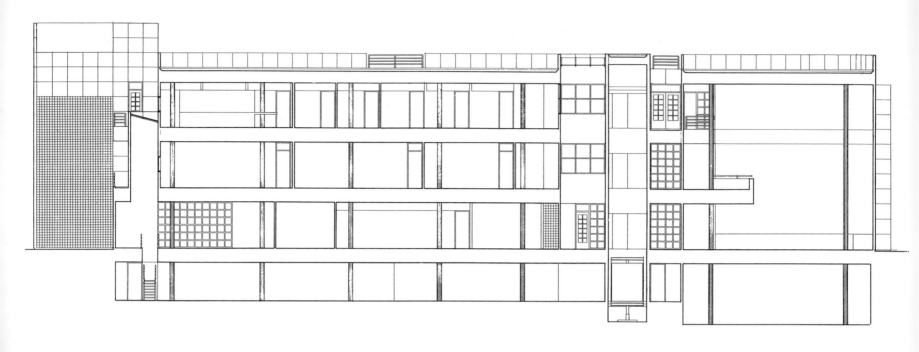

Longitudinal section through front corridor

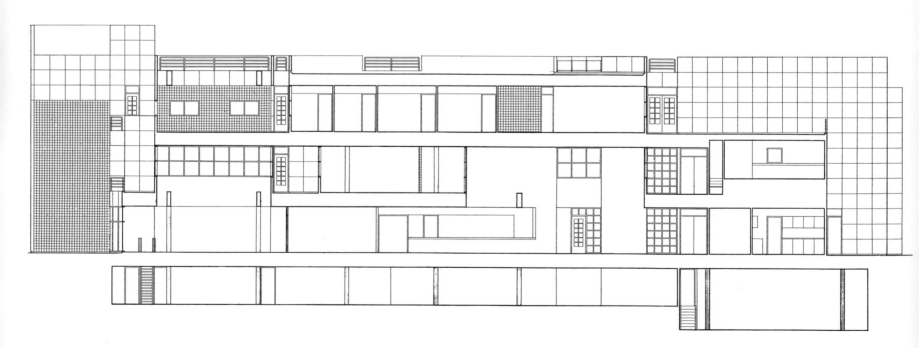

5| 10| 15| 30|

Cross section through meeting room and chapel facing north

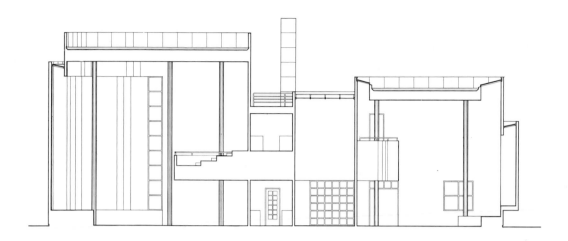

Cross section through chapel and meeting room facing south

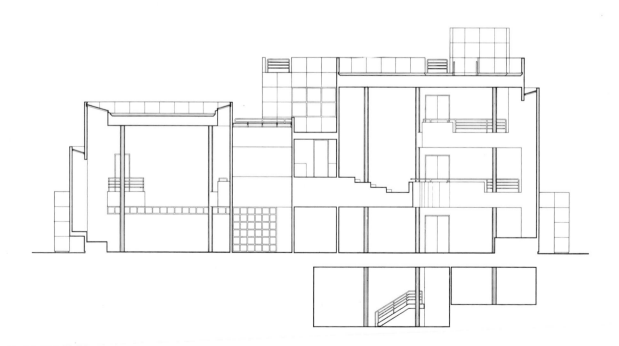

The layered, screenlike front facade gives the institution an image of openness. The projecting volume of the chapel not only accentuates the independence of that space, but also functions to allow natural light to enter from above. The projecting volume of the library, at the opposite end of the building, performs the same function, as well as relating these two major spaces of the building. The glass-block screen wall seen in the photograph above at right houses an interior stair and serves to anchor the east end of the entry facade.

247

The parti is an L-configuration, the dominant block of which is set back from and parallel to the primary street front. Three major public spaces, of two or more stories, are located at the extremities of the L: chapel, meeting room, and library. A three-story lobby occupies the center of the composition. Smaller private spaces such as offices, study cubicles, and seminar rooms fill out the remainder of the plan, some of them with overlooks or pulpit-like projections into the public spaces. The only major departures from the overall orthogonal scheme occur in the section or plan of the public spaces: the rounding of the chapel skylight and the echoing curves of the meeting room's exterior corner and the library's undulating glass ribbon-wall.

On the exterior, the need to provide a transition from the surrounding context into the ordered life of the institution provided an opportunity to explore notions of architectural sequence and promenade. As in some early Christian churches, the seminary is entered through a cloistered courtyard, which the L-shaped plan surrounds on two sides. A path from the street and a major gate wall on axis with the entry initiate the processional way. The elaborate layering of walls, canopies, and openings draws the visitor successively inward and across the building's threshold.

Within, light becomes the animating and all-encompassing symbol of the building's purpose as a place of intellectual and spiritual illumination. The fall of light along axial vistas and on curved white wall surfaces guides the visitor through the sequence of circulation, linking the public spaces at either end. Framed views through different grids of cross-mullioned glazing refract and integrate the natural and man-made worlds, and the juxtaposition of the glass grids with the grid of reflective white panels creates a continuous dialogue between materiality and transparency. The spirit of the building as a religious center is evoked by the luminosity and pristine qualities of its architecture—by the pure configuration of light and space.

250

The three-foot-square panel grid is halved to produce the one-foot-six-inch-square window size, which is further broken down into the six-inch increment of the glass block. The interworking of these square grids of different sizes horizontally and vertically relates spaces that have a large-scale definition to those of smaller scale. The theme of the square contrasts with the linearity of the system of circulation.

The meeting room is a cubic volume with light coming in at the edges of the curved wall (see the enclosure diagram on page 240). Interestingly, the seating arrangement on the ground floor works as well on the diagonal as on the orthogonal. The view at right shows the toplit three-story entry area.

*The light cast on the altar comes
from a piece of blue glass in the
recessed window above.*

The window in the glass-block wall of the director's office continues the play of materiality and immateriality manifested throughout the building.

Clifty Creek
Elementary School

Columbus, Indiana
1978–1982

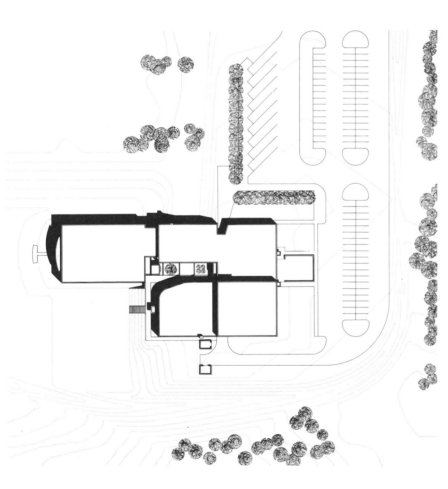

A public school for kindergarten and grades one through six, Clifty Creek is built on a sloping twenty-two acre site three miles from downtown Columbus. The three-story wing at the lower end of the site stacks the classrooms for the three instructional levels hierarchically (first floor, grades one and two; second floor, grades three and four; third floor, grades five and six) under one roof. On each floor two symmetrical suites of four 900-square-foot classrooms are partitioned with movable walls, allowing combined use of two classrooms when desired, and each couplet shares a glass-walled area where students can work by themselves while still under the supevision of the classroom teacher.

The compact classroom wing communicates by means of a system of ramps with the specialty and service areas of the school, organized in a large eroded square in plan. Each quadrant of this square contains a different activity center: library, cafeteria, gymnasium, and art and music rooms, and each has its own entry or entries. The double-height, north-lit library is adjacent to the classroom wing, and its central location in the plan is designed to encourage student use. The library also contains a free-form balcony for story-telling and more intimate reading. The ramp system runs directly along the south side of the library, and is flanked by a glass-pane wall affording views into an outdoor courtyard.

Across from the library, and separated from it by the courtyard, is the cafeteria, with its kitchen and services on the south side and a curved stage area at the west end for group presentations. The cafeteria's canted glass-pane north wall, facing the similar wall of the ramp opposite, allows views back and forth and makes for a transparent interpenetration of the two spaces, giving the stepped courtyard space in between a compressive energy.

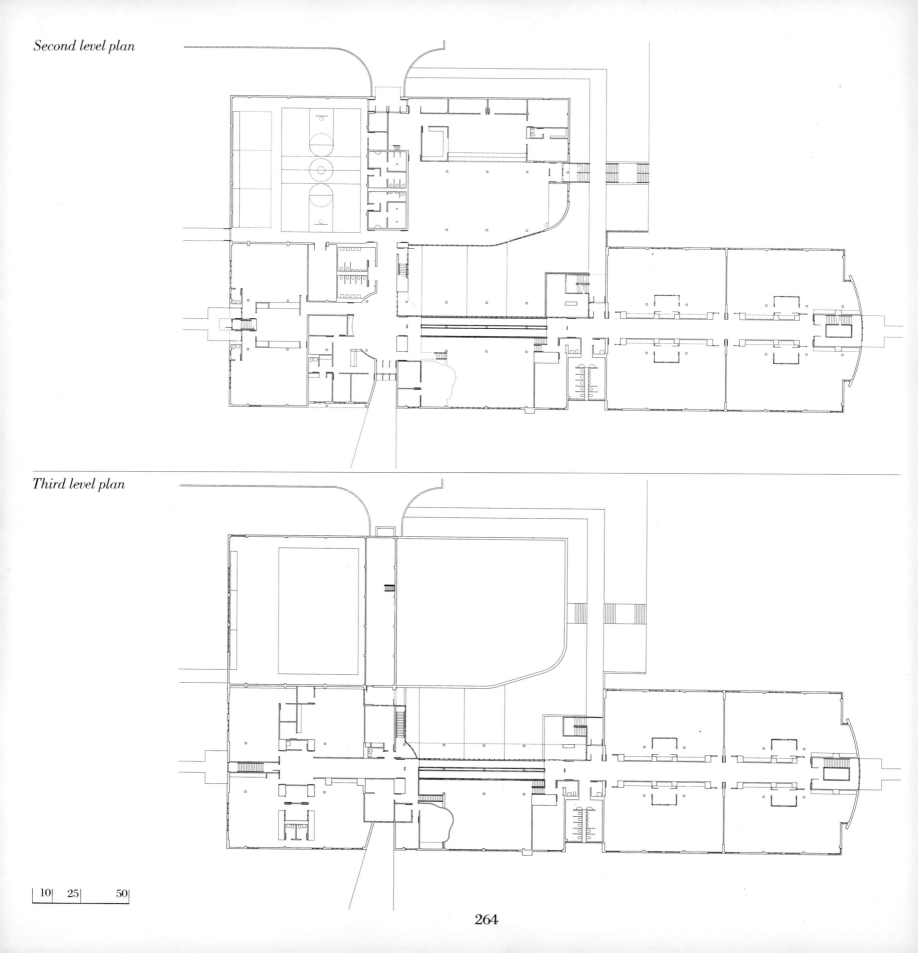

| 10 | 25 | 50 |

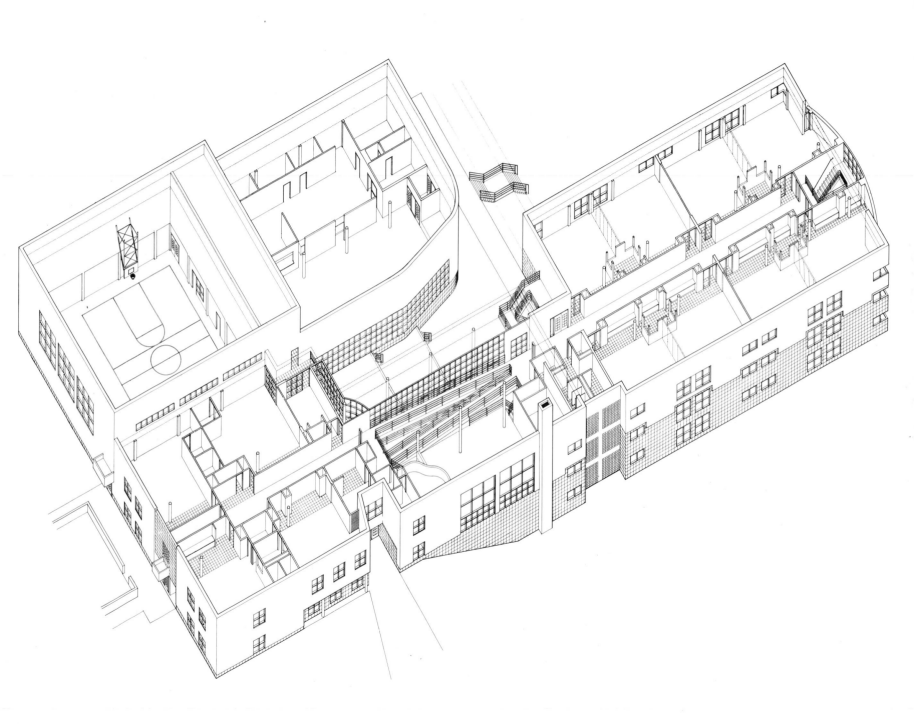

The southeast quadrant contains physical education facilities. The northeast quadrant, containing art and music rooms and special classrooms, has a semicircular vestibule that feeds off the main entry, on the north elevation. This vestibule serves compositionally as the displaced center of the scheme. With the convex entry to the classroom wing at the west end of the building, it defines the main axis of circulation and primary horizontal datum. The terminus of this axis is indicated on the east elevation by a canopy over a secondary entry, while the horizontal datum is marked on the north and south elevations by a change in coloration and material. This combination of design gestures suggests one of the formal strategies at work: the pulling out of the academic wing from the square plan along the trajectory of the ramp; in other words, the possibility of reading the classroom wing as a displaced fourth quadrant and the library/ramp/courtyard space as a tensile intermediary "void." Such relationships make the architecture at once dynamic and unified.

266

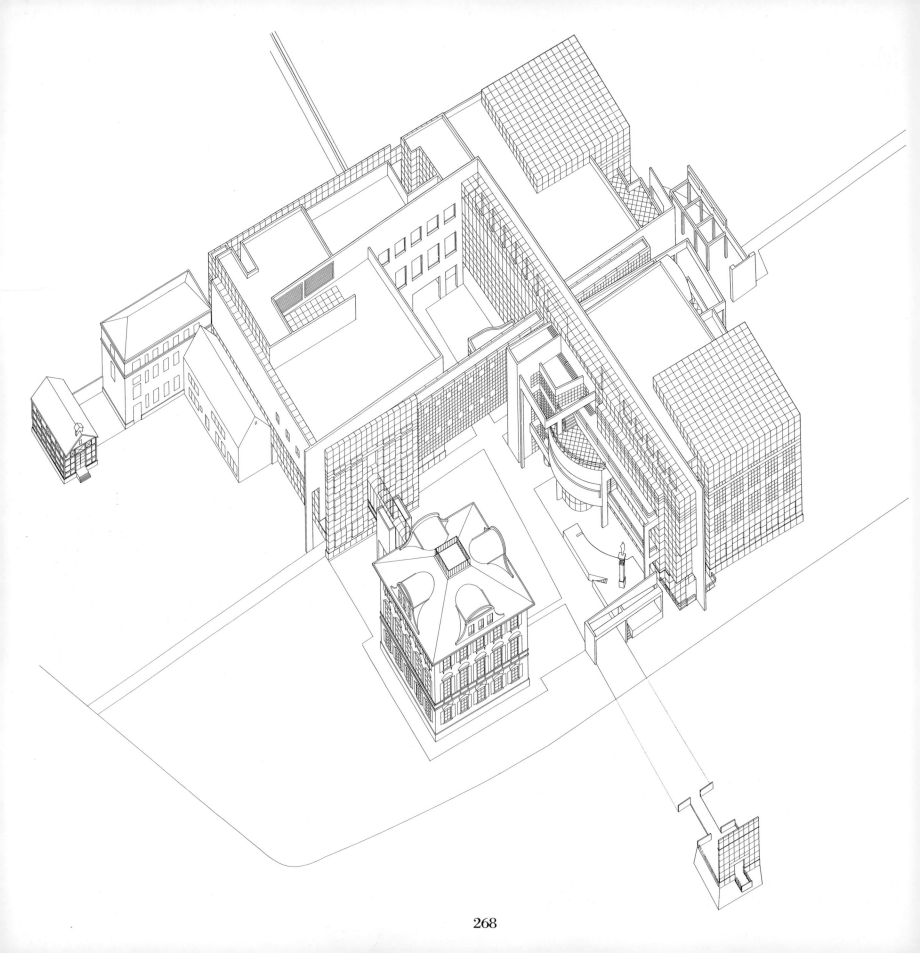

Museum for the Decorative Arts

Frankfurt am Main, West Germany
1979–1984

Urban form evolves between type and incident, fabric and discontinuity, history and the moment of design. This dialogue strongly influenced the design of the Museum for the Decorative Arts in Frankfurt am Main. The parti developed out of a notion of context that takes in not only geographic features but also historical and typological ones. In this sense, and in contrast to some of the earlier buildings for more rural or less historic sites, the museum is emphatically a public and an urban institution, a rejection of the modernist isolation of the building as a free-standing object distanced from its surrounds. The scheme here is meant to connect: to respond to, enlarge, and reinforce the public context and the urban fabric.

A repository for the city's collection of decorative arts treasures, in recent years overcrowded in a nineteenth-century palazzo, the Villa Metzler, the new complex joins and renovates the existing building, integrating it into an overall development of the site. The site is on the south edge of the Main River, in proximity to several other museum buildings which together form the Museumsufer, a venerable embankment of buildings fronting the water. Since the program readily fits into the east end of the site, the rest is given over to a landscaped park, intended to function as a "bridge" that uses its prestigious location to connect two previously poorly related parts of the city, the residential community of Sachsenhausen to the south and the center of the city across the river to the north. The park is designed as a recreational and green zone, connected by landscaped pathways and axial vistas to the museum buildings and openly accessible to the community. This treatment of the site is intended to diminish the separating effect of the frontal buildings along the Main, thus eliminating the present no-man's-land behind them.

The organizational grid of the new complex is derived primarily from two geometries: that of the Villa Metzler, a near-perfect cubic volume, and that of the slightly skew angle to the site of the river bank and existing buildings. The Villa is inscribed into one quadrant of a larger square plan, a sixteen-square grid that takes in the entire new complex. This grid is then overlaid by another of the same size, but rotated 3½ degrees to establish a frontal relationship with the other buildings on the embankment. The superimposition of these two basic grids generates the design at nearly every scale, giving rise to a shifting and subtle interplay within the highly ordered set of formal relationships.

Thus, for example, the quadrant plan contains two outdoor courtyards. One surrounds the Villa Metzler on two sides (comprising three of the sixteen squares) and is based on the original (unrotated) grid, but it is inflected by the major path of entry to the museum, a funnel-shaped path on the rotated grid that originates in a ceremonial portal at the edge of the river. This three-square courtyard has the important role of holding the Villa at an intimate but respectful distance from the rest of the complex, thereby preserving its jewellike integrity—a tactic that is just the opposite of that adopted in the Villa Strozzi renovation, where the masonry walls of the old building were closely integrated into the new structure. The second courtyard is an internalized one, straddling the two southern quadrants, and it is oriented on the rotated grid, a kind of displaced center of the two cross-axes of the site: the entry axis coming from the river, which skewers this courtyard on its way to the community behind the complex, and the park axis, which bypasses it on its northern edge.

269

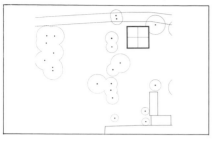

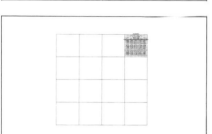

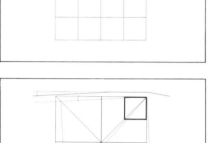

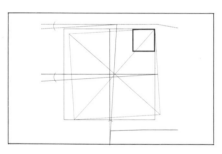

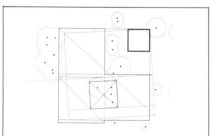

Analytical diagrams of the site and the overlaid grids

Early sketches showing development of the site plan

At the scale of the buildings themselves, the Villa Metzler's dimensions are replicated and extrapolated to produce many different modules for the new building. The Villa's 17.60-meter width and height become the basis for the exterior dimensions of each quadrant, while its elevational dimensions become the source of the 1.10-meter width and height of the metal-panel grid; similarly, the proportions of windows in the Villa generate those of the new building. This process of extrapolation is not merely a formal game; it serves to lend the larger complex some of the Villa's domestic and intimate scale.

Within, the building is dedicated to the Enlightenment concept that the museum is a place of education as much as of display. The visitor is conducted through a prescribed didactic sequence of spaces, proceeding counterclockwise through the history of the European decorative arts. As in the design for the New York School Exhibition, the architecture frames the exhibits in multiple ways, allowing for the possibility of discovery and surprise as one views objects through different apertures, but at the same time always deferring to the objects themselves, permitting them to create their own environments and not overwhelming them. Intimate niches are provided for viewing small, precious things, while focused paths of light indicate the general sequence of movement through the building. The rococo and neoclassical collections are housed in the Villa Metzler, reached from the second floor via a glass-walled bridge. Throughout, the whiteness, the delicacy of the structure, and the quality of the light suggest the similar qualities of German Baroque architecture, one strong source of inspiration for this building; even the white porcelain-enameled panels of the exterior here evoke the fine examples of Meissen and Bavarian china that constitute a major feature of the collection.

While the vocabulary and technology of the building are decisively modern, history is a constant presence, through the collection itself, but also through the dialogue between the architecture and its context. Fragmentary objects like two quasi-Gothic towers to be placed at the park entry allude to similar structures depicted in a nineteenth-century painting of the site when it was part of the vineyard owned by the local parish; a statue column in the entry courtyard, taken from the city's repository of artifacts, alludes to the eighteenth-century origins of the museum as a type, when Etienne Boullée first envisioned it as a "temple of fame for statues of great men." But the primary dialogue remains the architectural one, in which the stucco and stone of the Villa Metzler and the metal panels of the extension beside it reveal much about the culture and history that have produced their juxtaposition.

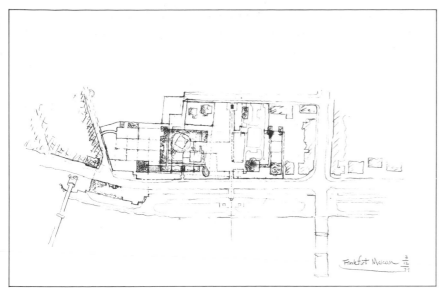

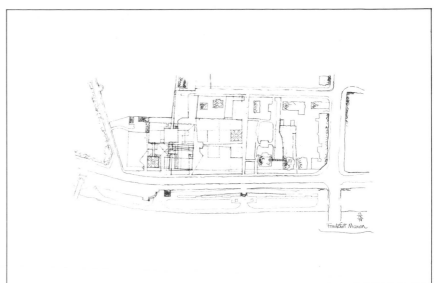

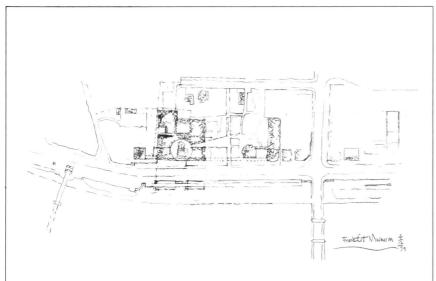

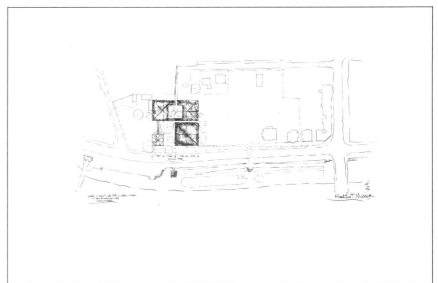

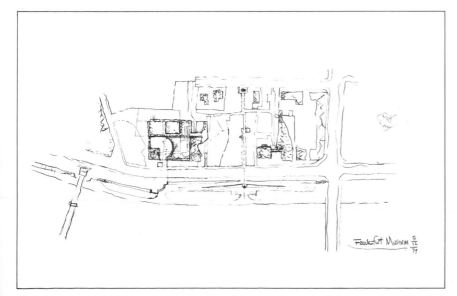

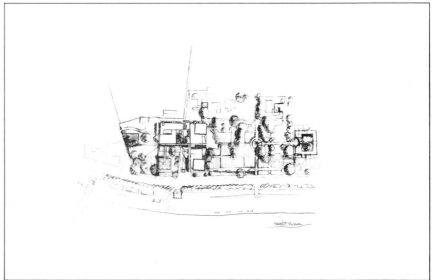

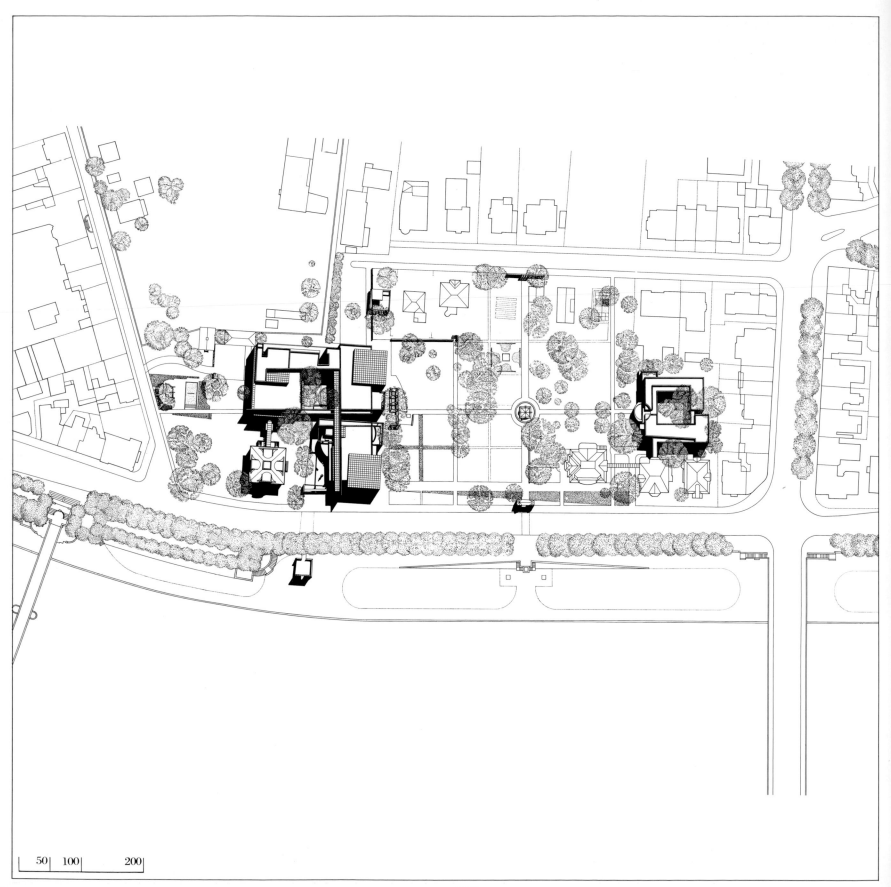

50 | 100 | 200 |

Site plan including proposal
for an extension to the museums
of Anthropology and Musical
Instruments

Axonometric cut-away of
circulation

Axonometric cut-away of
exterior spaces

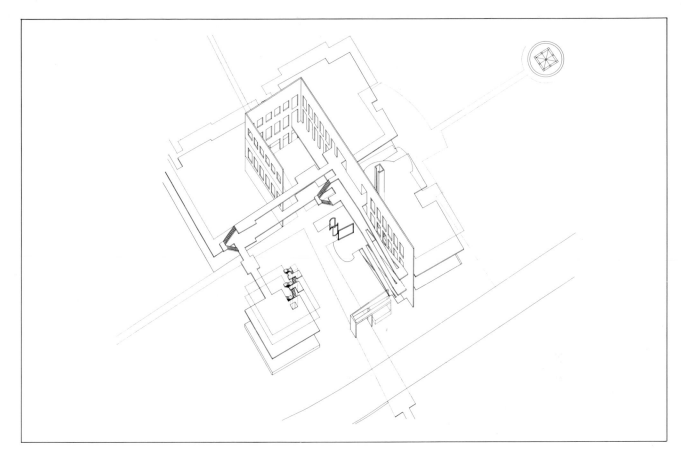

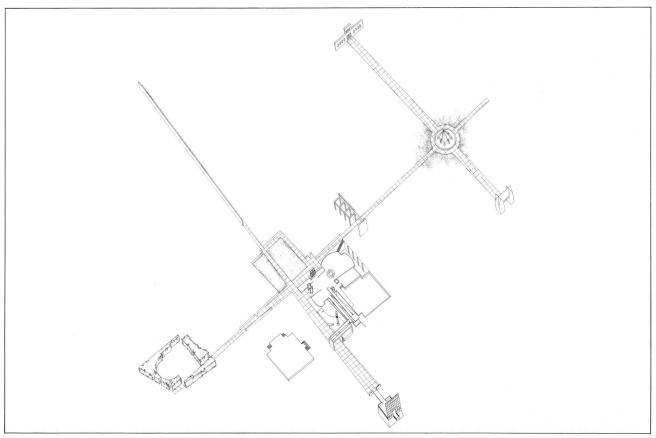

Ground level plan

20 50 100

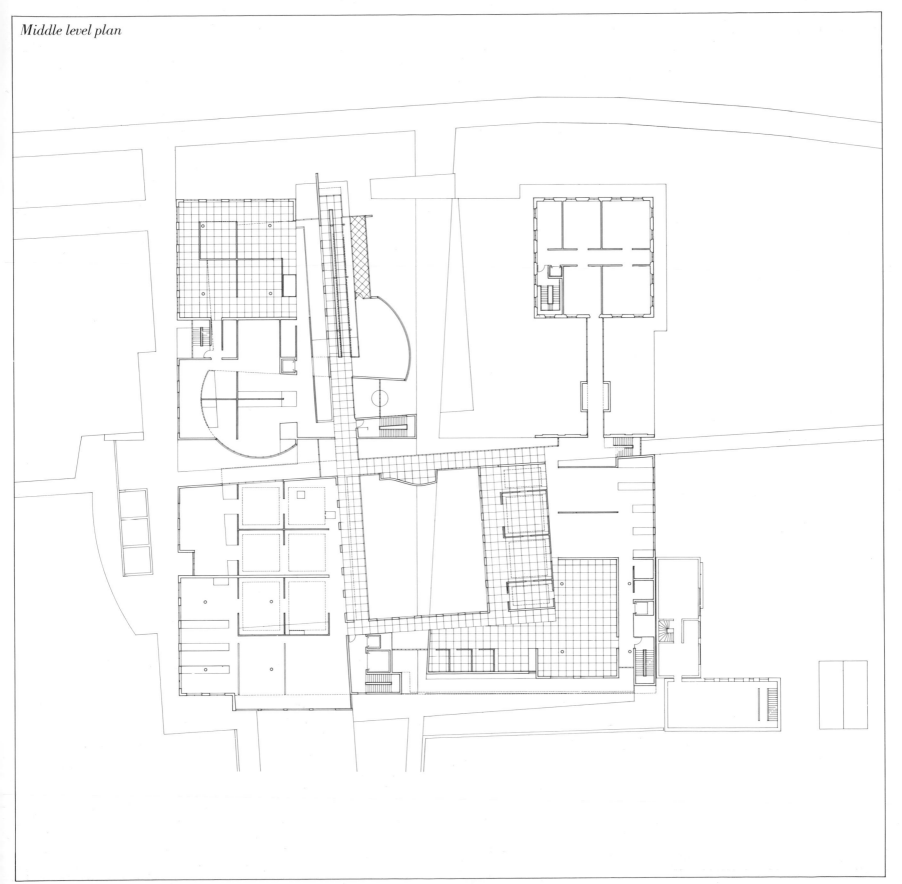

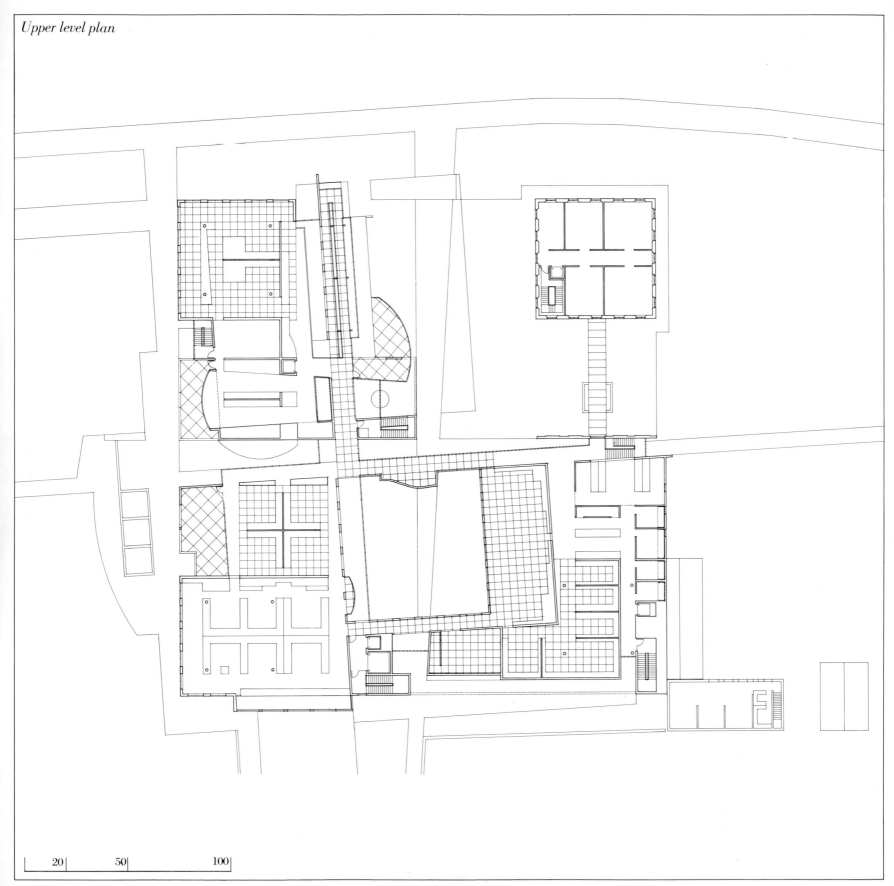

20   50   100

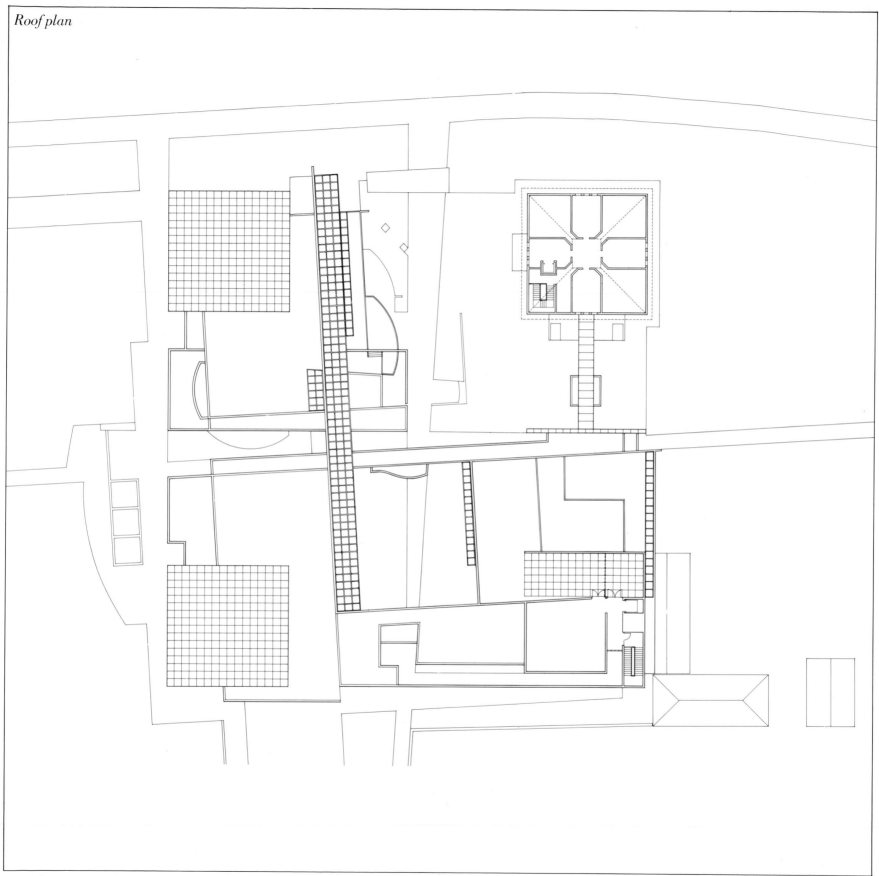

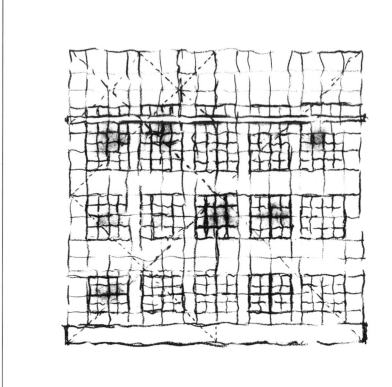

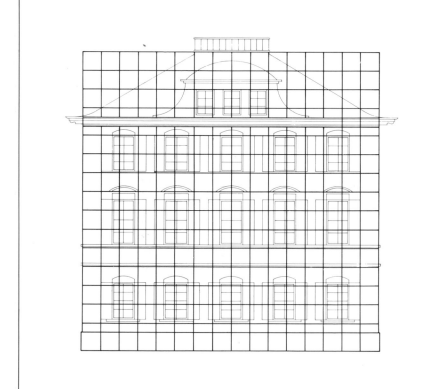

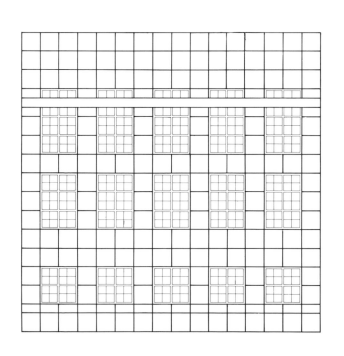

Facade study of Villa Metzler
Facade study of new building

Facade of Villa Metzler with
overlaid grid
Panel and fenestration grid of
new building

West elevation study
North elevation study

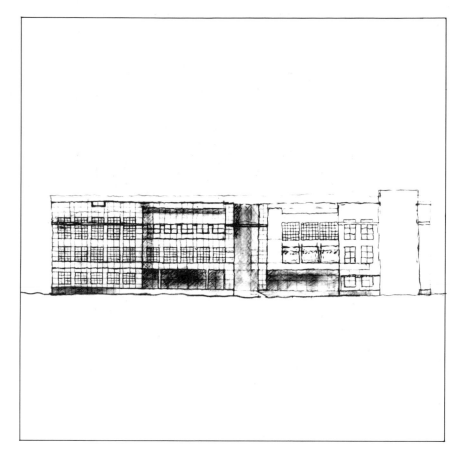

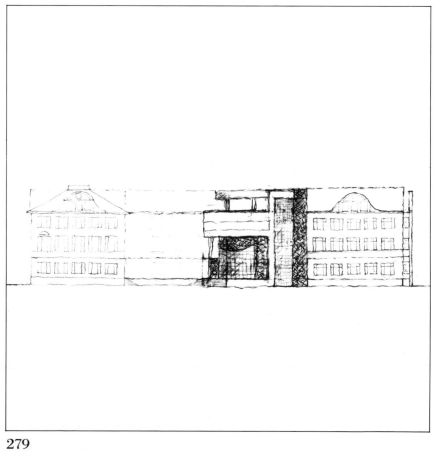

279

North elevation

Section through Villa Metzler and new building facing south

South elevation

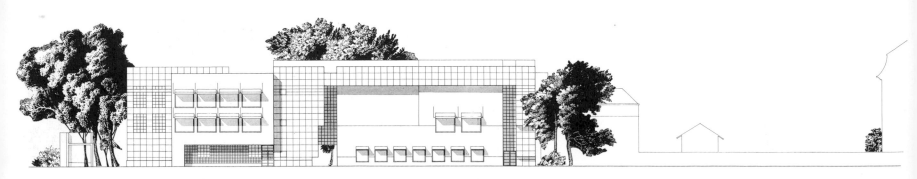

20| 50| 100|

East elevation

Section through garden and entry courts facing west

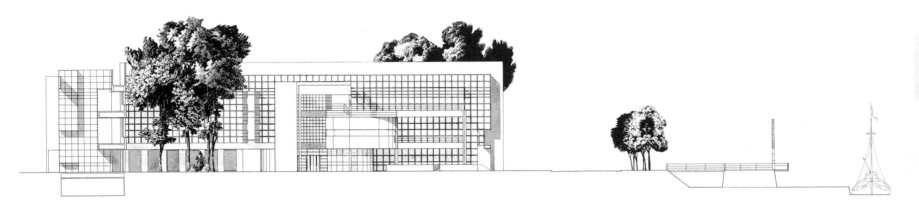

West elevation

281

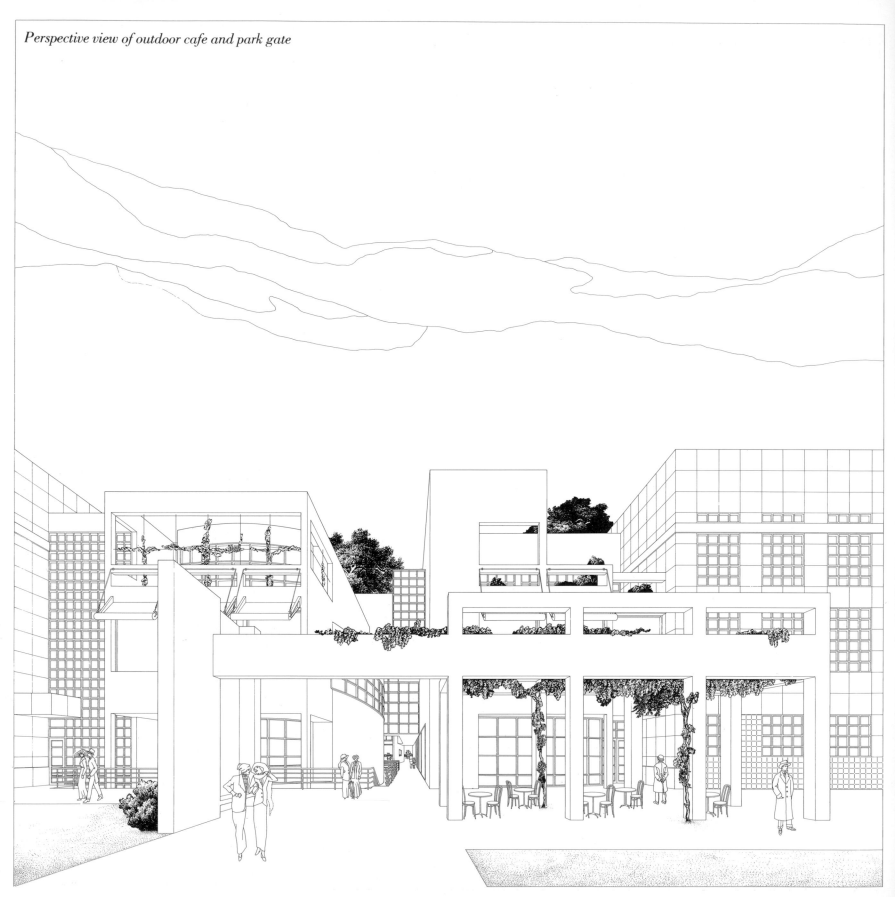

Perspective view of outdoor cafe and park gate

Perspective section through museum galleries

Axonometric view
of upper level galleries

Perspective view of the museum
seen from the park

284

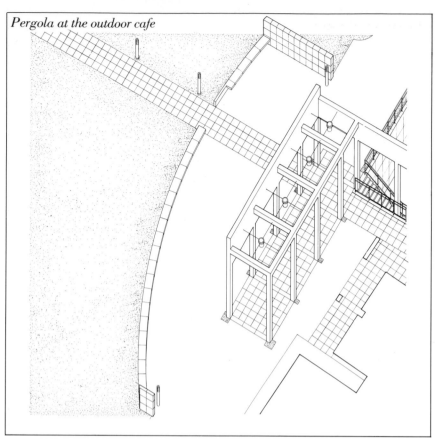

Pergola at the outdoor cafe

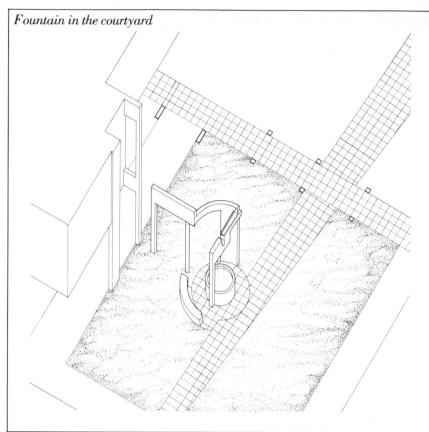

Fountain in the courtyard

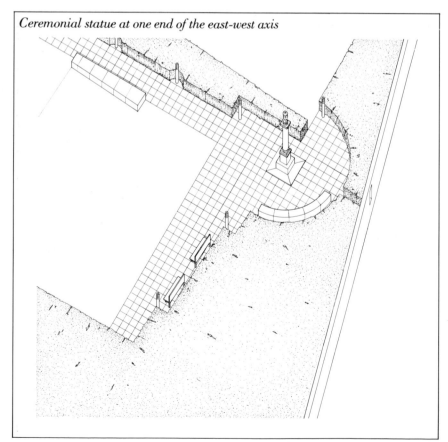

Ceremonial statue at one end of the east-west axis

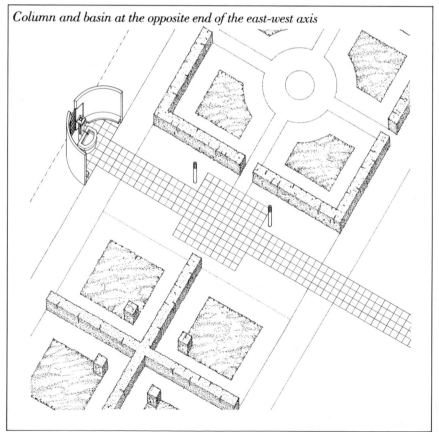

Column and basin at the opposite end of the east-west axis

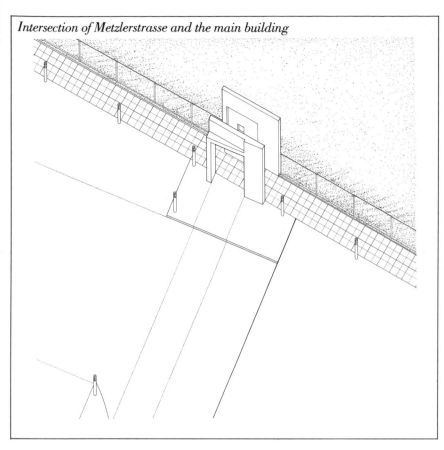

Intersection of Metzlerstrasse and the main building

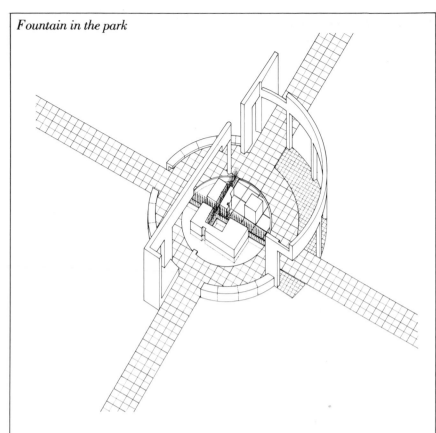

Fountain in the park

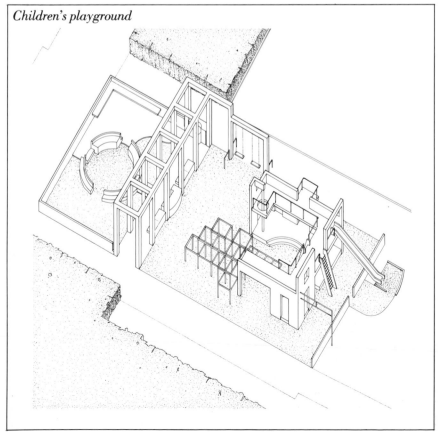

Children's playground

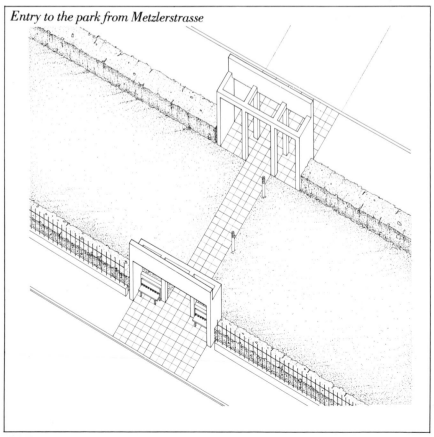

Entry to the park from Metzlerstrasse

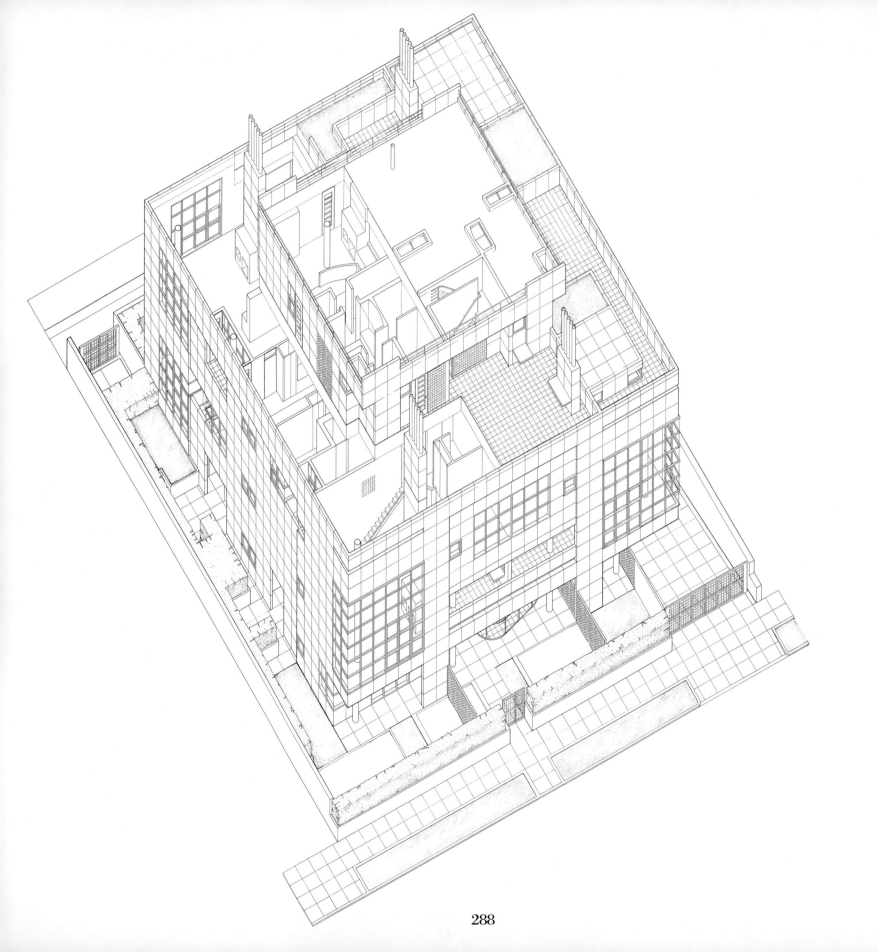

Somerset Condominiums

Beverly Hills, California
1980

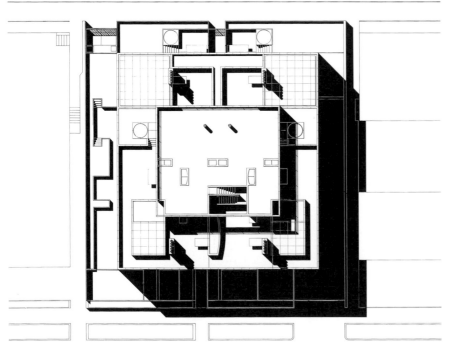

Luxury housing for a compact site on a quiet residential street in Beverly Hills, this square, four-story detached block contains six duplex units. On each of the first three floors, two units are entered, so that the middle two floors each contain the lower level of two duplexes and the upper level of two duplexes. This staggering of the units in section, accomplished by means of rotating the placement of the entries around a central circulation core in plan, is the primary innovation of the building. Not only does it afford maximum space and privacy to the residents, but it imparts a rotational energy to the cubic "doughnut."

In the case of each apartment, one enters at the living-room level and ascends by a stair to the bedroom level. Four of the duplexes have a double-height living room; the two entered on the third floor have large penthouse terraces. From the street, a hedge and gate serve as a barrier between the sidewalk and a columnar portico leading into a curved, glass-walled lobby. Zoning regulations mandated the building's height as well as a ten-foot setback on all the upper floors from the alley in back and from the two buildings on either side. This reduction of the ground-level footprint created a need for especially tight planning, and for this reason the units, while luxurious, are compact. It is the square geometry and central circulation core that make the maximizing of the floor area of each unit possible.

As a result of the square and more or less bilaterally symmetrical floor plans, as well as the relatively neutral site conditions, each facade is largely symmetrical, and the two side elevations are similar to each other. The grid of square metal panels expresses the internal geometry and responds to the floor plans, while the size of the individual panel establishes a domestic scale for the fenestration and the overall building.

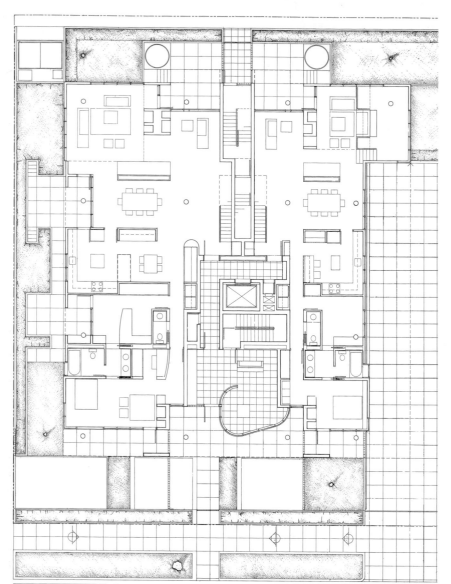

Ground level plan

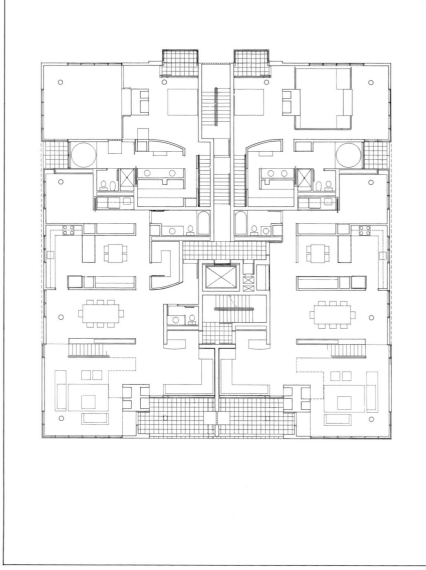

Second level plan

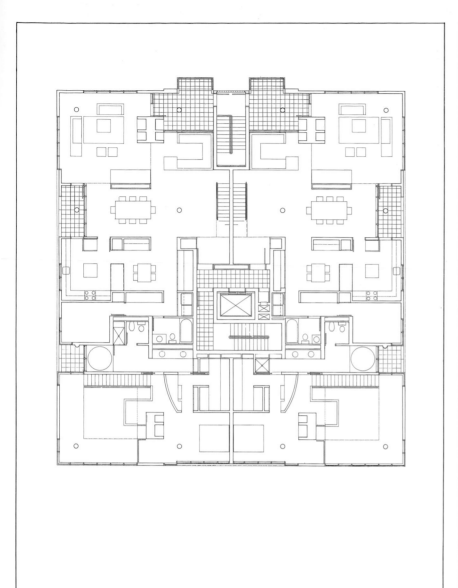

Third level plan

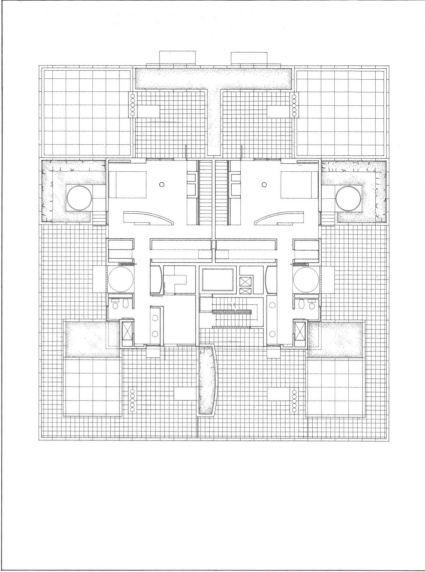

Roof level plan

East elevation

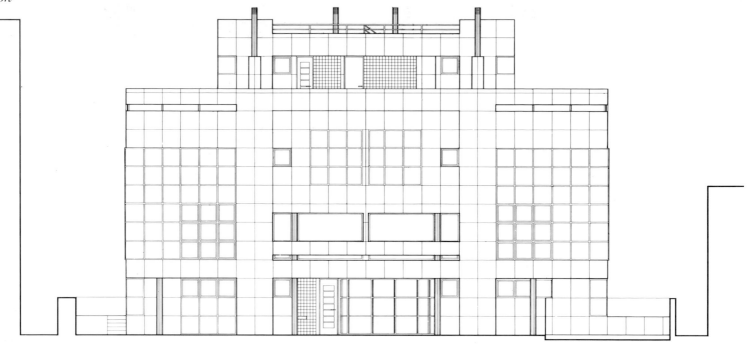

West elevation

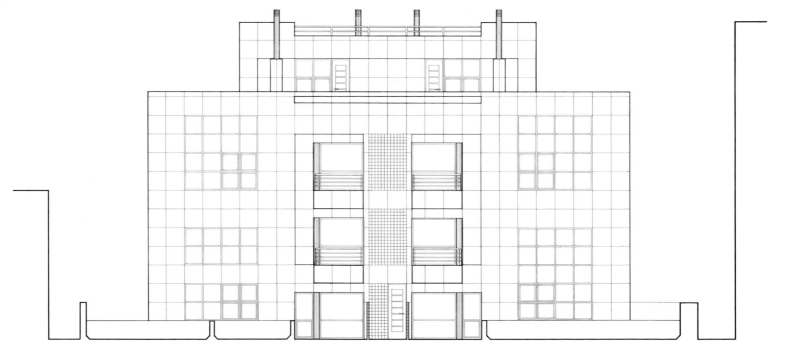

South elevation

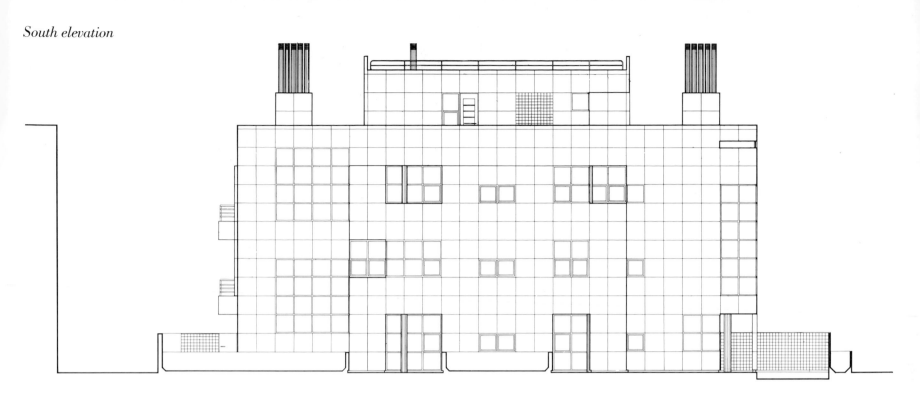

North elevation

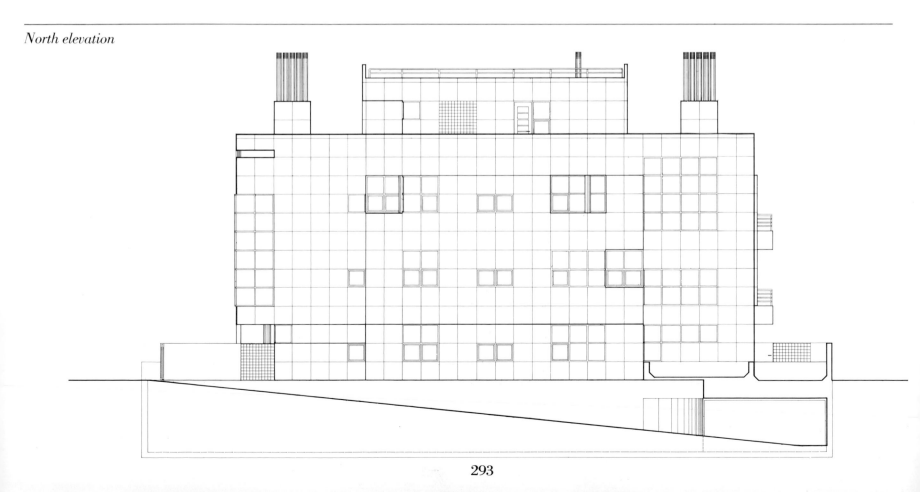

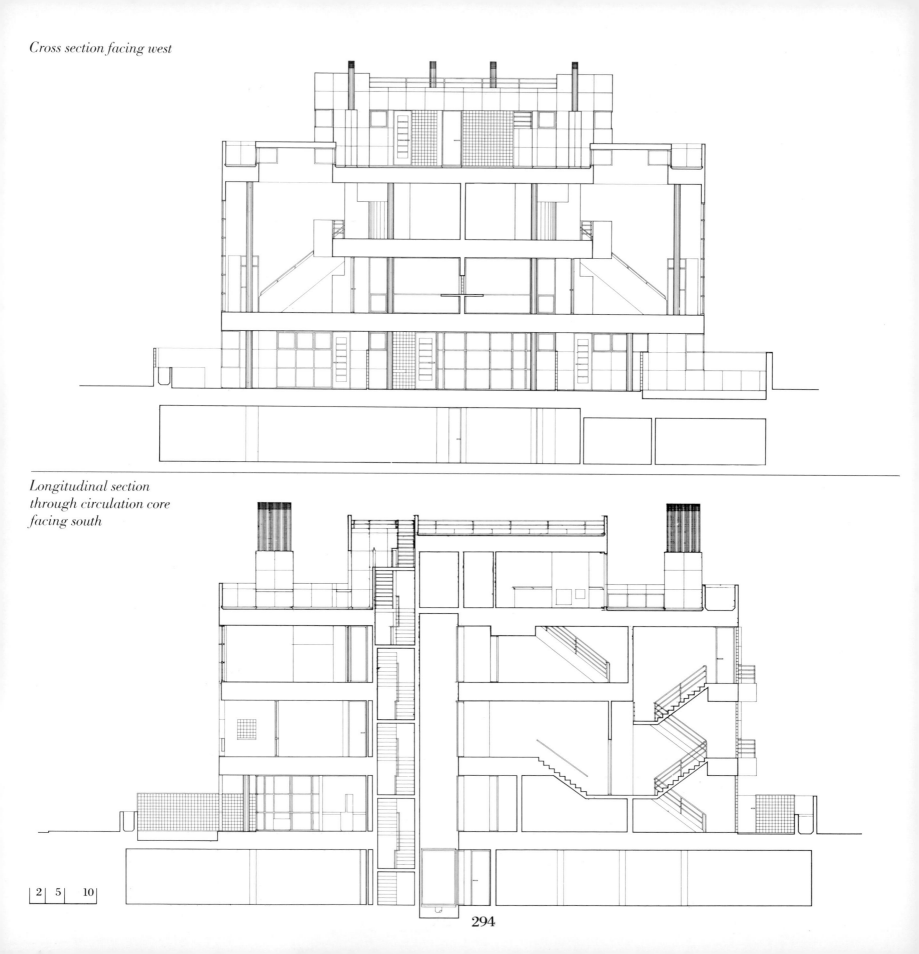

Cross section facing west

*Longitudinal section
through circulation core
facing south*

2 5   10

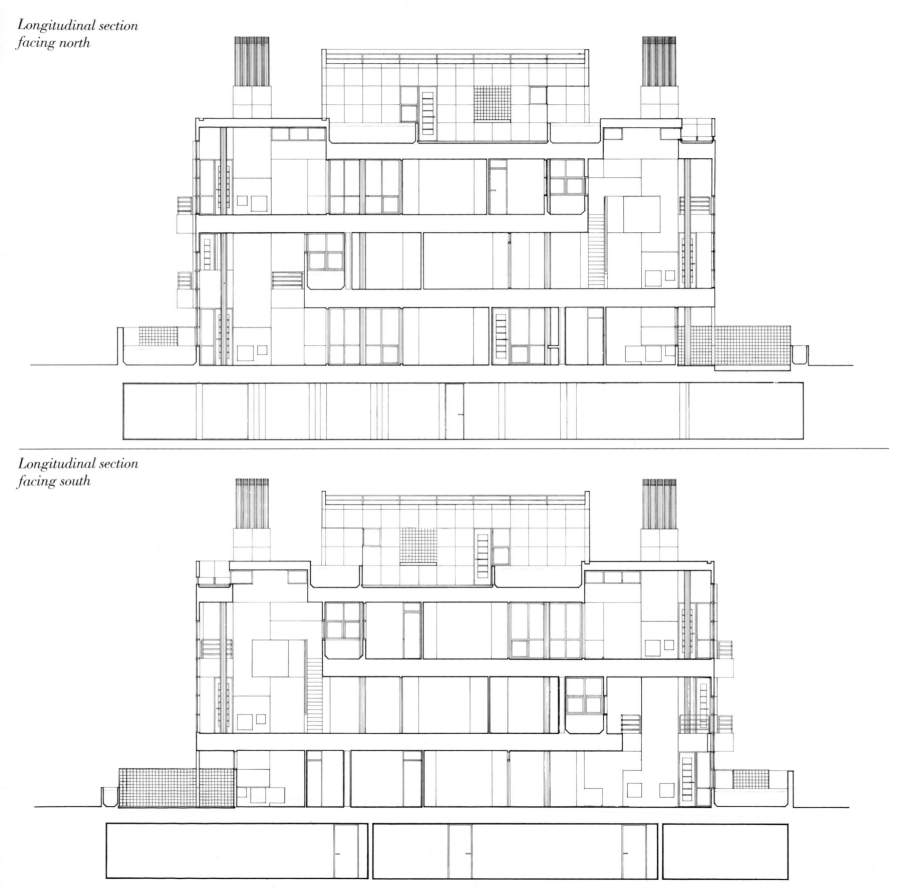

Longitudinal section facing north

Longitudinal section facing south

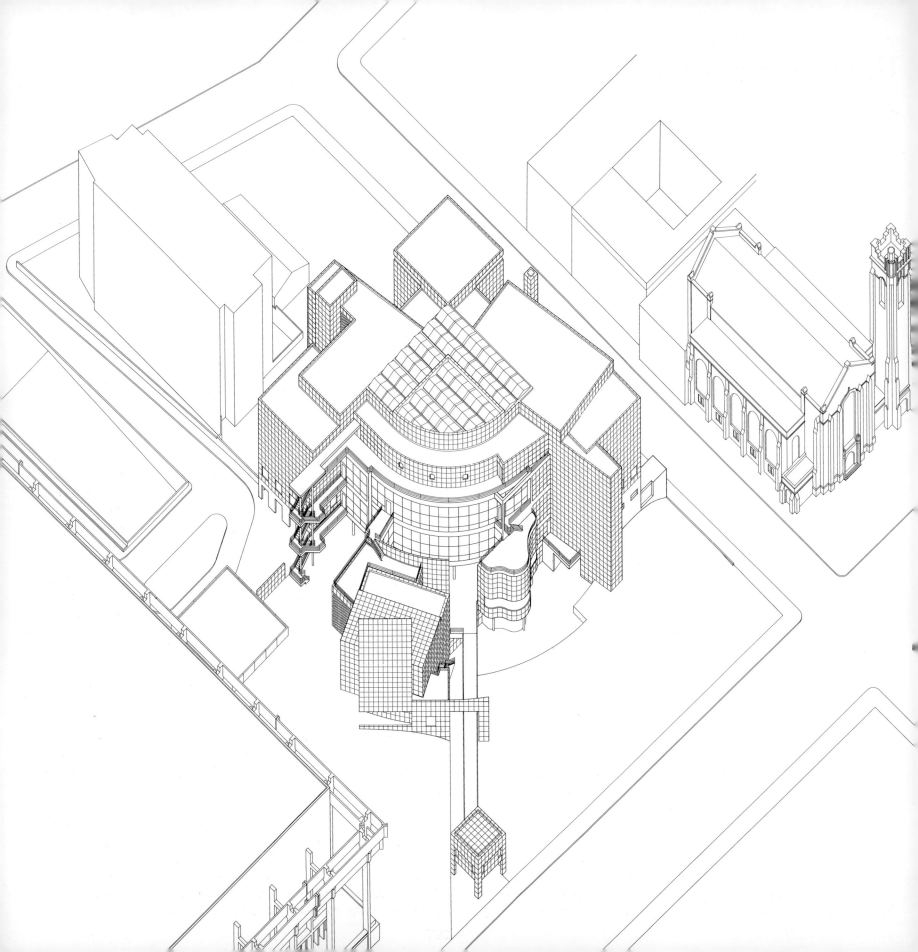

High Museum of Art

Atlanta, Georgia
1980–1983

The High Museum of Art is a major public building and art repository for an important city. In this respect it resembles the Museum for the Decorative Arts in Frankfurt. But whereas the Frankfurt museum is designed to complement the neoclassical villa which is its centerpiece, the Atlanta museum is an entirely new building that responds in another way to the typological and contextual aspects of the museum program. The city's consciously progressive building tradition as well as its role as a developing cultural center had a strong influence on the design.

The corner site, at the junction of Peachtree and Sixteenth streets about two miles from downtown Atlanta and adjacent to both the large Memorial Arts Center and the First Presbyterian Church on Peachtree, places the museum at an important location for Atlanta's future development and within a pedestrian-oriented neighborhood with good public transportation access. The parti consists of four quadrants with one carved out to distinguish it from the other three—a basic diagram not unlike that of Frankfurt, though completely reinterpreted; here the missing quadrant becomes a monumental atrium, the lobby and ceremonial center of the museum.

As the treed frontage on Peachtree is attractive, and as traffic patterns prefer an entry on this thoroughfare, the building faces this side of the site, sitting adjacent to the Memorial Arts Center. It is set well back from the street to allow the green space in front to be preserved. One enters by way of a long ramp projecting along the diagonal of the site. This ramp takes one past a screen wall and a portico into the main level of the building.

As in the Atheneum, the extended exterior ramp is both a symbolic gesture reaching out to the street and city, and a foil to the tensile—here quarter-circular—interior ramp which is the building's chief formal and circulatory element. The diagonal of the entry ramp

plunging into the heart of the building disrupts the classical four-square symmetry of the plan, setting in motion a set of more turbulent geometries which successively inflect the architectural order.

The cubic volume at a sixty-degree angle to the building which one passes on the left of the entry ramp is a two-hundred seat auditorium. It is treated as separate from the main body of the building for reasons of access and security, but by its location it reinforces the entry and forms part of the processional sequence. This volume is entered at the end of the ramp through a neck between itself and a convex wall, and exited by way of a ramp running in reverse alongside the ingoing ramp, producing a continuous circulation loop.

At the end of the ramp on the right is a piano-curved element; this is the main entry and reception area, from which one passes into the four-story atrium. To some extent the light-filled atrium space is inspired by, and a commentary on, the central space of the Guggenheim Museum. Ramped circulation and gallery spaces encircle it, making it the fixed point of reference for movement up and around the galleries. As in the Guggenheim, the ramp system mediates between the central space and the art itself, which may be seen and reseen from various levels, angles, and distances as one moves upward. In the Guggenheim, however, the ramp is made to double as a gallery, inducing a propelling motion that is inappropriate to contemplative viewing. The sloping floor plane, ceilings, and walls not only are uncomfortable but, by suppressing the right-angle datum, make the display of paintings especially difficult. In Atlanta, the separation of circulation and gallery space overcomes these problems while maintaining the virtue of a central space governing the system of movement. This separation also allows the atrium walls to have windows which admit natural light and offer framed views of the city, while the galleries can receive both natural and artificial light depending on the requirements of the art displayed.

Site

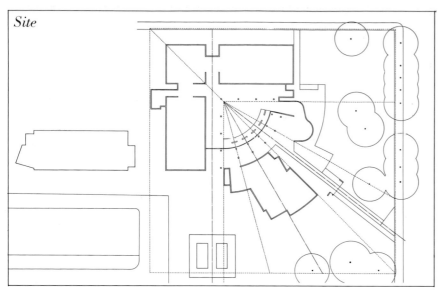

Entry

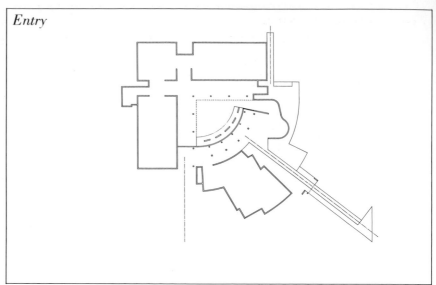

Program

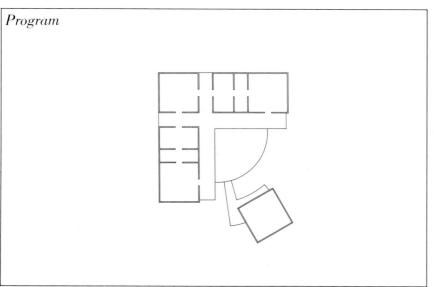

Circulation

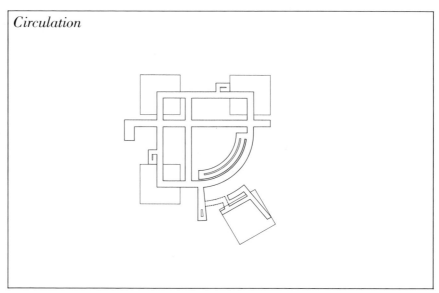

Structure

Enclosure

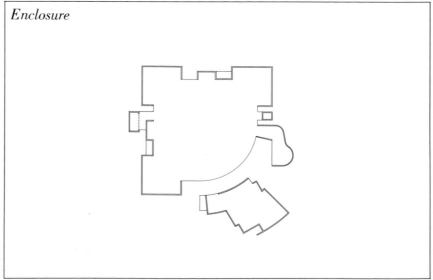

Studies of plans and sections

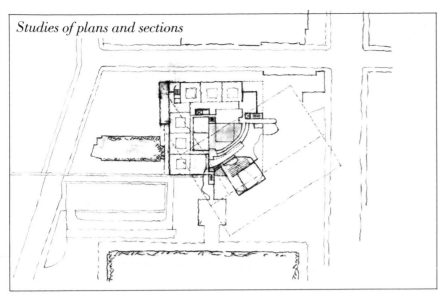

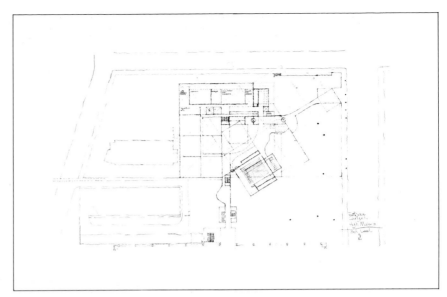

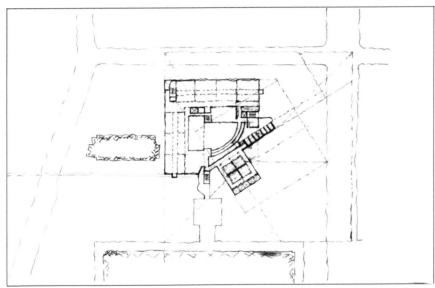

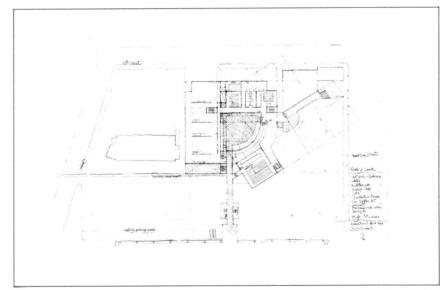

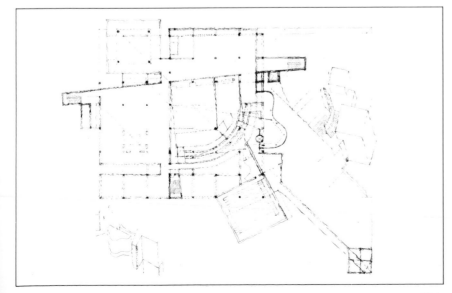

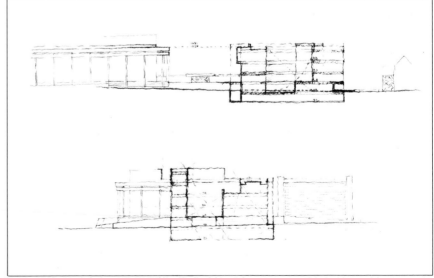

Ground level plan

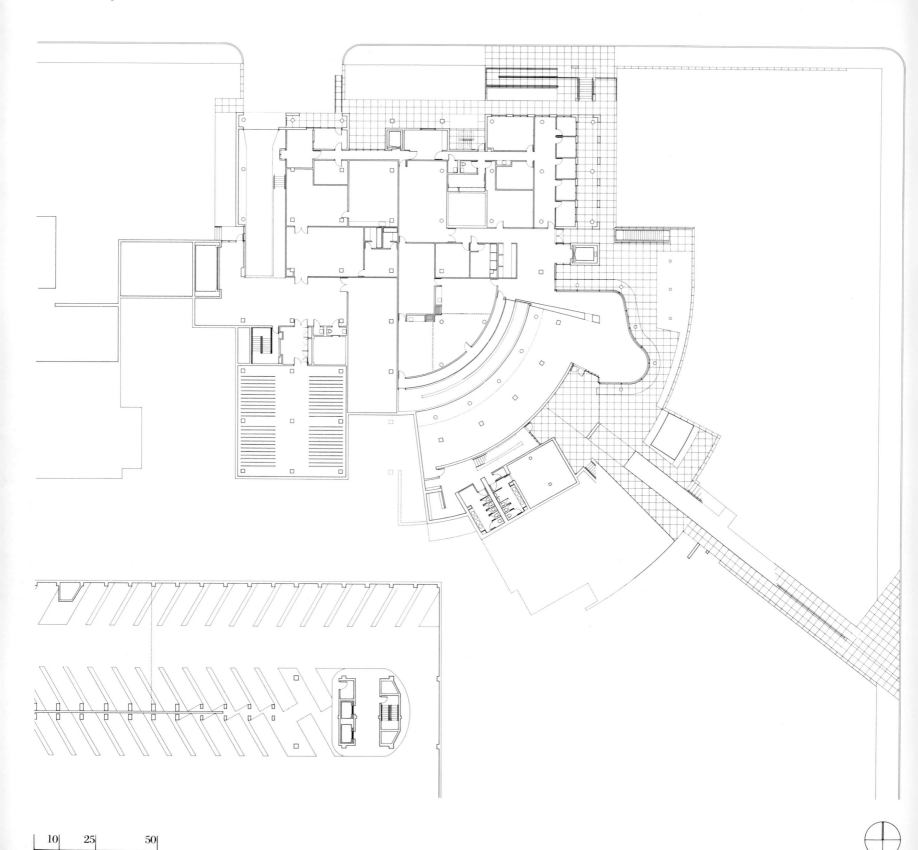

|10| 25| 50|

Entry level plan

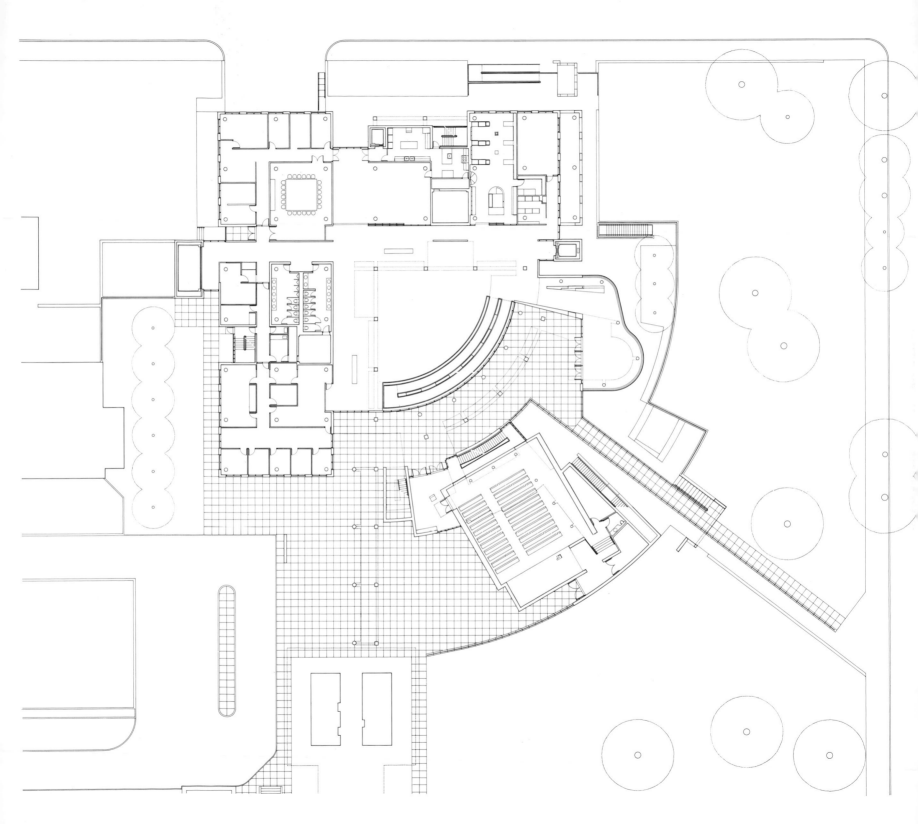

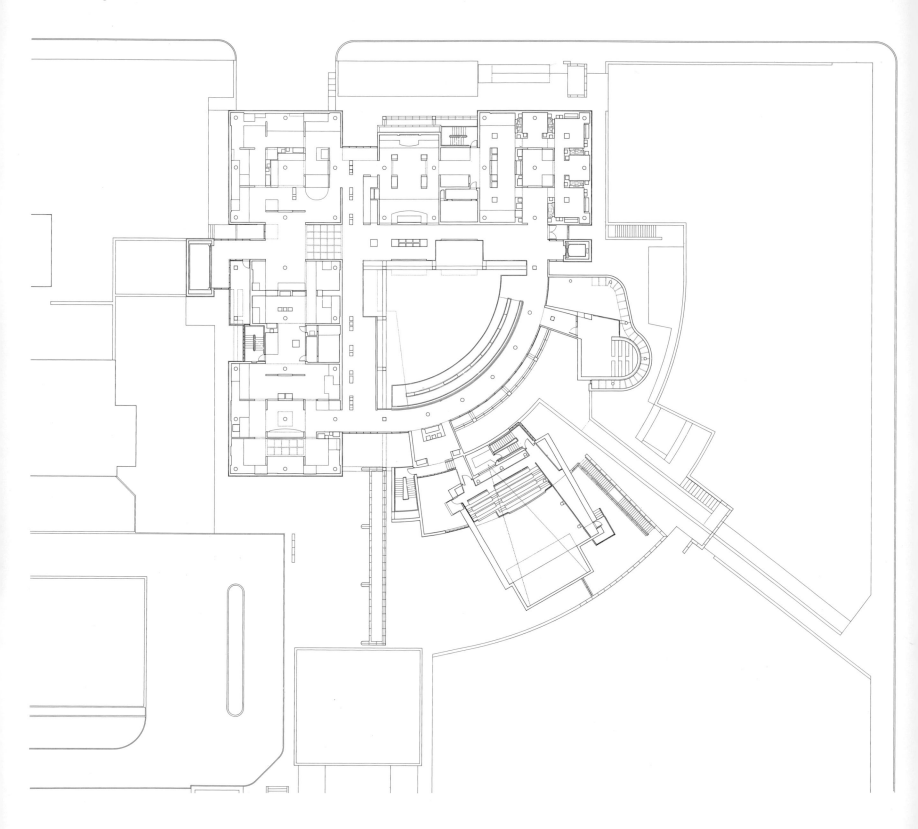

Third level plan

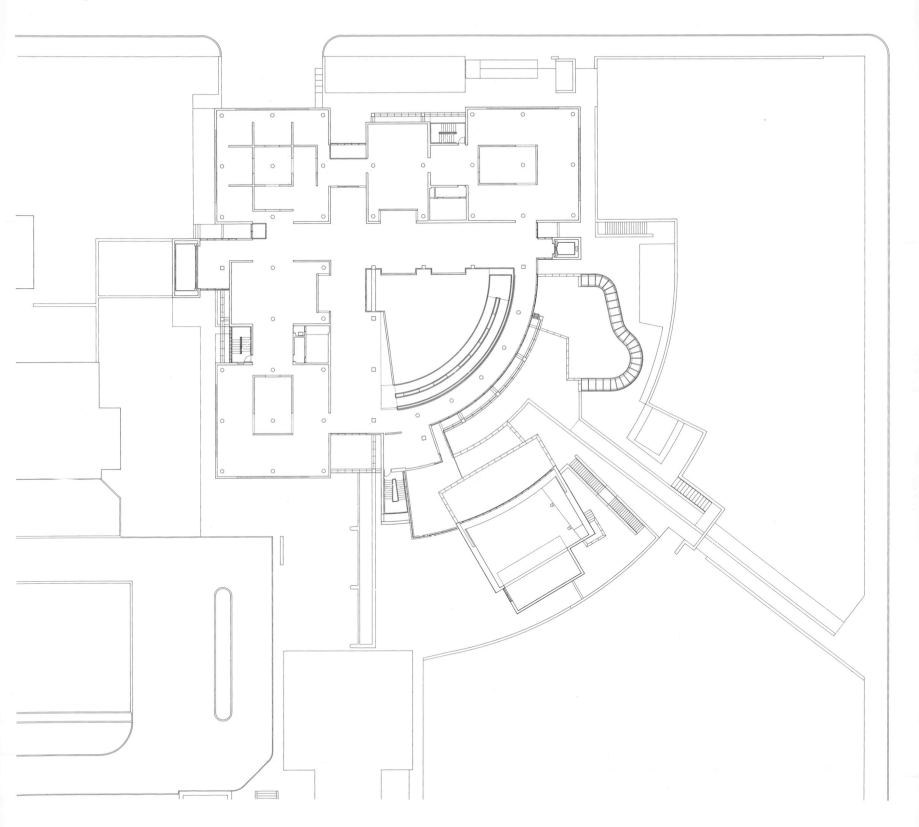

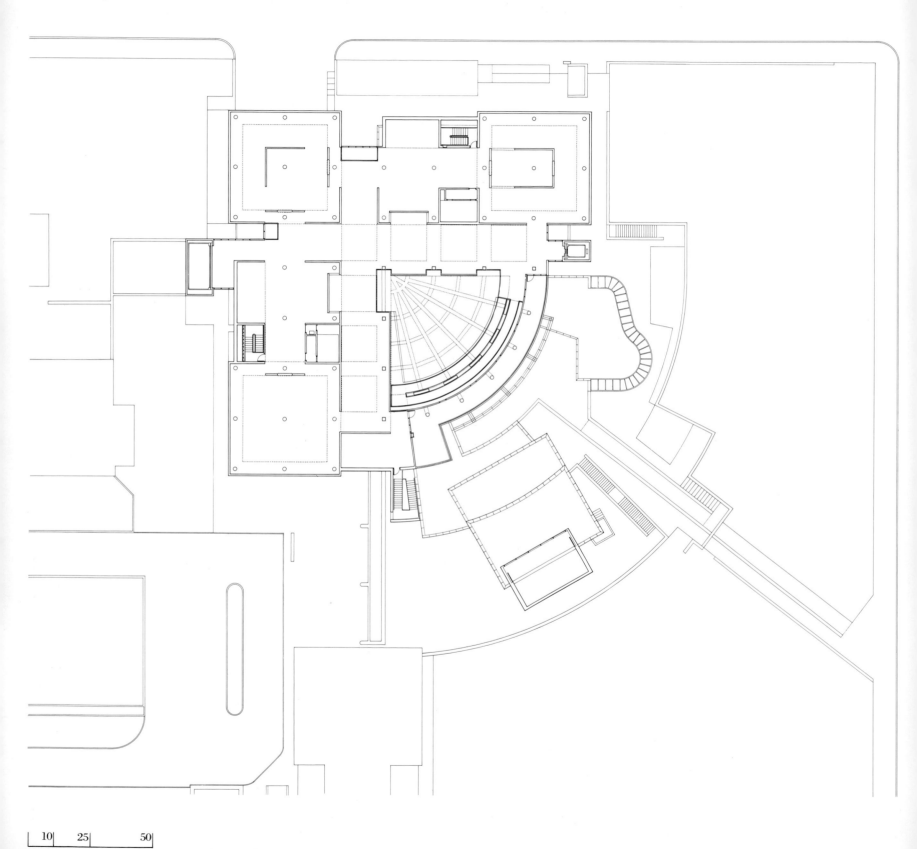

| 10| 25| 50|

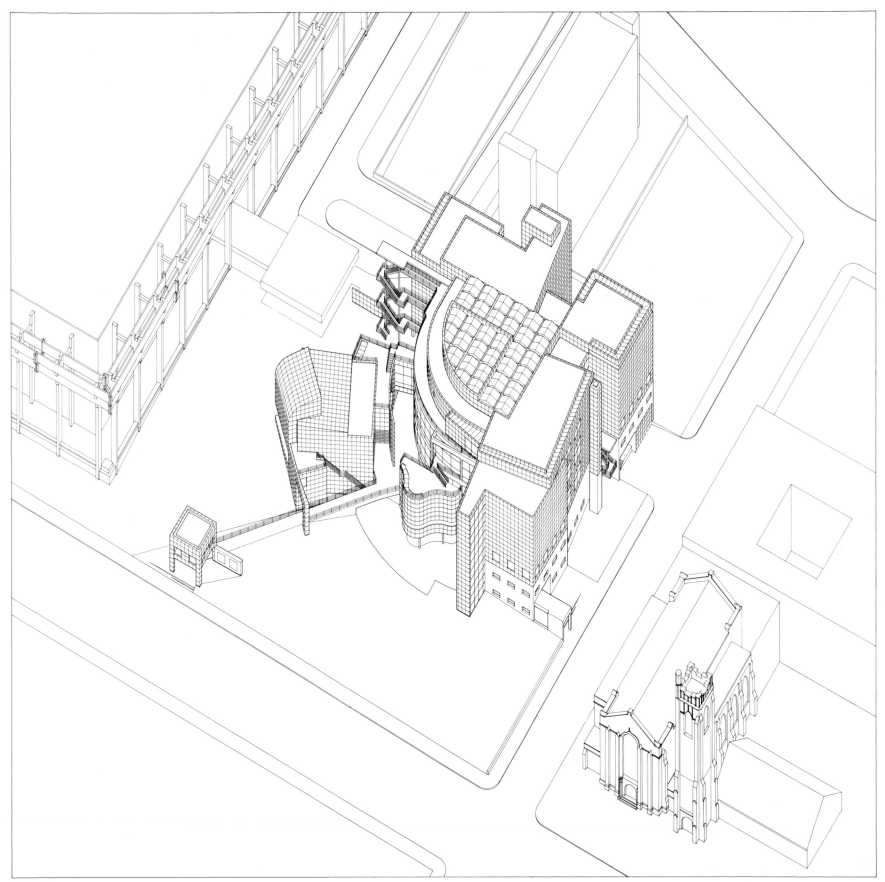

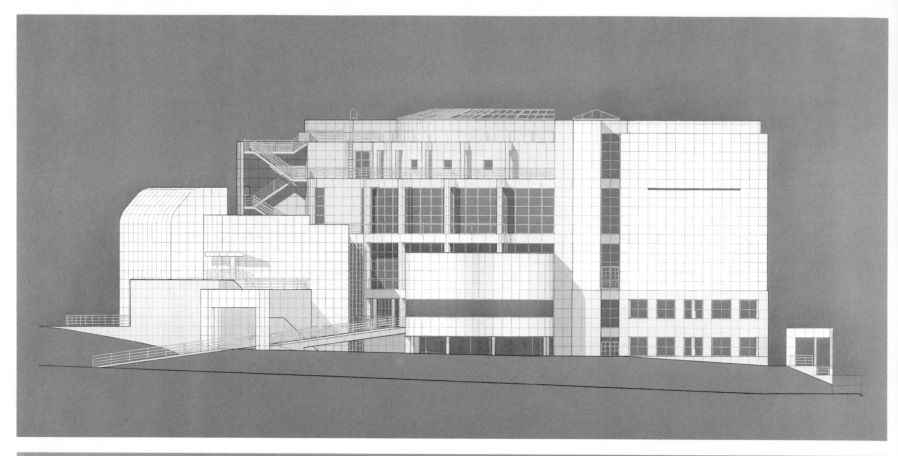

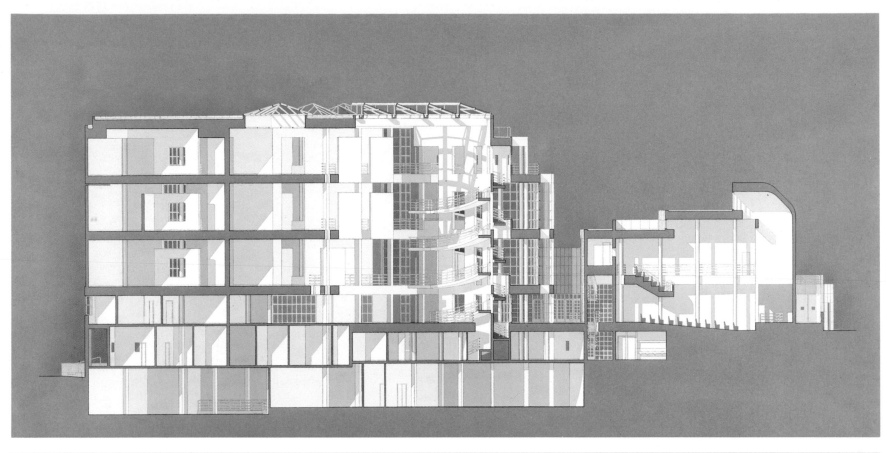

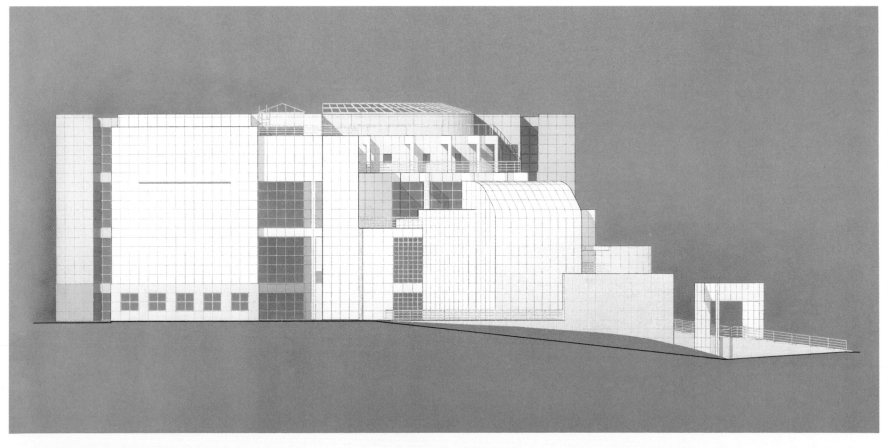

West elevation

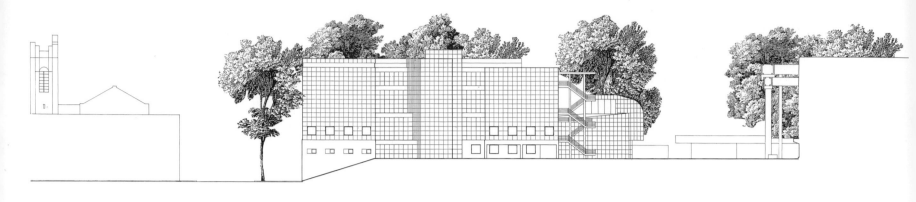

Section through west galleries facing east

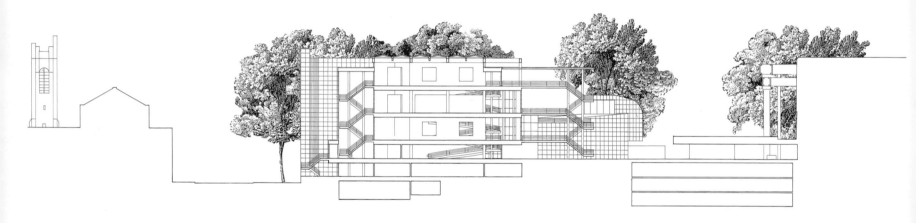

Section through galleries and atrium facing southeast

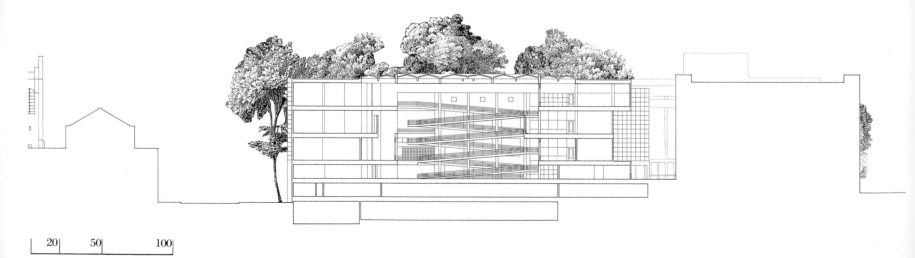

20 50 100

East elevation

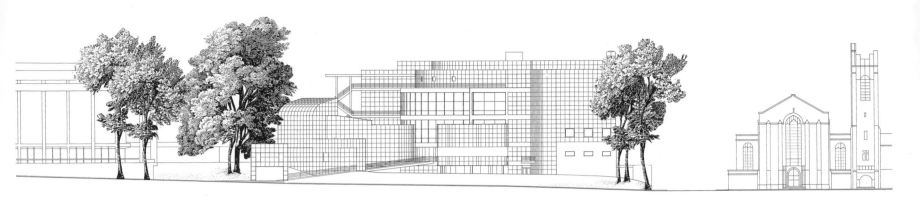

Section through atrium facing west

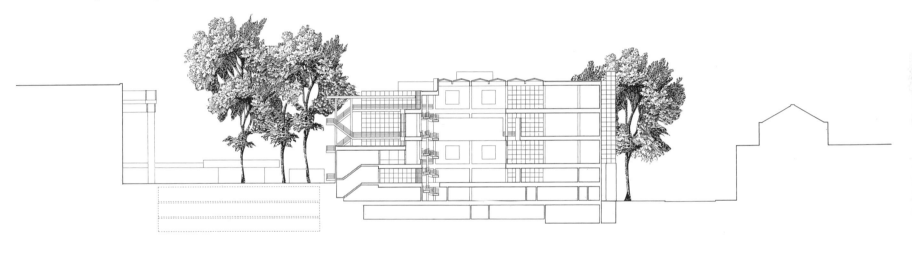

Section through atrium and auditorium facing northeast

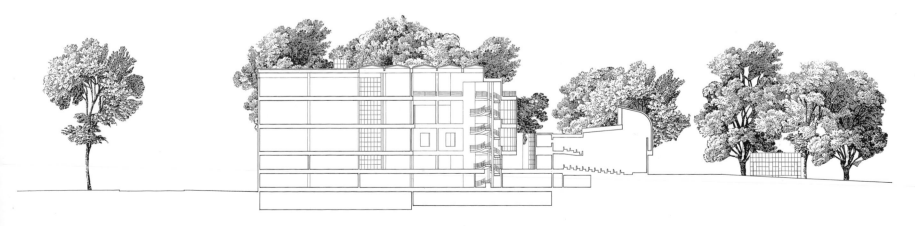

The galleries are organized to provide multiple vistas and cross-references, intimate and larger-scale viewing accommodating the diverse needs of the collection, and glimpses across the atrium from one exhibition space into another. This technique of creating multiple points for viewing art was initially conceived for the New York School Exhibition, where it worked very well, and used again in the museum in Frankfurt. Here the spatial variety, together with the clearly apparent relationship of the plan parts afforded by the atrium, helps alleviate the fatigue that one often experiences in large museums.

Programmatically, the 130,000-square-foot building is composed of 52,000 square feet of gallery space. Off the ground-floor court are a cafe with a kitchen, a museum shop, a members' lounge, and, behind a wall used for exhibiting new acquisitions, curators' and director's offices, staff spaces, and the board room. The counterclockwise ramp circulation to the upper-floor galleries takes one roughly chronologically through the history of art; stairs and an elevator provide alternative means of circulation. The top floor is shared by twentieth-century art and loan exhibitions; built-in flexibility allows the loan space to expand into the twentieth-century space in order to accommodate major shows. The auditorium, separate from the main building at entry level, may be entered from within at the second level, where the balcony access allows it to function as an integral part of the museum when desired. On the floor below the main level are the educational spaces—junior galleries, lecture rooms, workshops, department offices—which have their own entry off of Sixteenth Street, so that children coming by bus can be dropped off here and come directly into the building under cover. Storage areas and other service and mechanical spaces are also located on this level.

The structure consists of steel columns and frame and concrete slabs. The granite plinth acts as a horizontal datum for the ramps and, in elevation, as an anchor for the white porcelain-enameled steel panels cladding the galleries above. Light, whether direct or filtered, admitted through skylights, ribbon glazing, clerestory strips, or minimal perforations in the panel wall, is a constant preoccupation throughout: apart from its functional aspect, it is a symbol of the museum's role as a place of aesthetic illumination and enlightened cultural values. The primary intention of the architecture is to encourage the discovery of these values, and to foster a contemplative appreciation of the museum's collection through its own spatial experience.

The High Museum is the same height as the adjacent Memorial Arts Center, a building of the sixties to which very little other relationship could be made, seen at the far left in the photograph above.

The inclined ramp goes to the main entry of the museum. The flat path leads to the lower-level educational spaces and children's museum. The photograph at right is of the view as one moves from the car park area toward the outdoor arrival space where the main entry ramp culminates.

314

315

Half the length of the circulation ramp is inside the atrium space; the other half is outside it, with large windows looking both into the atrium and out to the exterior. From the entry level, one can take the ramp either up to the main exhibition spaces or down to the children's level. The main level of the atrium is for reception as well as public events.

Vertical views of the twentieth-century collection on the top floor, the nineteenth-century collection on the third floor, and non-Western art on the second floor make for an unconventional way of perceiving and contrasting three different periods of art.

319

The ramp's cantilevered landings and alternating points of entry to each gallery floor add interest and provide changing standpoints for viewing the works of art.

Views into the atrium space exist on every gallery level. Overhead, one can see the changing light through the radial skylight, whose form reinforces that of the quarter-circular atrium. Twelve-foot-square walls along one side of the atrium modulate the light coming from the skylight into the galleries behind them.

Within the permanent collection galleries, rooms within rooms allow for more intimate-scale viewing of smaller paintings and sculpture. In contrast, the galleries around the atrium are more open and provide a mixture of natural and artificial light.

The decorative arts installation was specifically designed for the museum's permanent collection in order to show each object to best advantage. Conceptually, the organization is similar to that of the rest of the collection in that perspectival vistas and views through framed openings exist throughout.

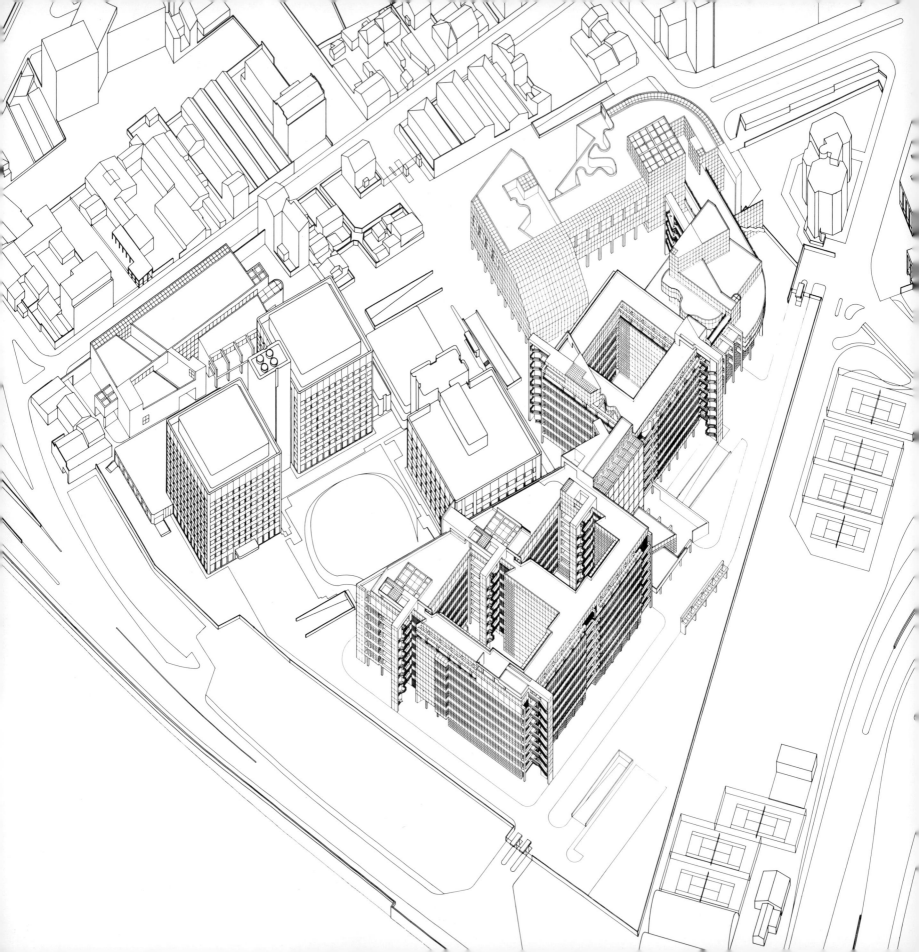

Renault Administrative Headquarters

Boulogne-Billancourt, France
1981

The proposed headquarters for the Régie Nationale des Usines Renault is located on a triangular site at Point du Jour just outside Paris city limits on the west bank of the Seine. Incorporating a group of office buildings built in the 1960s, the master plan takes its cues from the geometry of the site as well as from its orientation to the city of Paris. The program was especially challenging. Besides requiring an appropriate public image for a company dedicated to the development of advanced technology, it emphasized the provision of an environment for the center's fourteen hundred employees that would assure the highest quality of life in the work place. Too often the design of office buildings is little more than an attempt to maximize square footage or to erect a prestige-conferring object in a landscape of corporate one-upmanship. In this case, the standard of amenity specified—including an office with a window for every worker, an art gallery, employee gymnasium, full-service restaurant, and outdoor park space—as well as a flexible office layout that would promote communication between different levels of the company hierarchy, encouraged a search for an innovative solution.

Facing Paris across the dividing line of the Boulevard Périphérique on one side and the existing Renault office blocks on the other, the new administrative building has two major facades—a ceremonial public one directed to the community and city, and a private one directed to the company itself. Two corresponding geometries are used as ordering devices. The private facade, facing the existing buildings and creating an internal enclave with them, responds to and complements the older buildings, and its orientation and scale as well as the height of the complex as a whole are generated by these buildings' orthogonal grid and plan dimensions. The public facade is rotated twenty-four degrees from this grid; its geometry is derived from the street grid of Paris across the boulevard and from the perpendicular bank of the Seine, which the south facade of the building, along the Quai du Pont du Jour, parallels.

329

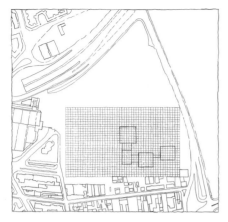

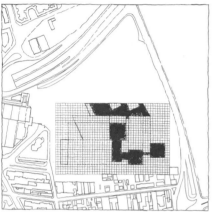

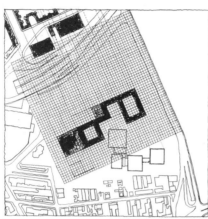

Schematic analysis of the site
Top left: existing buildings on the site and their grid extended as a field
Top right: diagonal grid generated by the edge of the Seine, and the geometry of Paris as it meets the edge of the site
Bottom left: the portion of the new building within the field of the existing buildings
Bottom right: the portion of the new building within the field generated by the city of Paris

The overlay of the two grids in the new design is seen in the site plan

Symbolically the existence of the two "fronts" emphasizes the dual corporate aspect, public and private, while formally the two orientations and two geometries fuse to create a rich architectonic vocabulary. The distinction between public and private realms permeates every part of the complex. It is articulated in plan in the contrast between rectangular, cellular, or repetitive spaces, which contain offices and rooms of defined function, and more free-form, freely planned spaces, containing social, recreational, and eating areas, lobbies and galleries, and the like. It is the public facade that governs the grid of the more rigidly defined system, while the grid of the facade oriented to the internal domain allows for freer composition. The eight-story building is organized vertically in a fairly hierarchical way: public spaces are concentrated at ground level, general offices are distributed throughout the upper stories, and the top floor is reserved for executive office suites.

The ceremonial public entry faces Paris and is reached by a private roadway whose principal access is off the Quai du Point du Jour. The main entry space is a skylit atrium with exhibition, information, and waiting areas. From here one gets glimpses both horizontally and vertically of the inner world of the corporation. To the right of this lobby, near an enclosed passageway leading to the older buildings, is the full-service restaurant, again freely defined and with its own internal courtyard. Next to the restaurant and sharing the kitchen and services in between is a cafeteria, which turns the corner of the site and opens out onto a formal landscaped garden and toward the site for a future automotive museum-showroom. The other public spaces on the ground level are located to the left of the lobby, but separated from the front wall of offices by two courtyards. They are related to the restaurant facilities by a setback alignment in plan and to the existing buildings behind by their orientation and grid. These spaces, which like the other social spaces lend themselves to free plan and curvilinear elevational treatment, balance the rectilinear articulation of the office spaces across the courtyards. Their functions include large conference rooms and a Research, Art, and Industry Gallery where Renault personnel or the invited public can view changing exhibitions of art and science.

The office space, comprising the bulk of the program, is designed to allow every employee maximum natural light and view, and to respond to the primary goals established by the program: a flexible layout, work space that is both functional and comfortable, and an inter-floor arrangement that encourages communication among employees. The typical office floor is organized as a "life unit" of fifty people, a working-group size that corresponds to the company's lateral structure. Each life unit is disposed around one of the large exterior courtyards—there are three within the complex—and may function either as a suite of offices or as an open office landscape. From every office space there is a view, either out to the city or into a courtyard, and no office is smaller than three meters by five meters.

330

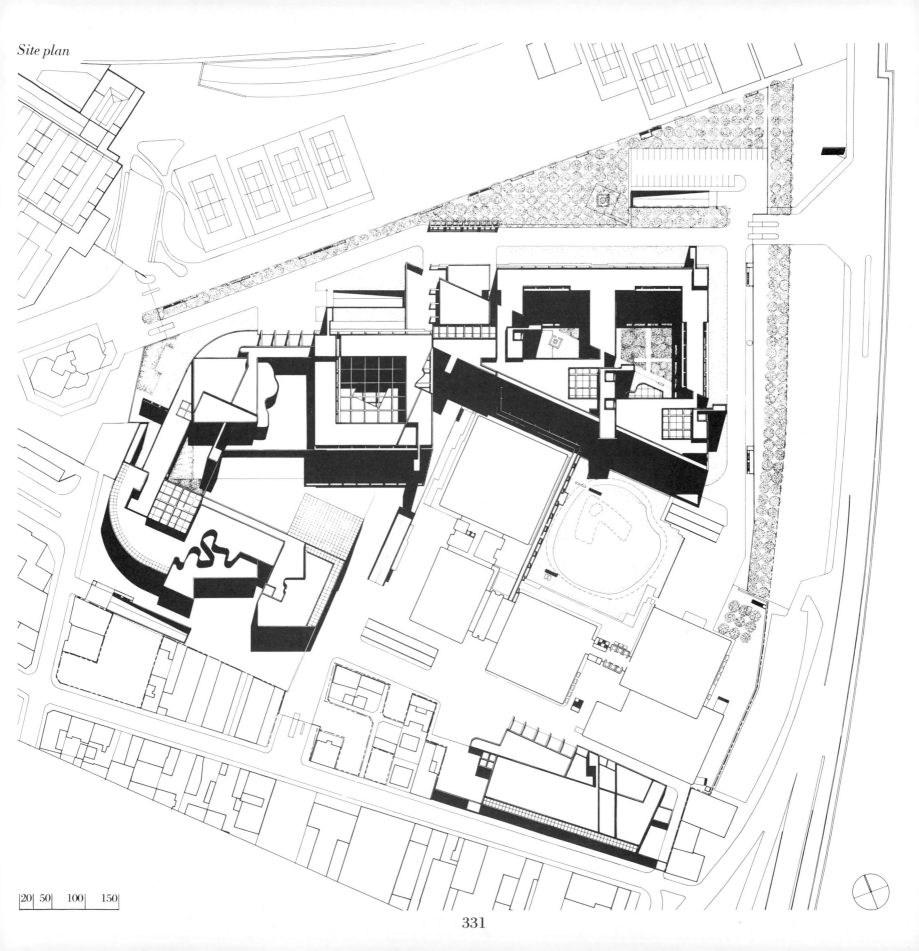

Site plan

|20| 50| 100| 150|

331

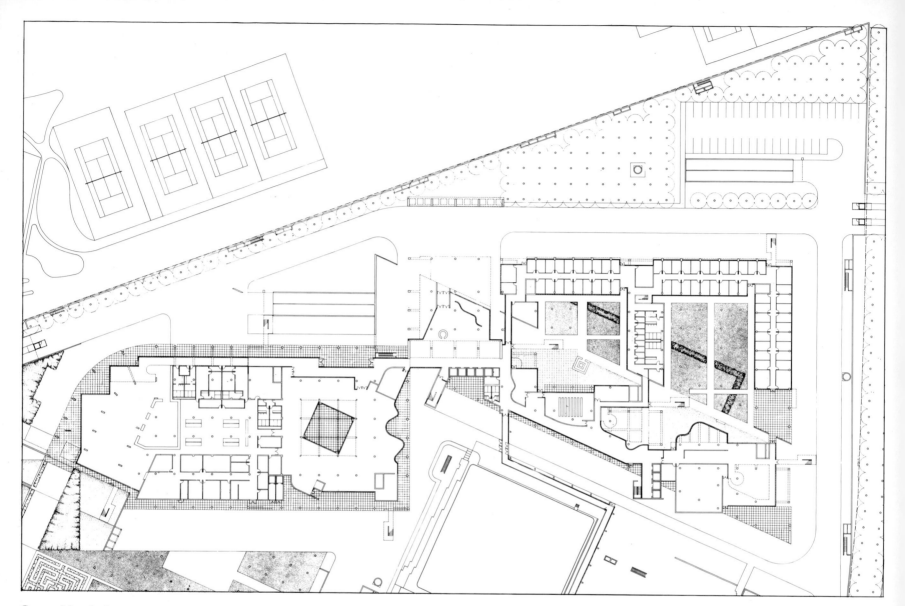

Ground level plan

20| 50| 100| 200|

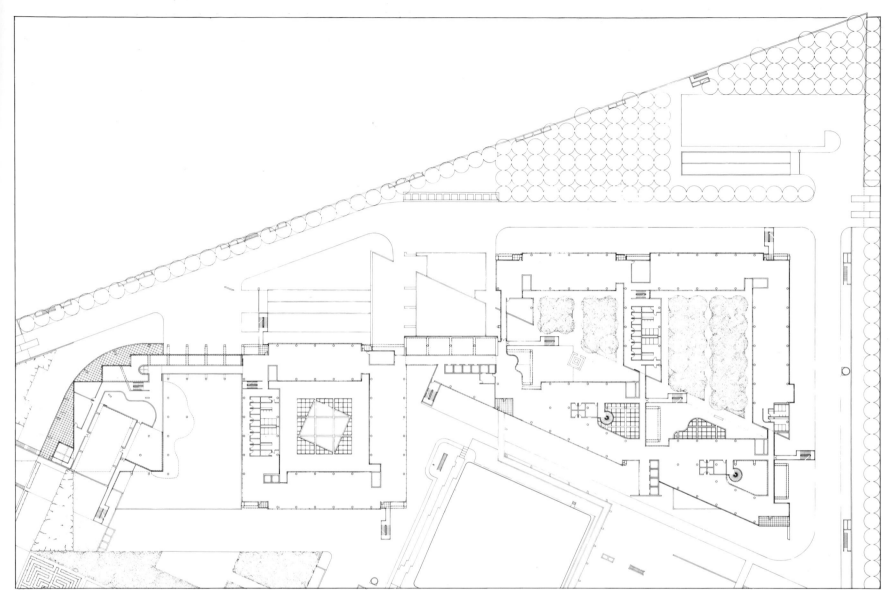

Second level plan
Transverse section through new and existing buildings facing west

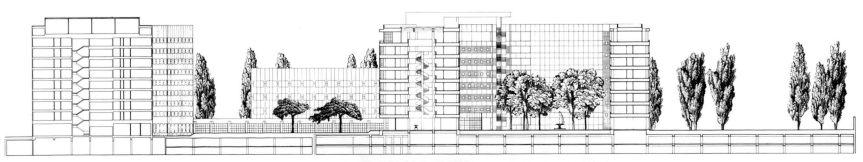

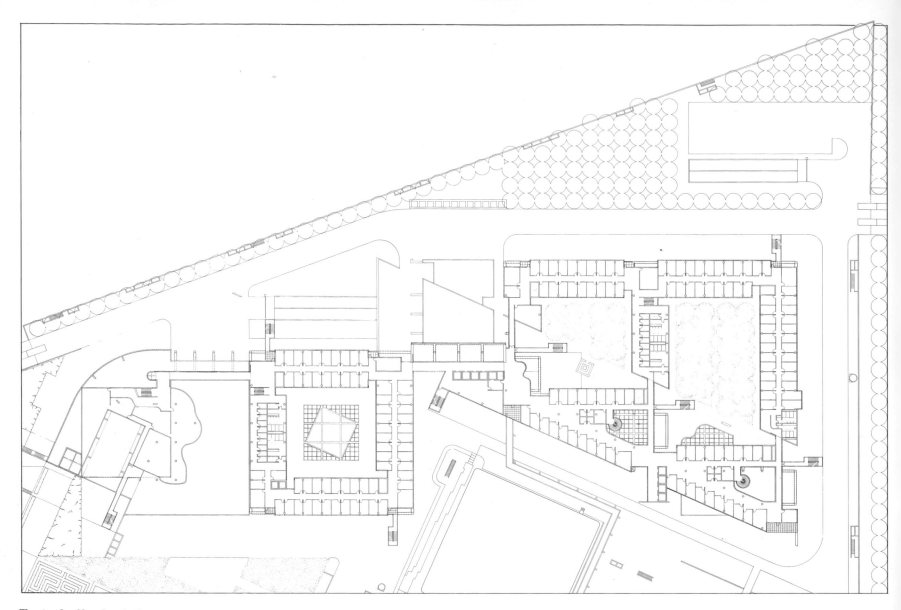

Typical office level plan
Longitudinal section facing south

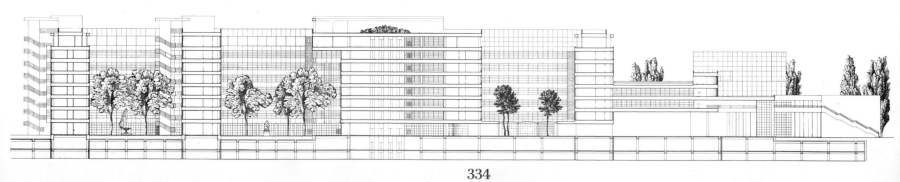

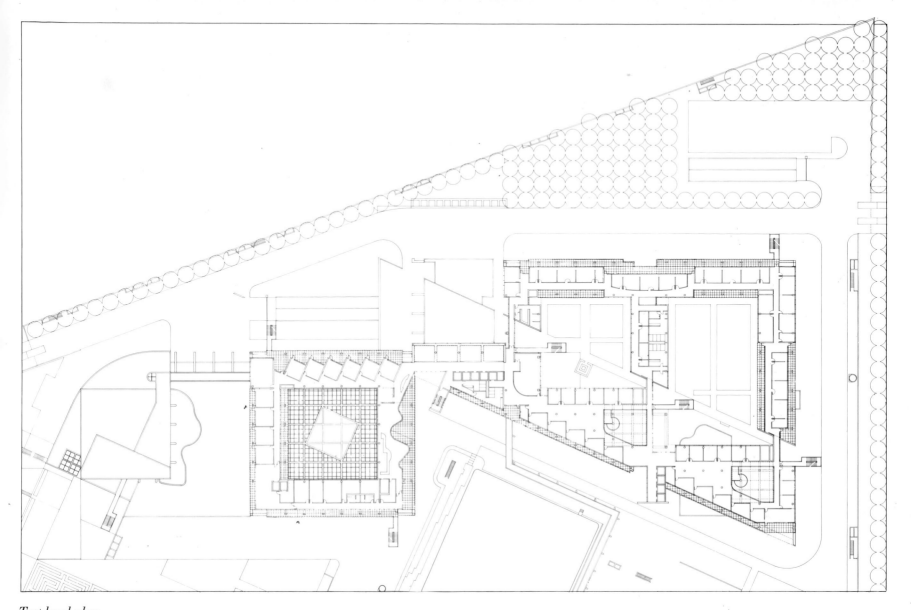

Top level plan

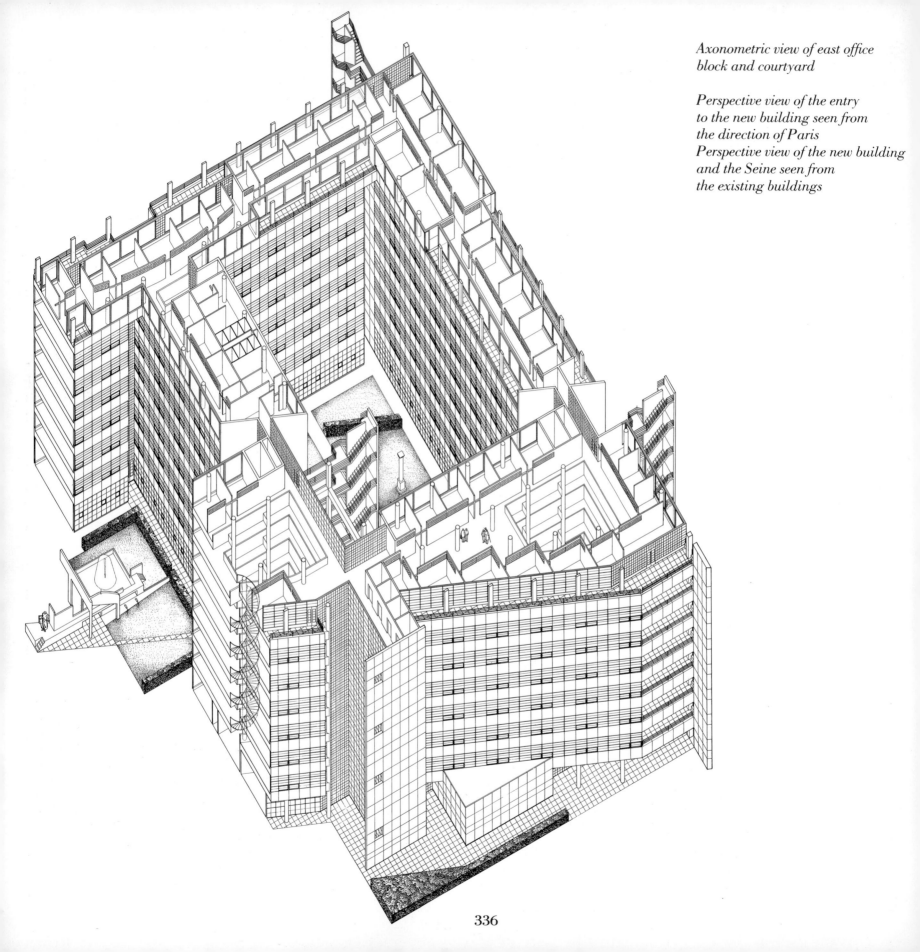

Axonometric view of east office
block and courtyard

Perspective view of the entry
to the new building seen from
the direction of Paris
Perspective view of the new building
and the Seine seen from
the existing buildings

336

The unusual requirement that every office space within the complex have its own window necessitated a building with a large perimeter surface, giving each employee a view to the Seine, to the city of Paris, to Boulogne-Billancourt, or to one of the open landscaped courtyards. The more sculptural edges of the building indicate the public-use portions of the complex: the two curved forms visible in the site model define a museum for the history of automotive design and a health club above a ground-level restaurant.

Building in a historic city like Paris involves certain restrictions, such as that of respecting an eight-story building height. This has both advantages and disadvantages. One advantage is the significant relationship derived from scaling the building to its context. On the other hand, one of the problems of designing an eight-story building of this size is the necessity to break down the monotony of what would otherwise look like a monumental horizontal extrusion. This was done here by pulling out fire stairs and insetting balconies to articulate each life unit and punctuate the facades. The exterior wall of the building was intended to be a metal-panel-and-glass unit prefabricated in the automobile factory, with gasketed movable windows and an automobile-type finish—an image much like that of Renault's cars, representing the advanced technology of this multifaceted company.

The world headquarters building for Renault is not an office building in the conventional sense in that it houses numerous communal functions not usually found in such a program, encompassing uses both interior to the company and oriented to the city at large.

The life units are conveniently linked both horizontally and vertically. Vertical circulation is via banks of elevators and internal staircases which open into skylit atria that also allow horizontal access to contiguous units. The atria are located along the main artery of circulation on each floor and are intended to be primary elements fostering sociality. The top level of the building is the executive floor, and here, as in each of the life units, each director's suite is distinctly defined but still related to the whole. As throughout the building, privacy exists without isolation, and the plan responds to the needs of both the individual and the larger group, accommodating variations in usage as well as fixed functions.

The facades combine materials matched closely in color and texture: porcelain-enameled steel panels, glass blocks, glass. The concrete structure behind allows for a free facade that can become a giant windowed screen, admitting light where glass is inserted, or blocking it where a metal panel, an "opaque window," is introduced. The cladding harmonizes with the existing office buildings, which also have a metal-panel skin.

The major exterior elements of the complex, the gardens and courtyards, are conceived of as a formal, highly ordered landscape that echoes and comments upon the architectural order. Manicured flower beds and ornamental orchards intended for two of the courtyards, and a close-cropped carpet of grass would extend uniformly up to the foot of the facades. Axes are emphasized by fountains or sculpture. As in the great gardens of French classicism, a close accord exists between the natural element and the architectural one—in the interplay of open and closed spaces, transitions and contrasts, geometry and irregularity. Thus, the gardens impose themselves on the architecture, which in turn limits and contains them. This encounter between built and natural worlds produces a poetic effect in which conventional definitions and boundaries are overcome. Order gives way to discovery and delight, offering the worker place for his creative dreams and imagination.

Historical development of the site

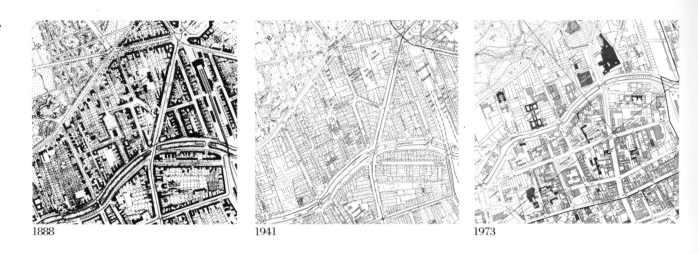

1888   1941   1973

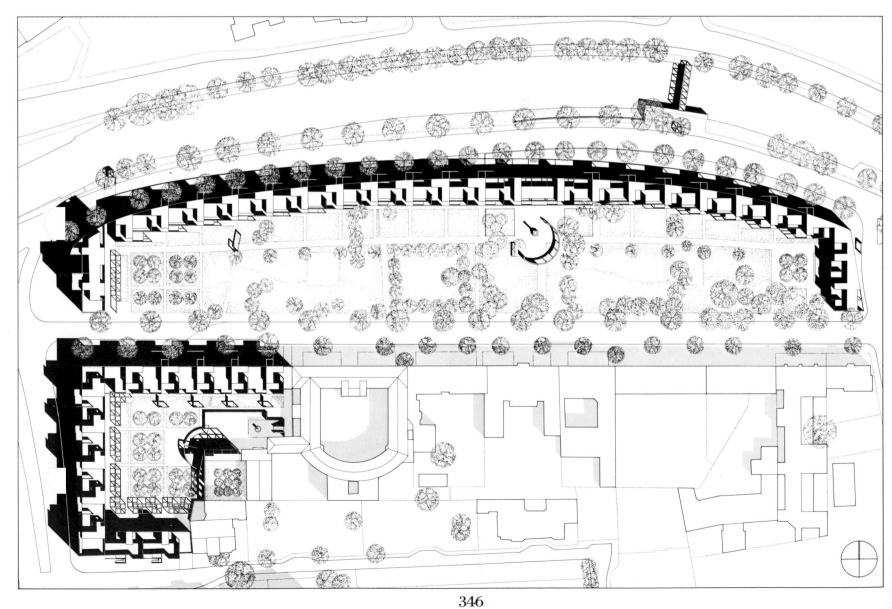

Internationale Bauausstellung Housing

Berlin, West Germany
1982

In 1888 this two-block site in Berlin between the Landwehrkanal, Potsdamer Strasse, and Flottwellstrasse had a completely built periphery. Along the crescent-shaped bank of the canal, the Schöneberger Ufer, it took the form of a wall of four- and five-story housing, the front plane of which followed the contour of the water and, with adjacent blocks of similar housing, gave a continuous edge to the canal. Behind the crescent housing was a mostly open area of private garden plots and a minor street, Am Karlsbad, separating the shallow canal block from the interior one behind. In the years prior to 1941, the open area behind the crescent was densely infilled with housing, Am Karlsbad became a thoroughfare, and a wall of large-scale, mixed-use buildings developed on the south side of the street. By the end of the war, however, most of the housing had been destroyed, and today, despite the survival of the older housing on the block to the east, the canal block consists of an open sports ground and parking lot, while on the interior block, no longer served by a through-street, only about half of the buildings remain. On the opposite side of the canal, the city structure suffered almost complete destruction. Since 1945, it has evolved into a large open green space with scattered monuments such as Hans Scharoun's huge State Library located directly across from the site, Mies Van der Rohe's National Gallery diagonally opposite, and Scharoun's Philharmonic Hall further north.

The housing proposed here is an attempt to resurrect some of the density and urbanistic quality present in the two earlier plans. It does so by defining a new canal wall of building that serves both as an edge to a densely built block south of it and as a response to the undefined space across the canal. From the nineteenth-century plan, the crescent-shaped row of housing with open space behind is revived, while from the later plan is derived the transformation of Am Karlsbad into a through-street with a continuous wall of building on the south side. The placement of additional housing around the perimeter of the interior block creates an enclosed quadrangle courtyard that is completed by existing housing and commercial buildings.

On the canal block, at both ends of the crescent, a corner piece turns and completes the block, the more monumental end piece on Potsdamer Strasse, a major traffic artery in the city, reestablishing an orthogonal street grid and nine-story building height along this elevation, and functioning with the building adjacent to it as a gateway to Am Karlsbad. The ground-level space along the Potsdamer elevation is given over to shops, with housing above. From the canal elevation, public access to the interior of the development is through a passageway under three of the housing units, the center unit widened by a bay to mark it as the portal and apex of the curve. Slightly further along the crescent, a pedestrian bridge over the canal is proposed, restoring a connection that existed prior to the war.

The housing itself consists of one-bedroom and two-bedroom apartments, all with individual winter gardens facing into the courtyard. The perimeter scheme affords each unit private views inward as well as more public views outward to the street and the city. The overall scheme as well as many of its details—for example, the way the entry stair to each unit is treated—represents a typology of housing which is in the best tradition of older Berlin residential building. At the same time, the scale and density proposed for the blocks is an attempt to restore some character and definition to the damaged urban fabric.

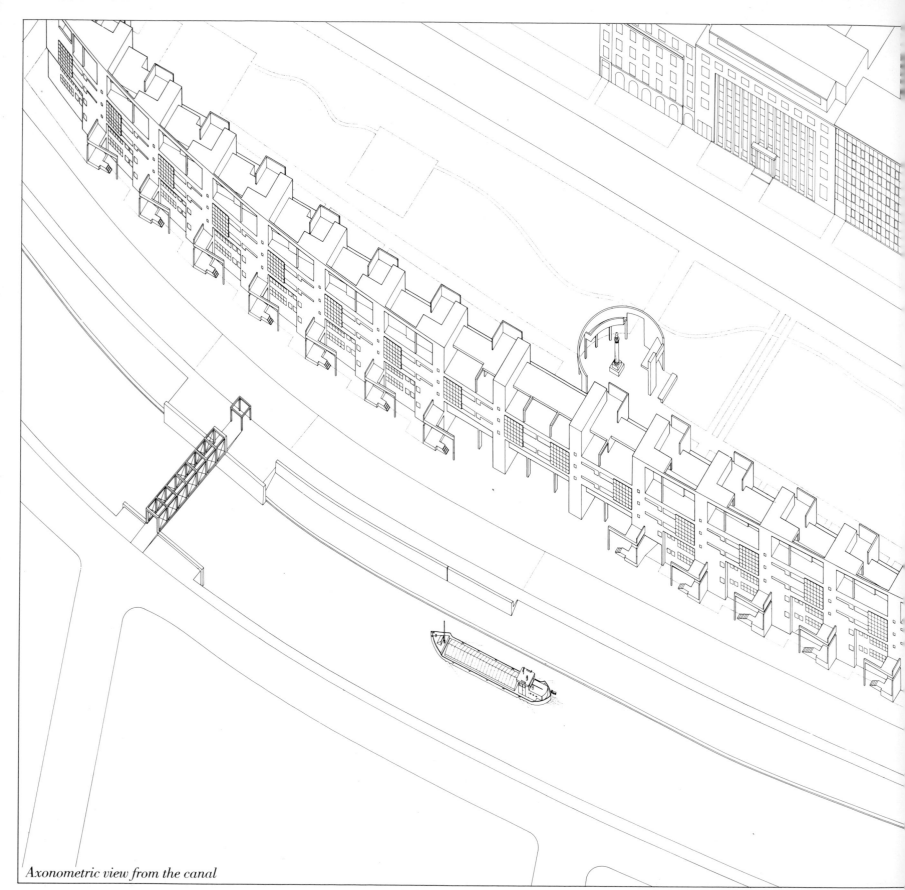

Axonometric view from the canal

Partial ground level plan

20 50 100

350

Partial second level plan

West elevation

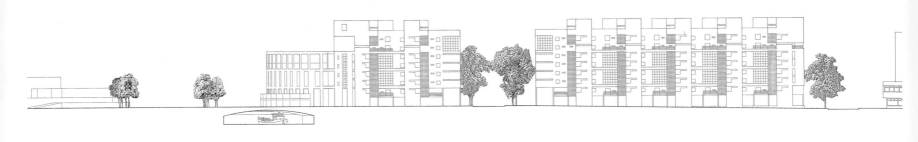

Cross section facing east

Cross section facing west, with Mies van der Rohe's National Gallery seen across the canal

20 50 100 200

Partial north elevation of canal housing

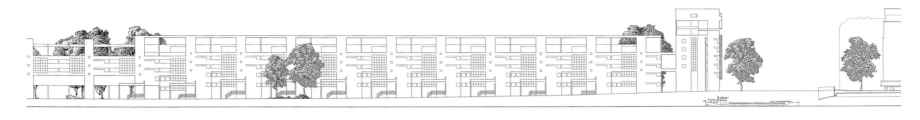

North elevation of Am Karlsbad housing

Partial south elevation of canal housing

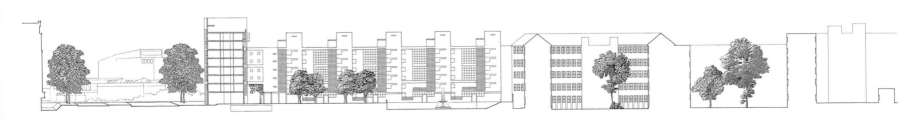

Axonometric view

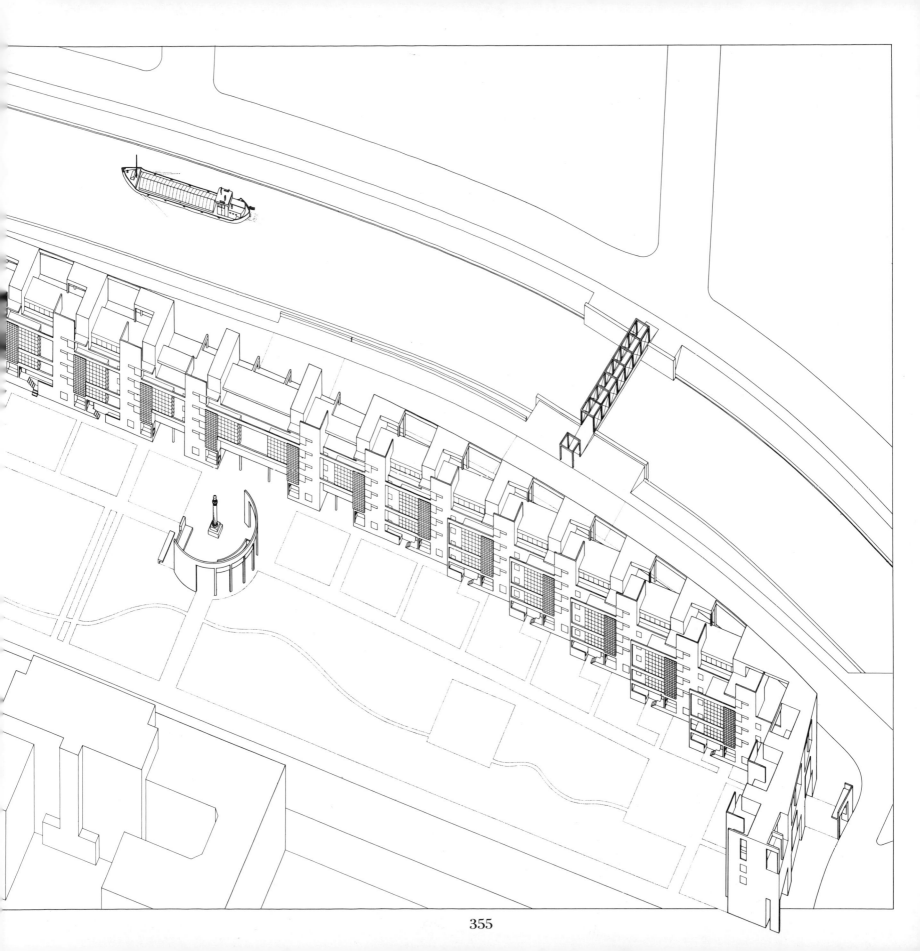

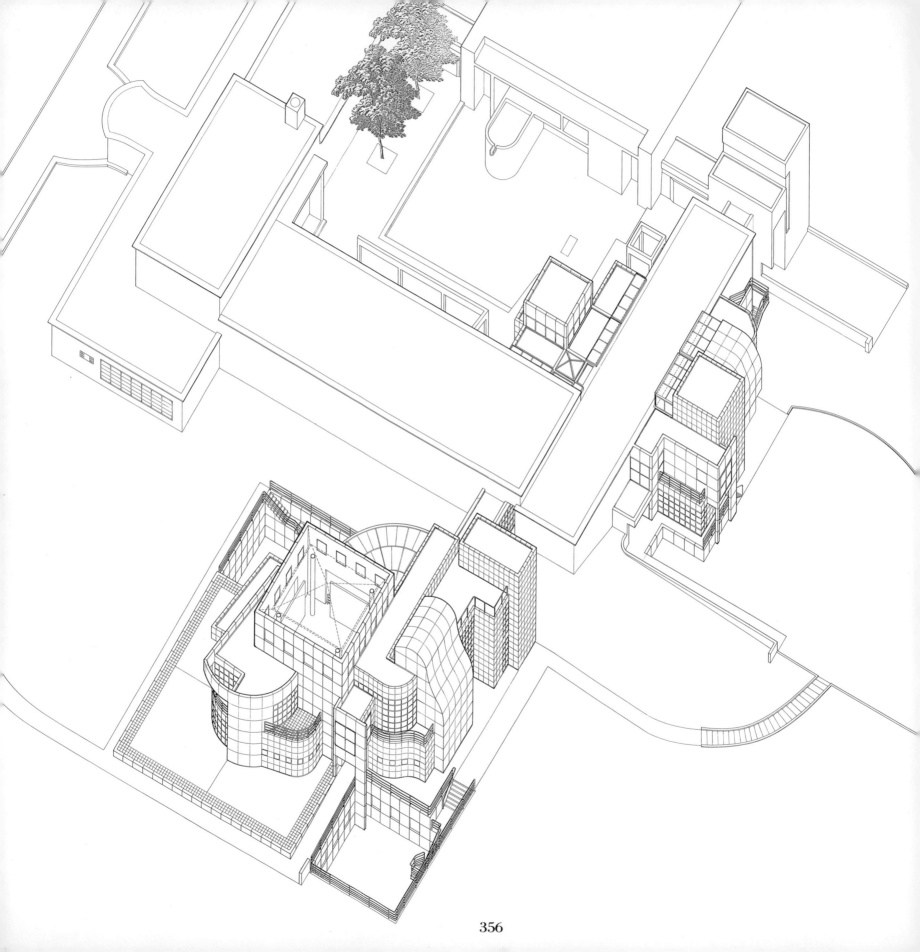

Des Moines Art Center Addition

Des Moines, Iowa
1982–1984

The Des Moines Art Center was designed in 1948 by Eliel Saarinen. It consists of a U-shaped sequence of gallery spaces, all of one-story height except for a double-height gallery in the west wing and a two-story education annex attached to it. In 1965 I. M. Pei designed the first addition to the center, on the south side of the site facing a public park, closing the U-plan to create a sculpture courtyard. Because of the slope of the site and the addition's proximity to the education wing, the Pei building could rise two full stories without overwhelming the low profile of the existing complex. The site for the present addition to the art center is mostly on the north side of the original building. In this case, as the chief view of the Saarinen building is toward its long masonry wall on the north, visible from Grand Avenue, the main thoroughfare, to visitors coming from downtown Des Moines, the problem was to design an addition that would respect the older building's horizontality.

The program called for permanent exhibition spaces as well as temporary ones to house large traveling exhibitions, additional service spaces including a maintenance room and loading dock facilities to provide a direct relationship to new and existing art storage areas, and a new public restaurant that could also function as a meeting room. An analysis of the site and program suggested dividing the new addition into separate volumes that would allow for expansion in required areas, rather than introducing a third large building mass. On this premise, three new additions were located with respect to the existing operations, the interface between the new and old designed to allow efficient functional coordination. Enclosed connections to the additions reinforce the existing axes in the Saarinen plan, and become the binding threads of the museum complex. This organization also enabled some hundred-year-old trees on the north part of the site to be preserved.

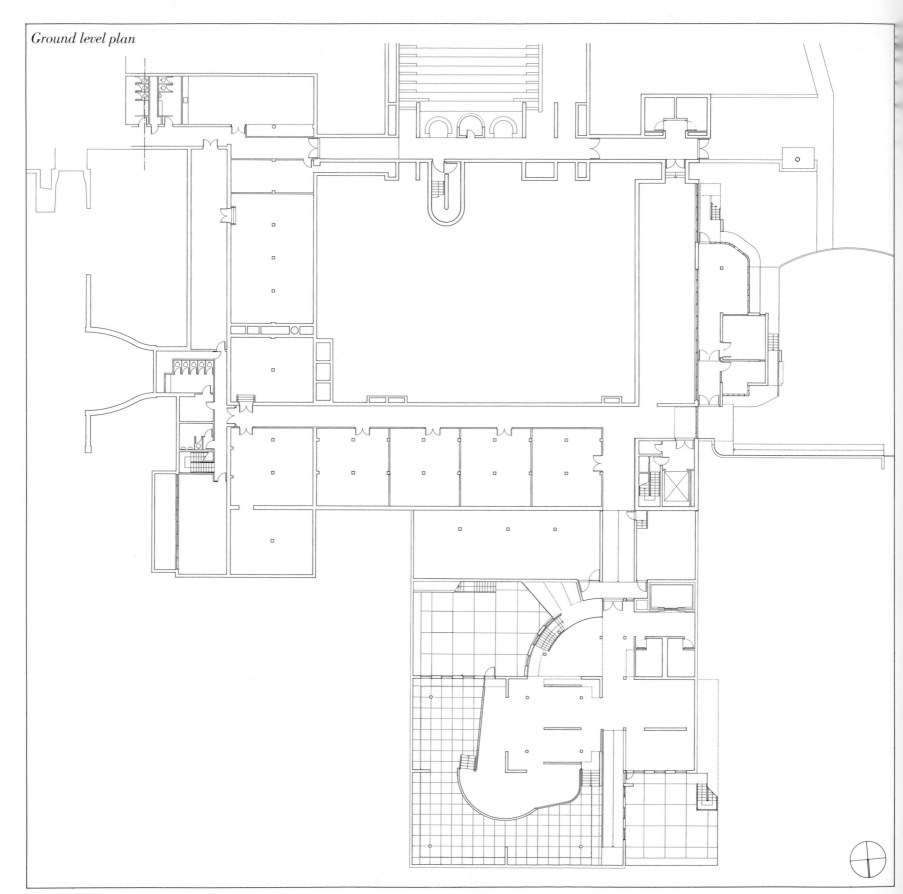

Ground level plan

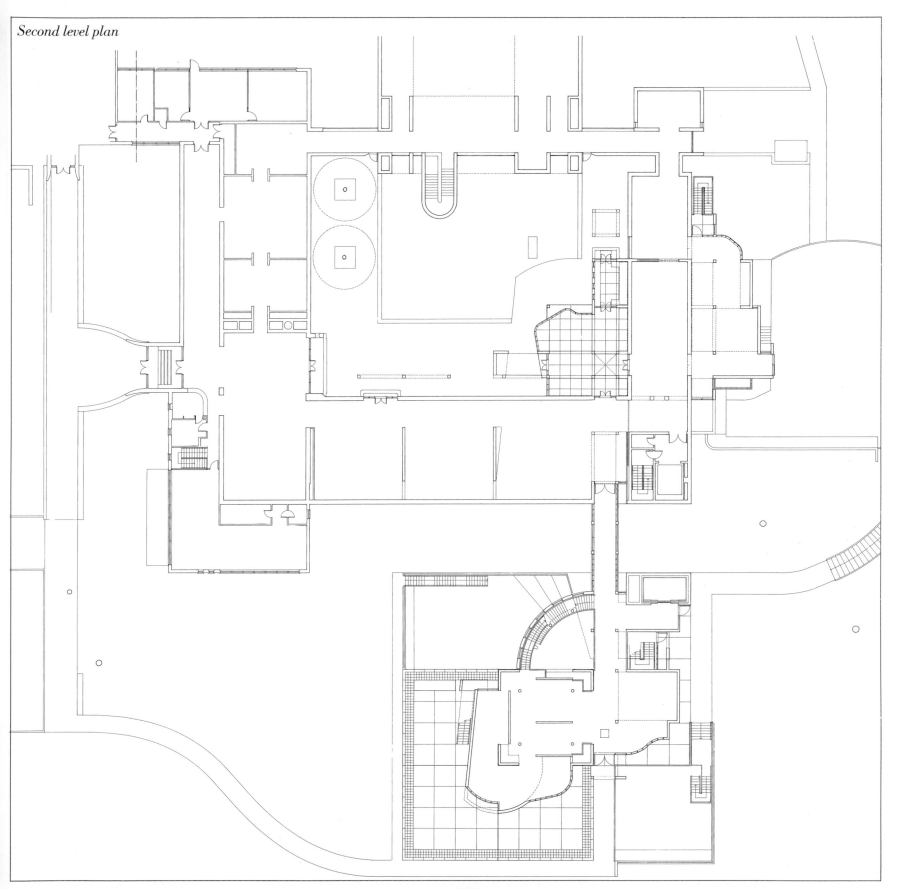

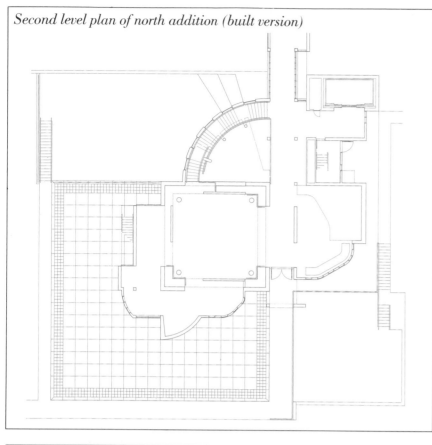

Second level plan of north addition (built version)

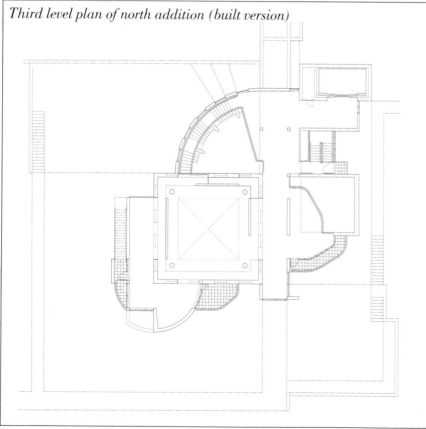

Third level plan of north addition (built version)

The east-west entry axis of the existing museum is reinforced architecturally by the new courtyard pavilion, which also acts as a pivot point for the intersecting north-south axis. This pavilion, which contains the restaurant/meeting room and opens to the courtyard during the warm months, activates this previously little-used outdoor space. The courtyard becomes, in effect, a stage for the juxtaposition of the three different phases and manners of architecture represented in the building.

The glass-enclosed connection along the north-south axis provides access to the new north addition, which houses most of the new gallery space—the twentieth-century collections and changing exhibitions. This addition, volumetrically separate from the Saarinen building and located so as not to obstruct the preferred view of it, compacts its program into a vertically organized pavilion. The largest of the three levels is below grade and has two associated terraces, excavated to provide controlled natural light to the temporary exhibition galleries there. The plan is an eroded nine-square grid, with the central square pushed up to provide a four-column central atrium, lit by clerestory windows and perimeter skylights. This central volume is sheathed in granite and roofed by a flattened pyramid that acts as a foil to the butterfly-section roof of the Pei addition. The north-south section through the whole complex reveals the new building's relationship to the Pei addition: together the two bracket the Saarinen building, which becomes a centerpiece made all the more important by the strong volumetric and stylistic contrasts.

The third addition is attached directly to the west wing of the Saarinen building. This allows for an expansion of service spaces at the lower level, and for an enlargement of the west gallery space at the main level. An opening cut in the existing west wall at the main level extends the east-west axis into the addition, where a series of new galleries provides the necessary space for the museum's collection of African art.

The surface grids—four-foot squares of granite and two- and four-foot squares of metal panels and glazing—reflect the internal hierarchy of primary and secondary spaces. This is the first project in which granite is used as a primary building material (it was used as a base in Frankfurt and Atlanta). Here its role is to indicate the importance of the central volume of the north addition. Its pink-beige color is chosen to blend with the exterior masonry of the Saarinen building. The curved forms throughout the scheme, which echo each other in plan and section, are clad in porcelain-enameled steel, thin and reflective walls that contrast with the solidity of the granite. They serve to give the additions an animation that counterpoints the linear sobriety of the Saarinen galleries.

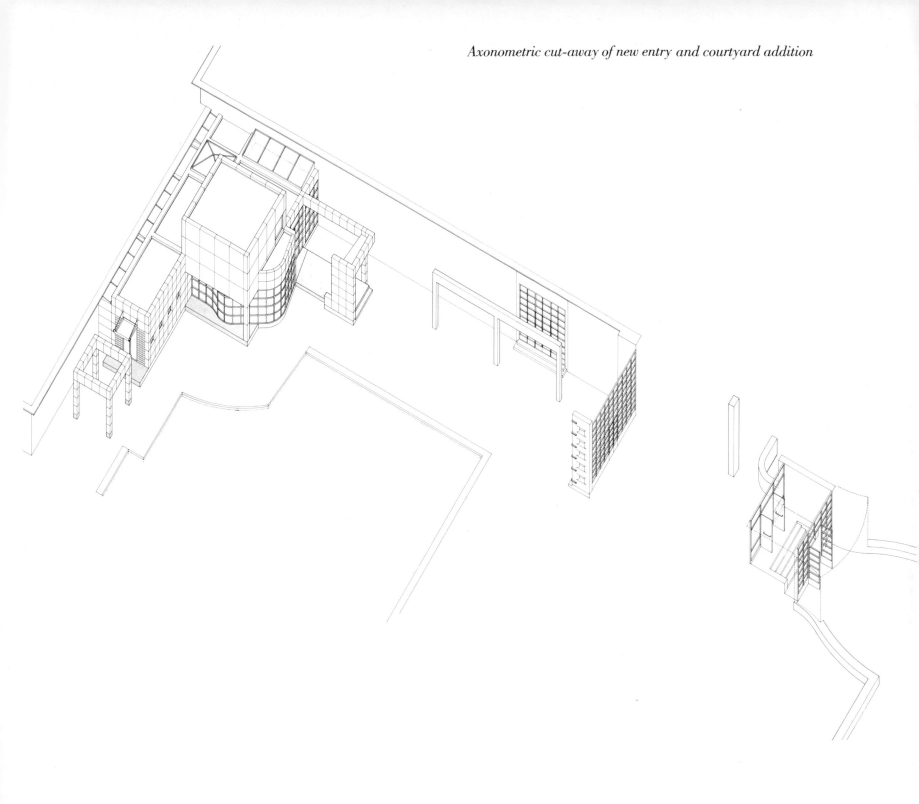

South elevation

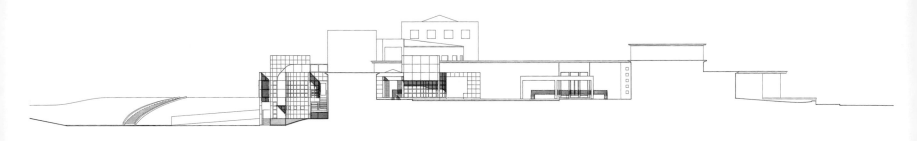

East elevation

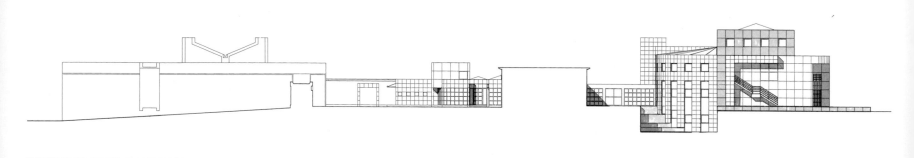

North-south section

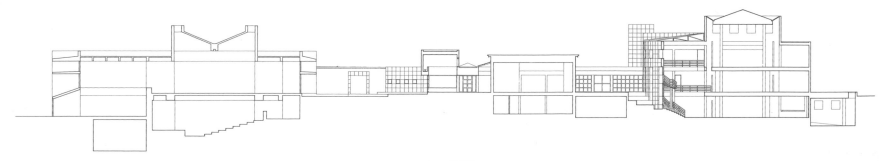

West elevation

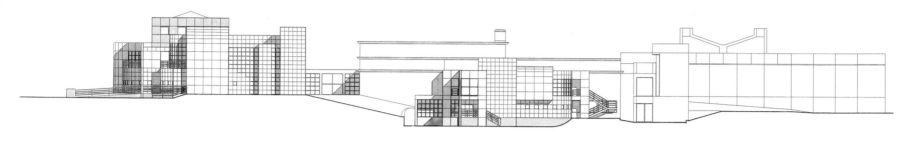

North elevation

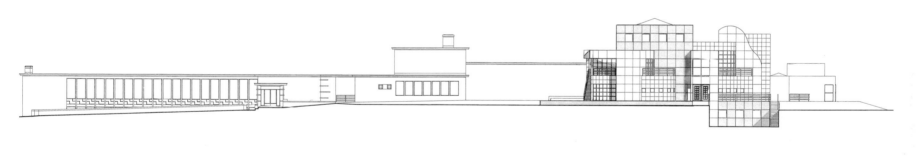

East-west section

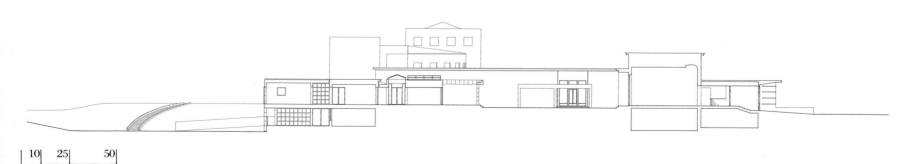

|10| 25| 50|

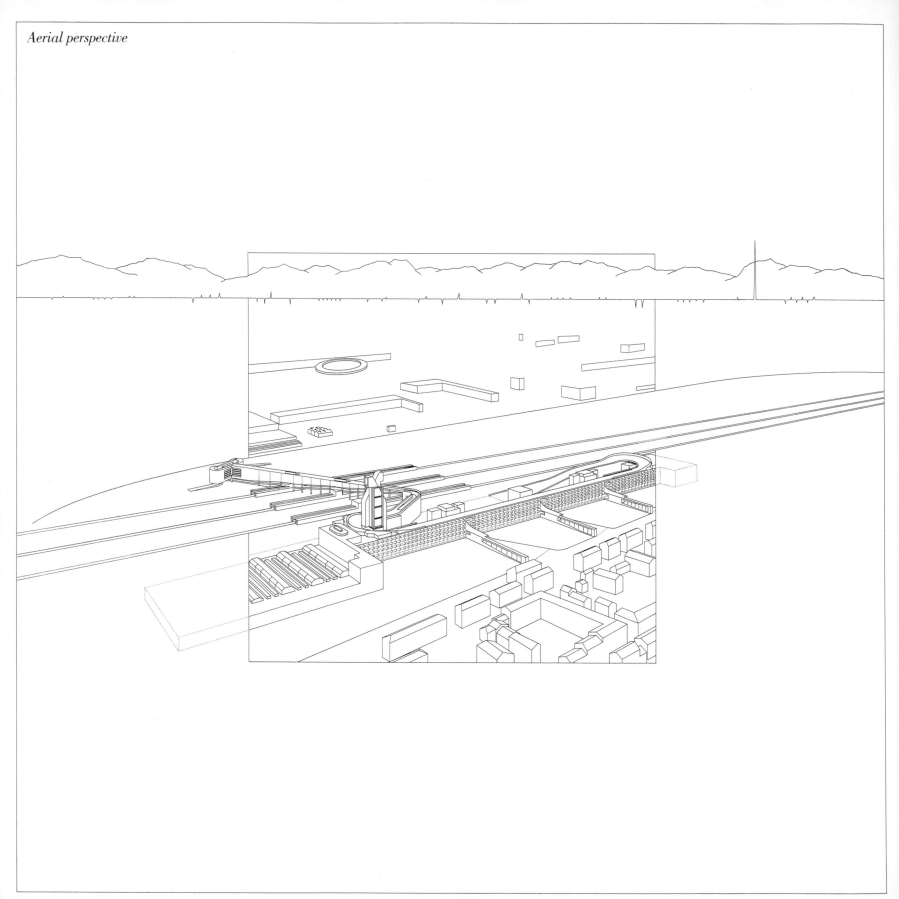

Aerial perspective

Lingotto Factory Conversion

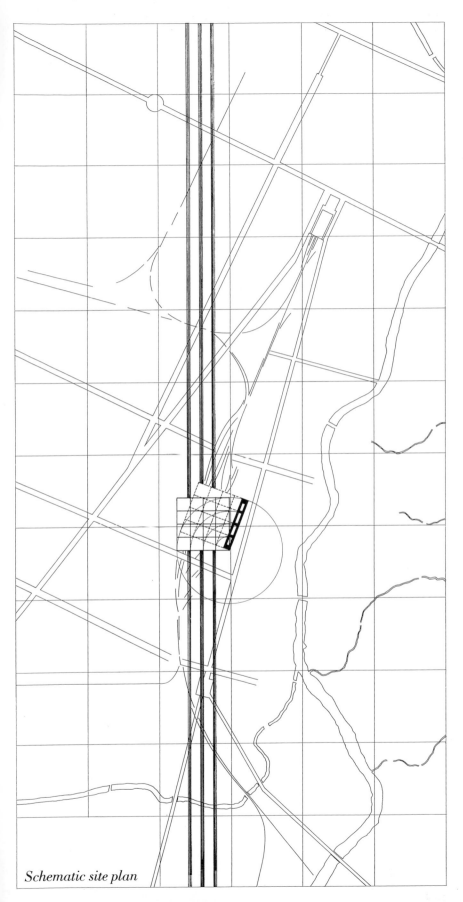

Turin, Italy
1983

Schematic site plan

The main building of the Lingotto factory in Turin, formerly the Fiat automobile works, is a long, linear, five-story block made up of a series of square structural bays, six meters on a side. Four bays wide by seventeen long, the building's overall width is thirty-two meters, and its length is punctuated three times by vertical circulation cores. The roof track, originally used for testing the assembly-line-produced cars, unifies the building volume from the exterior, giving it a monolithic insularity in its site. Situated parallel to the railroad tracks to its west, the building was conceived as a paradigm of the ideal, total factory based on a Taylorized system of production. In fact, in 1925, only two years after the "total" building was completed, the construction of new shops had to be undertaken in response to ever-increasing demand. The obsolescence of the original building over the years, especially its multilevel organization, contributed to its further decline in a period of economic recession. The purpose of the present project is to rehabilitate the building both functionally and formally. In converting the factory into a residential complex encompassing five hundred dwelling units as well as shops, a museum, and a connection to a new railway station, the intention is to open it to the city and outlying districts, and to restructure the building's machine scale into dimensions optimal for habitation.

Under the present proposal, the west side of the building would be opened up perpendicularly to the railroad lines to form a seven-story gateway bridging the tracks and spanning twenty-seven meters to Zino-Ziti Street. Three cubes designed as stations to handle three different kinds of traffic (north/south, east/west, national/ international) are located at intervals along this new bridge, and are reached by a car and taxi drive, a one-way route that begins on the roof track of the factory building and proceeds in three successive segments to the three stations, terminating in a great double ramp that accomplishes the descent to street level. Within the seven-story bridge are offices for railway business and administrative services.

Marseille Unité
d'Habitation
Le Corbusier
1947–1949

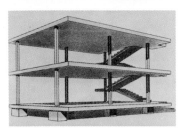

Maison "Dom-ino"
Le Corbusier
1914

Smith House
1965–1967

The elevated autoroute

Project for Algiers
Le Corbusier
1931–1934

Sequential perspectives
of the elevated coastal
highway into Algiers

Le Corbusier found
confirmation of this
scheme on the roof of the
Lingotto Factory in 1934

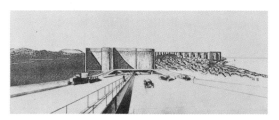

The east side of the building, facing Nizza Street, retains its monolithic appearance as a five-story wall, punctuated only by the three main entries to the new housing. These entries are actually bilevel automobile ramps that bisect the building perpendicularly on the axes of the existing circulation cores, leading to services and shops, pedestrian stairs and elevators, and an interior street, which occupies the second of the four latitudinal bays on two of the five stories and runs the length of the building, giving access to individual parking spaces directly underneath the main level of each of the five hundred dwelling units.

The dwelling units themselves are dimensioned on a 3-by-3-by-2.10-meter grid, a module derived by halving the original 6-meter automobile grid; prefabricated elements—metal posts and beams installed between floor and ceiling by hydraulic jacks—are superimposed within the old structure to define the new human-scale matrix. The double scale of the structural grid is further inflected by the diagonal (20.5 degree) orientation of the block bridging the railway tracks. In plan, each unit consists of an east and a west zone. These face each other across an enclosed bridge that is oriented on the diagonal grid and crosses the interior street—a microcosmic version of the railway bridge. The east zone of the apartment contains the collective spaces, including the kitchen and a double-height living room with library overlook, while the west zone contains the single-height, private spaces. Narrow passages in between the housing units permit the infiltration of natural light and ventilation. A consistently used vocabulary of elements and materials—glass block for straight partitions, white porcelain-enameled metal panels for curved partitions, a trellis of black steel outriggers pinning the interior facades to the old structure, and three types of stairs, all of white steel and each with a specific use—lends the interior landscape formal clarity and lightness.

Externally, two other major elements complete the new composition. A double lookout tower for railway traffic control rises within the southern elbow of the roof track. This high vertical forms a hinge with the horizontal gateway spanning the railway lines and stands as a landmark against the sky, serving to distinguish the horizon line of the roof track from that of the city. Finally, the complex to the south of the track building, which formerly housed the factory's press center, is to be converted into a racing-car museum.

This rehabilitation of one of the landmarks of modern industrial architecture is intended to revitalize a declining part of the city by creating an energetic new nexus of urban activity. Beyond this, through its formal integration of residential and industrial typologies and combination of housing, transportation, and cultural uses, it seeks to reinterpret the relationship between the technology of the automobile and the needs of modern urban life in a positive way.

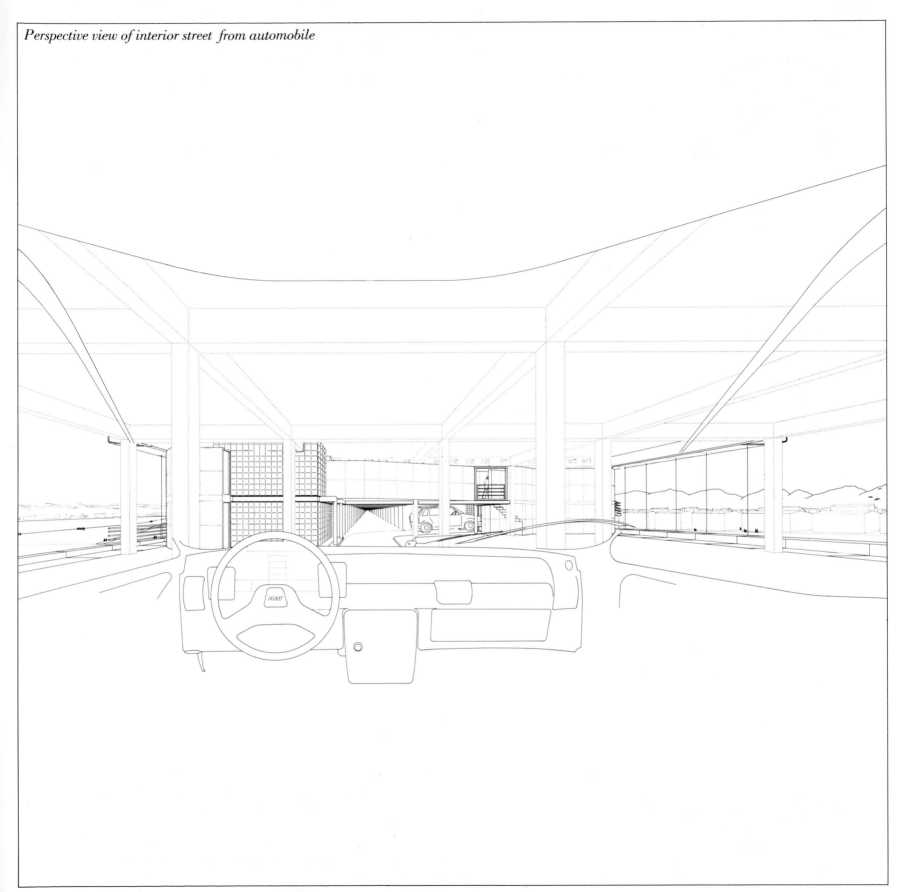

Perspective view of interior street from automobile

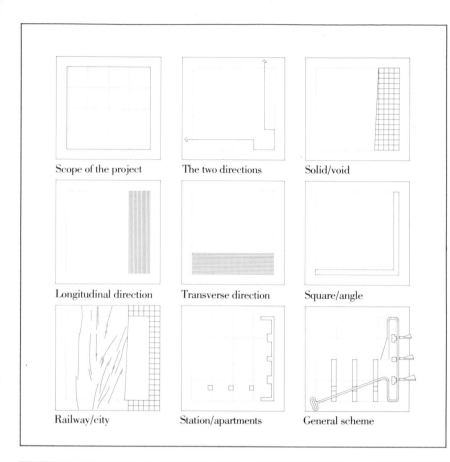

Scope of the project

The two directions

Solid/void

Longitudinal direction

Transverse direction

Square/angle

Railway/city

Station/apartments

General scheme

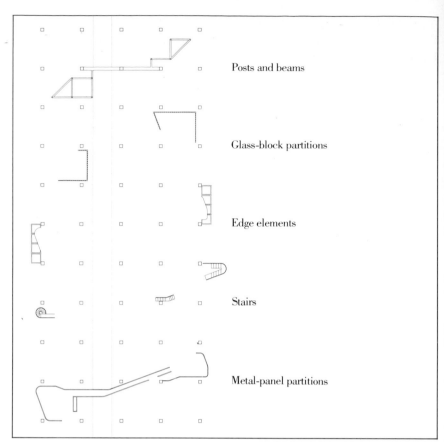

Posts and beams

Glass-block partitions

Edge elements

Stairs

Metal-panel partitions

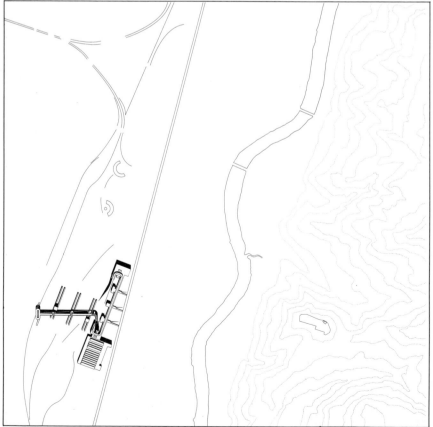

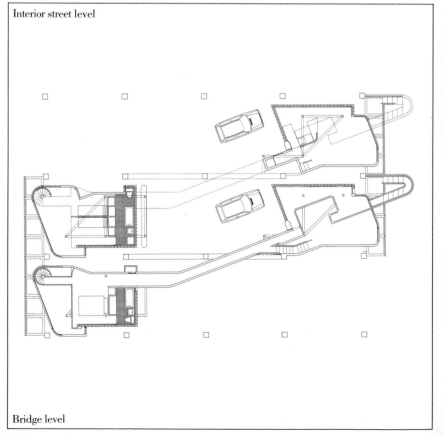

Interior street level

Bridge level

Analytical diagrams
Site plan
Vocabulary of infill elements
Apartment plans

Axonometric view
Plan and perspective view
of rail traffic control tower

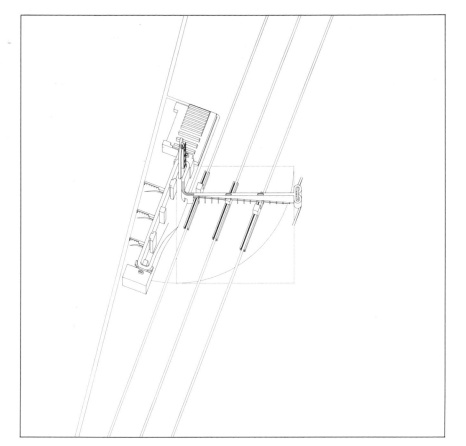

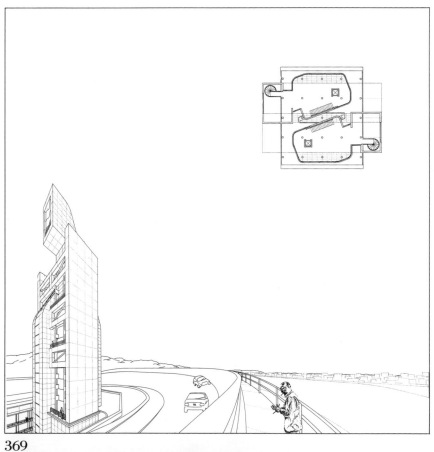

Perspective view of entry plaza

Office Building for Siemens

Munich, West Germany
1983

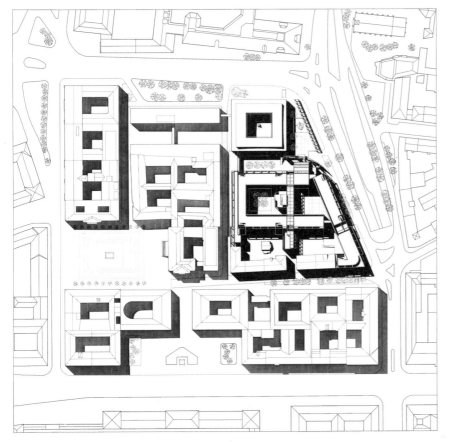

Intended to occupy one of the few remaining open sites in the historic center of Munich, the new Siemens office building is located on the block adjacent to the company's present headquarters and will become the centerpiece of an office complex incorporating old and new buildings. The main frontage is on Oskar-von-Miller-Ring, which lops off the site's north corner, eroding the city's orthogonal grid. This intersection has historically been a "problem point" in the city, resisting the strong axes emanating from Karolinenplatz to the west and Ludwigstrasse, a monumental boulevard lined with neoclassical buildings by Leo von Klenze and others, one block east.

The building is designed to respond to its site in several ways: by integrating the existing buildings into a coherent complex; creating a strong edge along Oskar-von-Miller-Ring so that a continuous street wall is maintained along the ring road encircling the old city; and using the site as a bridge between the inner city south of the site and the sector north of the ring road. The four diagrams at the lower left on the following page suggest how these intentions have been conceptualized. The first illustrates the two geometries to which the composition responds, the orthogonal grid of the city and the diagonal cut of Oskar-von-Miller-Ring. The second diagram illustrates the three main elements of the parti: a linear volume along Oskar-von-Miller-Ring, a U-shaped volume in the interior of the block, and a circulation spine which cuts through the center, picking up a vector from the city grid and recreating a street that existed in earlier urban plans. The third diagram shows how this massing fits into the context, the new structure reinforcing the built perimeter of the block, continuing existing building lines, conforming to the scale of its surroundings, and creating four courtyard spaces that relate typologically to the older buildings. The fourth diagram relates to the framing of the whole site, showing how the definition of the edges of the buildings as well as the open spaces between makes for a homogeneous reading of the entire complex.

371

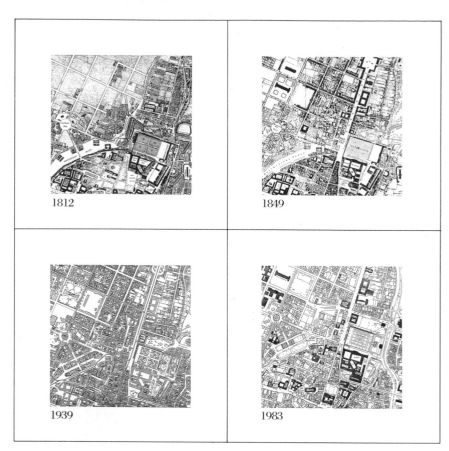

1812

1849

1939

1983

Site analysis

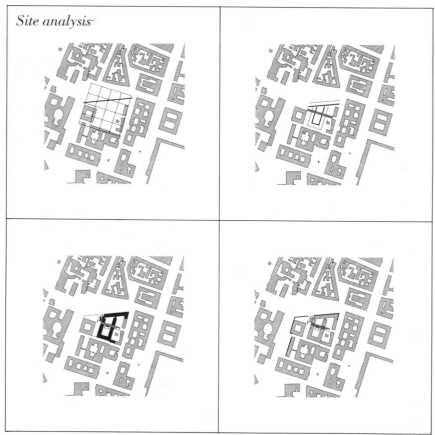

The building itself affords its users an efficacious space for working and a transition from the activity of the city to the quiet of the landscaped courtyards. The building's disposition around the four courtyards offers a natural principle of organization for its suites of offices as well as a way of segregating areas of greater and lesser security. The ground level is the one most closely related to the rest of the complex and to the city. The entry plaza on the north is intended to serve both the new building and the contiguous existing building. It contains a reflecting pool on the cross-axis of both buildings and, along the Oskar-von-Miller-Ring edge, a pergola which picks up the height of the first-floor soffit line of surrounding buildings. Its location also makes it the southern terminus of the street directly to the north, Amalienstrasse, which houses Munich's arts academy, and connects it diagonally to the existing plaza on Brienner Strasse to the south. Adjacent to the entry plaza is a driveway that also serves both the new and existing buildings, allowing employees and visitors to be dropped off directly in front of their destination. From here, in the case of the new building, one enters a glazed lobby whose transparency invites unobstructed views. Surfaces are provided for mounting publicity and exhibitions. The glass spine containing the circulation ramps and elevator banks is directly reached from this space, and its openness and central east-west location in plan facilitate orientation within the building. The ground floor also contains a cafeteria behind the elevators, facing into one of the courtyards, and a row of stores fronting Oskar-von-Miller-Ring, as well as suites of offices off double-loaded corridors. The upper floors contain more office suites, all with centrally located service areas, and exhibition-conference rooms stacked above the lobby. From the second floor, a glass bridge connects the new building with the existing one. The roof level on the Oskar-von-Miller-Ring side contains a setback sixth floor of offices with roof terraces.

The office floors are organized around the interior courtyards, which vary in definition. The courtyard facades consist of thick stone walls with single, square windows punched in to emphasize their massiveness. In contrast is the treatment of the exterior elevations, whose screenlike glass, steel, and aluminum-panel articulation presents a modern face to the world. The deliberate recall of a classical building tradition on the interior elevations is intended to create a historical and typological link with the Bavarian classicism of the context, as well as to emphasize the distinction between the private and public sides of the corporation. At the same time, the recessing of the base and top portions of the facade on the exterior gives a strongly tripartite reading, producing a differentiated wall plane and playing once again, this time in a modern vocabulary, with the classical context. In this way and others, the continuity and coherence of the overall massing accommodates the introduction on the smaller scale of variegated qualities of space and light, making for an architecture that is not only monumental but visually and functionally sensitive.

372

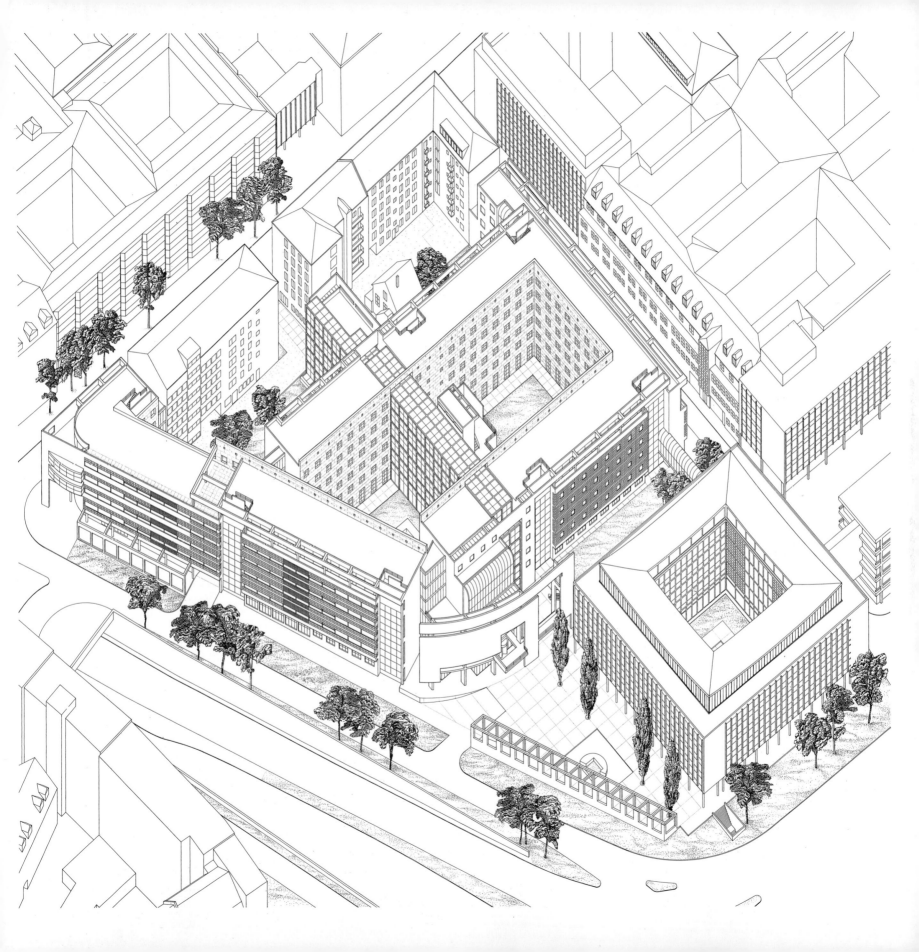

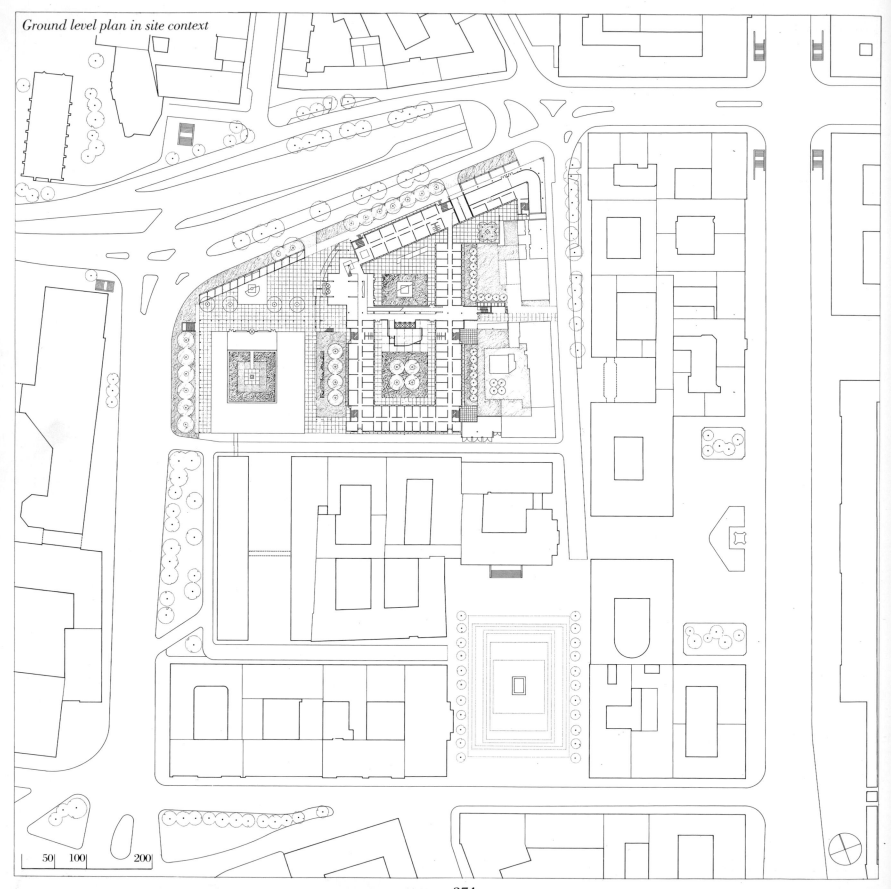

Ground level plan in site context

50 100 200

374

Ground level plan

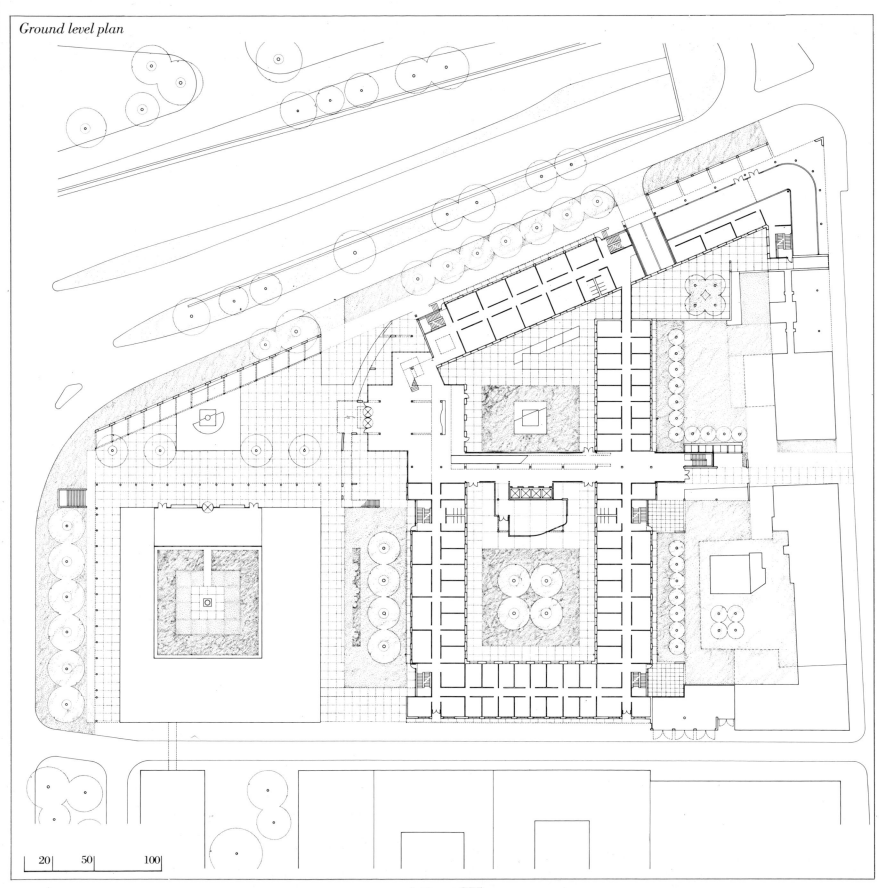

20| 50| 100|

North elevation

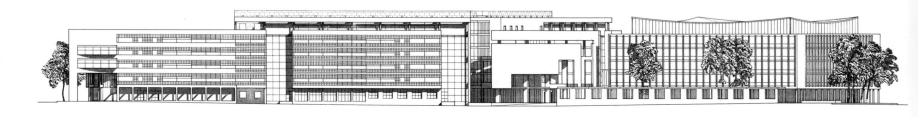

West elevation

South elevation

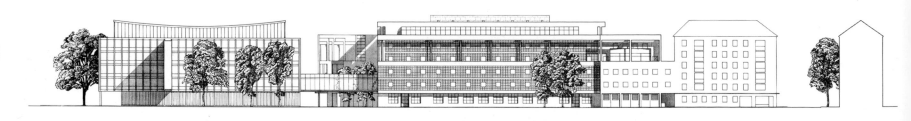

| 50 | 150 | 300 |

East elevation

Longitudinal section through courtyards facing west

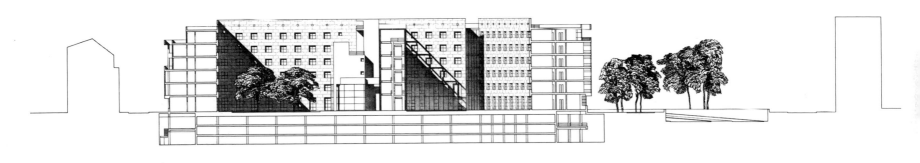

Cross section facing south

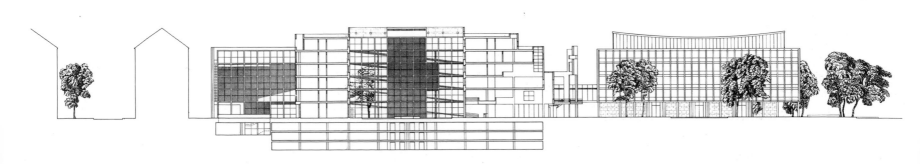

Postscript

Dear Richard:

I have decided to write you a letter instead of a postscript. It is, or can be, at once a private letter made public and a public letter made private. There are certain moments when friends must be critical as well as supportive—critical so that certain explorations can take place, supportive so that new explorations can begin. Old friends are like the old earth plates. They are solid, they move, they adjust, causing cracks and fissures so that a world still can stay intact.

In fact, lately I have been thinking about your work in relationship to the society in which we live. It seems that we have both been caught between two sides of a coin (perhaps minted by others). I no doubt should build more, you no doubt should research more. But what to build more and what to research more is the paradox, the dilemma.

Recently I met an old friend. I had not seen her for over thirty years. The body physical was there although it did not look the same as I remembered it; still, certain distant outlines could be seen, faint vibrations could be felt. I tried to get through the outer form presented me. That is, I tried not to look through, but to get over into the inside space, so to speak, to the soul. It was a strange experience. I tried to squeeze myself through the sockets of my companion's eyes. It was difficult, almost impossible, until a moment of recognition, of simultaneity, occurred. At that moment, there was an image of the stars in the heavens. For the first time in my life, the stars were not the fixed ones that I had seen throughout my life. They were actually moving out, back into black space. Not until that moment of transcendence when I tried to enter another's soul was I able to see physically the movement of the stars back into space.

Recently, too, I visited the National Archaeological Museum in Athens with Gloria. We stood fixed for some time looking at the metal Poseidon, the one where Poseidon's eyes have been removed. All that remain are the empty eye sockets, which appear to be black; yet although contained, the space in the black hollow of Poseidon's head seemed infinite, just like, perhaps, the black heavens. It was the impenetrability of the space which suggested its vastness. This conjured up the problem and meaning of black's antithesis to white. Before we left the Archaeological Museum we noted another phenomenon which haunted us, the tomb sculptures of Greek men and women. Combined with these human figures were gorgons, griffins, sirens, and other creatures. I came to the realization that these other creatures were unimaginable. They simply could not have been imagined: they were . . . just as husband and wife and child were. Gloria pointed out that Troy had been a myth for hundreds of years before the fact of Troy was uncovered and seen as a reality.

In my postscript to your last book, I included a quotation from Melville's Moby Dick. It had to do with the concreteness of white. There are other aspects of white. Melville is very descriptive about them:
"This elusive quality it is, which causes the thought of whiteness, when divorced from more kindly associations, and coupled with any object terrible in itself, to heighten that terror to the furthest bounds. . . . Bethink thee of the albatross, whence come those clouds of spiritual and pale dread, in which that white phantom sails in all imaginations? . . . Therefore, in his other moods, symbolize whatever grand or gracious thing he will by whiteness, no man can deny that in its profoundest idealized significance it calls up a peculiar apparition to the soul."

Melville certainly looked at white in a special way. As he suggests, white can have the same fearful aspects as black. After watching a re-run of Kubrick's The Shining, a companion made the following observation: "Most horror films have a pervading darkness, shadows, blacks, chiaro-oscuro. Kubrick's Shining is filmed and flooded with light, light pervades, not shadows, light is everywhere. White light can produce a sense of foreboding."

Perhaps, Richard, through your particular use of white, through that white-light whiteness, you have indicated another meaning for our society and its programs, a meaning analogous to that of the dark white houses of Hawthorne's New England with their hidden, unrevealed aspects. We as architects must explore the possibility of monochromatic programs—programs unknown as yet, which do not necessarily reflect society as it is, but which, somehow, speculate on what a society might become.

We too are strapped to Ahab's whale . . .

John Hejduk, Architect
New York
May 1984

Biographical Chronology

1959–1961
Worked for Davis, Brody & Wisniewski, New
York (1959); Skidmore, Owings & Merrill,
New York (1960); Marcel Breuer, New York
(1961–1963)

Lambert Beach House
Fire Island, New York
1962 (year of completion)

 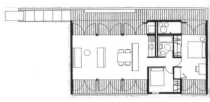

1963
Adjunct Instructor in Architecture at The
Cooper Union (to 1966)
Visiting Critic at Princeton University
Established private practice in New York
City

**"Recent American Synagogue
Architecture"**
Exhibition design and organization
The Jewish Museum, New York, New York

House for Mr. and Mrs. Jerome Meier
Essex Fells, New Jersey
1965

1964
Visiting Critic at Syracuse University
Awarded the *Architectural Record* Award of
Excellence for House Design

Monumental Fountain
Competition entry (with Frank Stella)
Benjamin Franklin Parkway, Philadelphia,
Pennsylvania

Dotson House
Ithaca, New York
1966

Renfield House
(With Elaine Lustig Cohen)
Chester, New Jersey
1966

On the southern dunes of Fire Island, elevated to twenty feet above sea level on wood columns to prevent hurricane tides from flooding the structure, this house opens to views of the Atlantic and the Great South Bay. Its extreme simplicity makes the presence of the ocean all the more impressive. Constructed in nine days exclusively of prefabricated elements for a cost of $11,000, the house is a precedent for later investigations of inexpensive, repetitive building systems using mass-produced or prefabricated parts.

The exhibition focused on contemporary synagogue design and the problems it raises in terms of reconciling traditional Jewish religious values with present-day social, economic, and architectural requirements.

This one-story house stands on a typical one-acre suburban lot. Its beige brick bearing walls provide privacy from the street, focusing inward on an enclosed courtyard. Skylights, clerestory windows, and a parapeted roof garden open the interior of the house to light and the seasons.

The fountain is composed of a three-dimensional cluster of polished stainless steel cubes, cantilevered off of two points and standing in the middle of a reflecting pool. The water travels up through the cubes before falling back down into the pool. The fountain of cubes forms an open V to frame the view up and down the avenue on the major axis, and an upside-down V to enclose it on the minor axis.

A contemporary house and barn built by a Cornell University professor and his wife and designed over an existing underground structure housing farm equipment, the new construction provides both a place to live and additional storage space for a small-scale working farm.

A renovation of an old house on a rural site, the interior was reorganized and almost totally rebuilt to provide a clear separation of family-use and sleeping spaces. The exterior—of wood, brick, stone, shingle, and slate—was modified by adding and subtracting elements, using white stucco and glass to transform and unify the existing surfaces.

1965
Visiting Critic at Pratt Institute

"Sona"
Shop for the Handicrafts and Handlooms
Corporation of India (with Elaine Lustig
Cohen)
1967

Stella Studio and Apartment
New York, New York

Smith House
Darien, Connecticut
1967

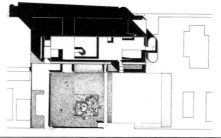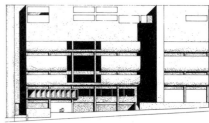

University Arts Center
Competition entry (with John Hejduk and
Robert Slutzky)
University of California, Berkeley, California

1966
Assistant Professor of Architecture at The
Cooper Union (to 1969)

Hoffman House
East Hampton, New York
1967

Mental Health Facilities
West Orange, New Jersey
The Jewish Counseling and Service Agency

This pilot shop for a non-profit export corporation sponsored by the Indian government was designed to accommodate the display of both large- and small-scale cottage industry handicrafts, from woven rugs, fabrics, and silk textiles to fine jewelry, wooden carvings, brass pots, and stone figurines.

A loft renovation for painter Frank Stella and his family, this large space was freely planned to allow a flexible and fluid interpenetration of living and working areas and to provide good viewing for large-scale paintings.

"What makes the Smith House so convincing is, above all, the manner in which it embraces space—both internal and external space. Le Corbusier, whose houses of the Twenties are the point of departure for most of the 'New York School' architects, once defined architecture as 'the knowing, exact, and magnificent play of forms in light.' The Smith House, in its crisp and complex whiteness, is such a play of forms. . . . People may wonder whether the elaborate rationalizations of early 20th-century Cubism are particularly relevant to problems of late 20th-century urban or suburban living. The answer, probably, is 'everyone to his (or her) taste.' It may be more practical and less demanding to live in a conventional 'ranch house' rather than a Work of Art; but it is also likely to be less rewarding. A house like this one, with all its obvious problems (some sacrifice of acoustic privacy, some special needs of exterior maintenance to preserve its pristine whiteness)— such a house is also a gift of a special sort of life to any family concerned with something more than basic shelter. For . . . as the weather and the seasons change, this sort of house will change with them—and no moment in its life will ever quite repeat itself."—Peter Blake, "Movement, Space, Direction," *The Daily Telegraph Magazine*, 5 October 1973

A competition project for a museum and arts center for the University of California at Berkeley, the building was intended to house the school's contemporary art holdings, including its collection of the paintings of Hans Hofmann. The two-phase proposal involved a loft-slab building whose space frame allowed it to be free of internal structure, and a triangular volume with a canted north skylight, to be added when the collection expanded.

"Compare two works apparently based on the same theme: House III by Eisenman and the Hoffman House of Meier. In the former . . . the two rotated solids present without commentary the result of the arbitrary act which has placed them thus. In the latter, what matters most is the jointing between forms, their synthesis. Models for this type of approach, however distant, seem to be found in the Kallenbach House of Gropius and Adolf Meyer of 1921 and in several designs by Luckhardt and Anker. In other words, Meier is proposing a method wherein the initial separation of components and the testing of a codified typology, by means of free variation, in no way obstruct their eventual synthesis. By means of this recovery of the 'function of the sign'—wherein we define 'function' in its broadest terms—Meier advances a tacit criticism of Eisenman's conceptualistic reduction of sign and structure. Geometry is no longer chained to its own harrowing silence, there is no search for 'deep structures,' or any attempt to extract multiple meanings from the signs, as Graves attempts to do. Meier's use of geometry also excludes any attempt to regain semantic values: the articulation of his signs is but a testimony to the presence of objects which display their function in absolute clarity."—Manfredo Tafuri, " 'European Graffiti': Five × Five = Twenty-five," *Oppositions* 5, Summer 1976

In an out-patient facility and day-care center for emotionally disturbed children and adults, the building's accessibility to the surrounding community and internal flexibility were primary architectural considerations.

Rubin Loft Renovation
New York, New York

1967
Visiting Critic at Yale University

Westbeth Artists' Housing
New York, New York
1970
The J. M. Kaplan Fund and *The National Council on the Arts*

Saltzman House
East Hampton, New York
1969

1968
Awarded the *Architectural Record* Award of Excellence for House Design; the American Institute of Architects New York Chapter Award for Outstanding Residential Design; and the New England Regional Council of the American Institute of Architects Honor Award

Fredonia Health and Physical Education Building
State University College, Fredonia, New York
New York State University Construction Fund

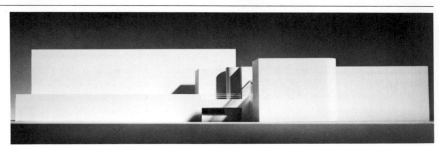

1969
Adjunct Professor of Architecture at The Cooper Union (to 1973)
Awarded the National Honor Award by the American Institute of Architects

Charles Evans Industrial Buildings
Fairfield, New Jersey, and Piscataway, New Jersey

Bronx Redevelopment Planning Study
The New York City Housing and Development Administration and *The New York City Planning Commission*

This loft renovation for a museum curator was designed to accommodate the reception of visitors as well as private living. As in the Stella loft, the flowing, skylit space allows for the display and grouping of large-scale paintings and freely incorporates art with the functions of daily life.

"Mr. Meier's solution is exemplary. There are, inevitably, some block-long corridors, but imaginative duplexes put them on fewer floors. There are good, and less good units, and those duplexes are a dream. There are both curious and creative tenant uses of the space, including a run on sleeping platforms. The range is from cluttered chaos to pristine, primitive simplicity. A bold and sensitive (yes, both) use of color turns hallways into abstractions that could not be bettered by painters. Mr. Meier thinks of Westbeth as a kind of Corbusian unité d'habitation, or at least a step toward it."—Ada Louise Huxtable, "Bending the Rules," *The New York Times,* 10 May 1970

"It is not by chance that, in the 1972 edition of the book on the Five, Meier is represented only by the Smith House of 1965 and by the Saltzman House of 1967. These villas have a layered structure, in which the relationship between volumetric order and transparency, and the analysis of possible geometric articulations, suggest certain analogies to the syntactic purity of Eisenman or even to some of the ambiguous metaphors of Michael Graves. Without doubt, the two villas invoke a 'charmed and magical' atmosphere in their absolute isolation from their context. This might even make them suspect of historicism. Nor is a sense of irony lacking: for example, in the Smith House, we notice the contrast between the weightlessness of the glass block and the mass of the chimney. There is more: the cut which exposes the internal structure of the Saltzman House, so reminiscent of Loos at the Tzara House, is there as if to challenge the ambiguous geometry of the prism with the great rounded corner built on the diagonal grid." —Manfredo Tafuri, " 'European Graffiti': Five × Five = Twenty-five," *Oppositions* 5, Summer 1976

"At Fredonia there was a reluctance to integrate fenestration into the body of the prefabricated cladding panels. Although there were technical reasons for ruling out pierced windows, what one seems to encounter in the renderings for Fredonia (as in all the Olivetti prototypes as well as in early elevations for the Bronx Developmental Center) is the remaining evidence of a conceptual struggle between the fenêtre en longueur *as the normative element inherited from the Purist tradition, and a Prouvé-like approach to the provision of an integrated skin. . . . As in the Hunstanton School in England by noted British architects Alison and Peter Smithson, the chief motivation in the Fredonia megastructure was a Brutalist preoccupation with circulation and services—every pipe being rendered in a different color, and suspended free with a verendell, wide-span structural truss. In more ways than one the Olivetti prototype was a scaling down of this processional* parti *to suit the more modest requirements of a series of office/showrooms. Yet the architect's own description reveals these designs as having been rather surprisingly dependent on the Fredonia scheme."*—Kenneth Frampton, Introduction to *Richard Meier, Architect,* 1976

"Meier's method is put to a much more trying test when he comes to design a prefabricated, standardized light industrial building for erection in industrial parks alongside main roads and highways. Since the buildings are inevitably clad in a light skin of standardized panels, the graphic-exercise aspect of the design is almost too easy for Meier, and he concentrates his attention on the problems of entry, on the molding of the volume: again, the formal vocabulary is deliberately restricted to the rectangle, the 45-degree diagonal, and the segment of the circle. With these elements Meier assembles an extraordinarily cool and elegant group of buildings, almost assertive in their understatement."—Joseph Rykwert, "The Very Personal Work of Richard Meier & Associates," *Architectural Forum,* March 1972

A master plan for the borough of the Bronx, this theoretical study attempted to define the parameters for growth and change with respect to public and residential space, athletic and park facilities, industrial and commercial functions, and transportation services. Once the existing operational systems were identified, connections were developed between them, emphasizing a network of overlapping and interdependent subcenters and proposing a new system of secondary connections. In deliberate contrast to earlier models like Le Corbusier's centroidal scheme of 1922 for a Ville Contemporaine, or his linear scheme of 1930 for Algiers, the network concept was aimed at containing urban sprawl and maintaining space standards.

Relocated to present office at 136 East 57 Street

House in Pound Ridge
Pound Ridge, New York

House in Old Westbury
Old Westbury, New York
1971

Monroe Developmental Center
(With Todd & Giroux, Architects)
Rochester, New York
1974
Facilities Development Corporation for the New York State Department of Mental Hygiene

Twin Parks Northeast Housing
The Bronx, New York
1974
The New York State Urban Development Corporation

Robert R. Young Housing
New York, New York
General Properties Corporation

1970
Member of the Jerusalem Committee Town Planning Subcommittee
Awarded the National Honor Award for Low and Moderate Income Housing by the American Institute of Architects; Municipal Art Society of New York Citation; and H.U.D. Honor Award for Design Excellence

Bronx Developmental Center
The Bronx, New York
1977
Facilities Development Corporation for the New York State Department of Mental Hygiene

"*Meier's organization is not unlike that found in John Hejduk's schemes for wall houses in which all elements of a conventional house are abstracted into separate entities. . . . It is as if Meier took Hejduk's abstracted categories out of their conceptual framework and put them back into a holistic, spatial setting. Where in Hejduk's wall schemes a single wall, used as a planar spine, is the generator of the given forms, in Meier's work this scheme, in a further spatial* twist, is turned outside in and thereby returned to the realm of spatial enclosure. A reflection of this categorization of forms into independent units is most obvious in the project for the House at Pound Ridge in which spatial containers are suspended within the contained space of the house proper. Meier's handling of architectural categories as strata that are layered within the building but are not two-dimensional in their total configuration, we might term a post-Cubist conception of spatial relationships.*"—Rosemarie H. Bletter, "Recent Work by Richard Meier," *A plus U*, April 1976

"*The fact that a circulation element is emphasized in the Old Westbury House must give pause for reflection. In a recent presentation of his works, Richard Meier, while discussing design tools, gave principal importance to circulation systems in the interior as well as on the exterior of his buildings. Graves and Hejduk also emphasize the 'circulation' component. Vertical or horizontal circulation systems played a precise role in Le Corbusier's small-scale architecture:* namely to reproduce within each single building the type of free relationship between street and buildings which he had postulated for interventions on the urban scale. Meier follows neither the Corbusian symbolism nor Hejduk's abstractions. Circulation systems, as well as the clarity of organization, bearing structures, and access points, are for Meier simply materials of design. They must be correlated in complex ways once their roles have been selectively analyzed. It is the complex web of their relationships which makes the architecture so compelling. In Meier's work, typological invention is the basis for an effort to completely recapture the functional aspects of language.*"—Manfredo Tafuri, "'European Graffiti': Five × Five = Twenty-five," *Oppositions* 5, Summer 1976

"*The Englishman Colin Rowe, critical of both Continental modernism and American Beaux-Arts, proposed that the Corbusian model of the city in a park could be bent to traditional urban patterns by means of architectural design, not utopian dogma. Critical to this solution was the replacement of the Zeilenbau system by the model of Le Corbusier's City of Three Million, because his city with its crankshaft blocks and open courts and its more comprehensive vision* allowed for a flexibility and grandeur denied by the German arrangement—for 'an order produced by encouraging variety rather than suppressing it,' in Rowe's words. At Twin Parks in the Bronx, Richard Meier gave Rowe's ideas architectural form by uniting low blocks and towers around courts and along streets in overlapping patterns that respond both to the neighborhood grid and scale and yet refer to Le Corbusier's grand design. No longer were the principles of European and American urban planning and housing design muddled by compromise and trivial detail; the systems now enlarged and augmented each other. . . . In this new conception, public housing was raised to the status of architecture on the highest level without denying its character as large-scale urban planning. By contrast the American architects and critics of the 1930s failed entirely to understand the European modernist principle of the inseparability of housing, planning, and architecture.*"—Richard Pommer, "The Architecture of Urban Housing in the United States during the Early 1930s," *Journal of the Society of Architectural Historians*, December 1980

Robert R. Young Housing was to be built just south of Westbeth. Intended to continue the midblock park begun at Westbeth, it would have provided a western edge to this part of Greenwich Village. The project has two scales: one related to the scale of Village housing, the other to its site facing the Hudson River. Unfortunately, local interest groups pressured the city to develop the site in another way, without any idea of its potential uniqueness.

"*In the Bronx State School the formal method which so strongly marked Meier's private houses as a formal device becomes a programmatic feature. It is clearly part of the program of the school to establish itself as a miniature, independent town, quite isolated from the wasteland of blight around it, and to turn in upon itself; the facades of the building, if one may put it that way, are clearly those which turn in on the courtyard: they are much more* complex, much more interesting than the external faces of the building—indeed, the southern face is almost entirely blank. . . . The elaboration of the interior, its formal richness, all help to emphasize the inward-turning character, almost as part of the building's therapeutic function.*"—Joseph Rykwert, "The Very Personal Work of Richard Meier & Associates," *Architectural Forum*, 1972

"*The clarity of conception and refinement of materials will surely make this one of Meier's most elegant buildings. It is not, in the end, machine imagery which speaks to us here, but a machine technology that has been turned into high art. Technology is briefly referenced to be almost immediately transcended. . . . Though we cannot escape the fact that the residents of the Center are separated from us—a separation imposed by modern society—the sophistication of* the design will make it possible to let treatment take place in a humane, non-institutional environment. The rest of us, who will see this building, sleeker than any recent corporate headquarters, from the vantage point of the mean, decaying area surrounding it, may indeed want to question the comparative merit of being outside or inside.*"—Rosemarie H. Bletter, "Recent Work by Richard Meier," *A plus U*, April 1976

1971

Member of the Cornell University Advisory
Council for the College of Art, Architecture
and Planning
Awarded the National Honor Award by the
American Institute of Architects and the
Citation for Excellence in Residential Design
by the New York Chapter of the American
Institute of Architects

Maidman House
Sands Point, New York
1976

Douglas House
Harbor Springs, Michigan
1973

Branch Office Prototype for Olivetti
Six locations in the U.S.A.
Olivetti Corporation of North America

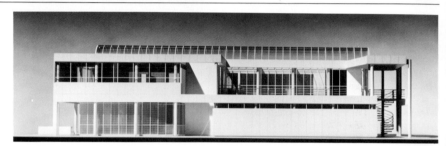

**Modification of the Olivetti Branch Office
Prototype**
Seven locations in the U.S.A.
Olivetti Corporation of North America

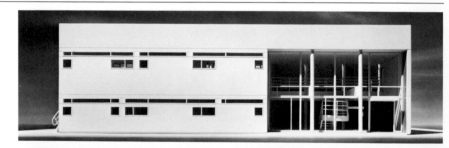

**Dormitory for the Olivetti Training
Center**
Tarrytown, New York
Olivetti Corporation of North America

Olivetti Headquarters Building
Fairfax, Virginia
Olivetti Corporation of North America

"European theoretical references become operative and produce an architecture in which one finds elements and technologies of the American tradition. No facile revival of one or of the other, but a complexity derived from a 'digestion' of both. A logic produced by the study of world history and an analysis of local needs, from which emerges the recall of the white houses of New England as well as the Yankee technology of wood-frame constructions. . . . Only white is used on the exterior; inside the colors are vivid, but measured out judiciously, in particular locations, as for example spaces not illuminated by natural light. They are used 'plastically' to accentuate, to render a spatial plane more important, or to 'mute' it, to render it less important, or else in an evocative way to create a state of animation, an atmosphere. . . . Thus we may say of Meier that the complexity of the relationships between the parti, the translation of a theoretical plan, and typological invention serve to render the architecture interesting, constituting a forceful reappropriation of the functional elements of the architectural language."—Robert Freno, "Le case bianche: Due ville unifamiliari dell'architetto Richard Meier," Gran Bazaar, July–August 1980

"In the Douglas House . . . Meier continues an investigation, begun with the Saltzman House and the House at Pound Ridge, of a language of 'oppositions,' of a denied dialectic between the total transparency of the front and the solid compartmented rear. . . . In section we find once again a 'machine age' modeling vaguely resembling Stirling's. But what matters more is that the building deliberately relates to its environment by means of an emphasis on external stairs. The two stairs and the elevated bridge, which lead directly from the hillside to the topmost terrace, form an independent circulation. The interior corridor and the hallways connect to this system. In this manner, the Douglas House establishes a dialectic between the independence of the object itself and its surrounding space."—Manfredo Tafuri, "'European Graffiti': Five × Five = Twenty-five," Oppositions 5, Summer 1976

"The rationalization also may be explained in terms of the language utilized, extracted directly from the rationalism of the twenties. The use of this formal repertory is explained in the case of the prototypes by the exigencies of the technological image sought, and by the lack of a concrete context, which made impossible any relation with a determined urban morphology. However, in the other [Olivetti] projects, this formal repertory is justified solely by the polemical posture . . . which transforms each project into a revindicated manifesto of the lost purity of the Modern Movement."—Rafael Moneo, "Proyectos no realizados para Olivetti," Arquitecturas Bis, July 1975

"The breakthrough in the Olivetti work, at a level of generality lying beyond this stylistic idealization of modular construction, came with the dormitory for the training center in Tarrytown, New York. This work definitely broke with Meier's prismatic, not to say orthogonal, prejudices, to respond in a direct manner to a sloping, heavily wooded site, preserving as many mature trees as possible, but at the same time affording an optimum view over the Hudson River. Apart from tree conservation, however, the ultimate form and orientation of this scheme were largely determined by height restrictions and tight zoning requirements. In any event, the result, remotely recalling both Aalto's Baker House for the Massachusetts Institute of Technology in Cambridge (1948) and Affonso Eduardo Reidy's Pedregulho Housing in Rio de Janeiro (1956), was a building whose very essence was organic—its broken curvilinear W-form in plan, layering in section over the site, to provide recreation rooms below the main datum to the west."—Kenneth Frampton, Introduction to Richard Meier, Architect, 1976

1972
Elected to the Board of Trustees, the Institute for Architecture and Urban Studies; and to the Board of Directors, the Architectural League
Awarded the Arnold Brunner Memorial Prize in Architecture by the National Institute of Arts and Letters and the Citation for Excellence in Residential Design by the New York Chapter of the American Institute of Architects

East Side Housing
(With Emery Roth, Architects)
New York, New York
Tishman Realty and Construction Corporation

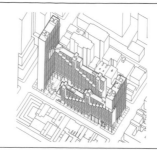

Shamberg House
Chappaqua, New York
1974

1973
Resident Architect at the American Academy in Rome
Awarded the Albert S. Bard Award by the City Club of New York

Paddington Station Housing
New York, New York

Museum of Modern Art at the Villa Strozzi
Florence, Italy
The Commune of Florence

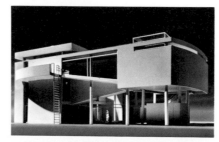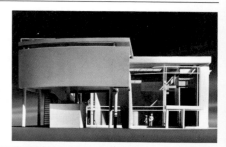

1974
Awarded the National Honor Award by the American Institute of Architects

Condominium Housing
Yonkers, New York
H Development Corporation

Cornell University Undergraduate Housing
Ithaca, New York

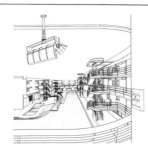

This project is a reinterpretation of the design for the Robert R. Young Housing, for another site in Greenwich Village.

"By placing the zone of enclosed rooms in stark opposition to the open, porous area, the particular quality of each increases in dramatic intensity. This impression is comparable to the afterimage produced by complementary opposites of light or color, where, say, in a green-red conjunction the green looks greener and the red redder. Similarly, in Meier's conception of the interior, continuity is not achieved by space that flows horizontally, but through the abrupt juxtaposition of density and void that forces us to perceive these contrasting spaces as a related whole in which one is forever incomplete without the other, producing a sharp oscillation of the two zones, rather than a harmonious resolution. This deliberate maintenance of a state of tension can be termed a Mannerist device, a Mannerism that is reinforced by other features of the design. For example, the series of bays established by the grid of steel columns is echoed in the vertical, paired window mullions along the northwestern window wall. However, the subdivisions formed by these mullions do not line up with the internal columns: they are shifted slightly toward the projected bedroom balcony, as if attracted by its mass. Further, the clear regularity of the window facade, where the pair of horizontal mullions corresponds in height to the second-floor balustrades and whose height is also related to the fascia above, is disturbed by the exterior balcony that billows out, an opaque, rounded object against the tautness of the glazing." —Rosemarie H. Bletter, "Recent Work by Richard Meier," *A plus U*, April 1976

Nine schemes (three of which are shown at left) were produced for a midtown Manhattan block to show various ways the block could be developed within the present zoning code to accommodate office and residential use. One of the requirements was that the space be flexible enough to accept either use, to be decided upon at a future date. Each scheme includes communal outdoor space for residents as well as space for commercial activities.

Overlooking the Hudson River from across a highway and railroad tracks, this housing takes the form of a slender thirty-eight-story accordion slab. It incorporates 1200 apartments as well as communal, recreational, service, and parking facilities. Five vertical cores decentralize services and humanize the scale at street level. The slab's undulating shape follows the contours of the land and allows for a variety of views from apartment to apartment.

"Arising out of all the suspended Olivetti work (Olivetti having been forced to abandon its building program because of economic pressure), this Cornell housing merits our serious attention for the break it makes with neo-Corbusian rhetoric. As with the equally fresh syntax of Twin Parks Northeast and the Bronx Developmental Center, it is a complex whose broad containment of open but modulated space has evident environmental if not urban implications. As with the Bronx Developmental Center, space resonates back and forth across the public realms of an enclosed arena, which in the Cornell housing is literally an esplanade about which one might fairly invoke the Hannah Arendt term, 'space of public appearance' (importantly, vehicular access would have been provided only for service). . . . The rationale for the Baroque undulation is again, as at Tarrytown, the preservation of mature trees. . . . As with the subtlety of its site organization, the rhythmic modulation of the fenestration has a delicacy matched only, in Meier's work, by the modulated skin of the Bronx Developmental Center." —Kenneth Frampton, Introduction to *Richard Meier, Architect*, 1976

1975
William Henry Bishop Visiting Professor of
Architecture at Yale University
Awarded the Citation for Excellence in
Residential Design by the New York Chapter
of the American Institute of Architects

Commercial Building and Hotel
Springfield, Massachusetts
Mondev International Corporation

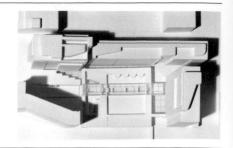

Wingfield Racquet Club
Greenwich, Connecticut
H Development Corporation

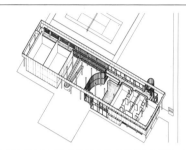

**Warehouse Rehabilitation for the Bronx
Psychiatric Center**
The Bronx, New York
1978
*Facilities Development Corporation for the
New York State Department of Mental
Hygiene*

The Atheneum
New Harmony, Indiana
1979
Historic New Harmony, Inc.

The Theatrum
New Harmony, Indiana
Historic New Harmony, Inc.

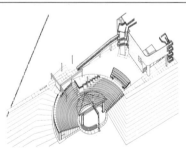

1976
Elected Fellow of the American Institute of
Architects
Awarded the National Honor Award by the
American Institute of Architects and the
Citation for Excellence in Residential Design
by the New York Chapter of the American
Institute of Architects

Sarah Campbell Blaffer Pottery Studio
New Harmony, Indiana
1978
The Robert Lee Blaffer Trust

In a projected shopping mall and hotel for a prime commercial location in downtown Springfield, with an existing department store and parking garage at opposite poles of the site, the intention was to bring new life and vitality to a decaying urban center.

This modest project is a recreational structure and clubhouse, with public functions along the entry side of the circulation spine and a squash court on the other side.

Located along the entry road to the Bronx Developmental Center, this warehouse is used for storage of hospital vehicles and equipment. A simple skin of black brick masonry was added to an existing structure, providing a strong contrast with the reflective silver panels of the Developmental Center.

"On the banks of the Wabash River, not far from the corn fields of Indiana, stands a dramatically handsome new building representing architecture's most advanced frontier. This gleaming white structure is as radical an addition to the rural American heartland as Le Corbusier's Villa Savoie was to the French countryside at Poissy half a century ago. . . . There is a remarkable fusion of architectural means with the programmatic result. But it is not possible, of course, to be aware only of this process. At the same time, one is also intensely aware of the building. It fulfills its purpose while it plays skillfully with a new aesthetic, advancing conventional modernist practice provocatively beyond established limits. Richard Meier does not deny or reject modern architecture in any way, as is the fashion now; he uses its vocabulary and achievements to move into a new phase of exploration of those things that architecture has always been about: the controlled and purposeful manipulation of light and space, and the rewarding relationship of pragmatic and sensuous purpose. This is the kind of development that has always marked the change from one period of art to another; it is the way Mannerism and the Baroque grew out of the Renaissance." —Ada Louise Huxtable, "A Radical New Addition for Mid-America," *The New York Times*, 30 September 1979

The Theatrum is an outdoor amphitheater for summer concerts which was to be built along the banks of the Wabash adjacent to the Atheneum. Seating would expand into the fields in the event of overflow crowds. Lighting is designed for night use. The sloping half-circle serves as a foil to the cubic volume of the Atheneum, and creates a stronger terminus to the ramp that projects from the Atheneum toward the town than exists at present.

"The isolation of each of his 'architectural objects' is emphasized by its whiteness: Meier has a strong predilection for white as a color for buildings. Whiteness operates as an isolant, so that each building is seen intensely on its own, whether its context is urban or rural. The surface of the building is always articulated, both inside and out, sometimes in apparent defiance of the construction, into a harmonious, but always somewhat mouvementé *composition, a composition to which plan and volumetric organization also conform. Within the building the grouping of volumes is always clearly related to a path—perhaps it would imply too much to call them a* promenade architecturale—*the sequence is not so much a discontinuous envelope for the movements of the inhabitants, but rather a chaplet of rooms strung on the continuity of the promenade; the sequence then folded in on itself, and enclosed within the orthogonal envelope of the skin."* —Joseph Rykwert, "The Very Personal Work of Richard Meier & Associates," *Architectural Forum*, March 1972

Weber-Frankel Gallery
New York, New York

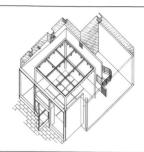

Suburban House Prototype
Concord, Massachusetts

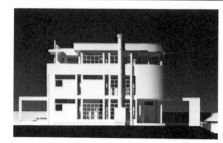

Alamo Plaza
Colorado Springs, Colorado
Mondev International Corporation

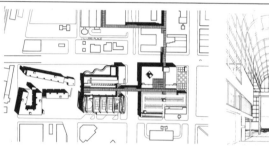

Opening Exhibition, Cooper-Hewitt Museum
New York, New York

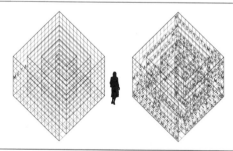

1977
William Henry Bishop Visiting Professor of Architecture at Yale University; Visiting Professor of Architecture at Harvard University
Elected Associate of the National Academy of Design
Awarded the Homes for Better Living First Honor Award, the National Honor Award, and the Bartlett Award by the American Institute of Architects; the R. S. Reynolds Memorial Award; the City Club of New York Albert S. Bard Civic Award for Excellence in Architecture and Urban Design; and the *Architectural Record* Award of Excellence in Design

Manchester Civic Center
Manchester, New Hampshire
Mondev International Corporation

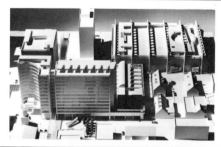

New York School Exhibition
State Museum, Albany, New York
State of New York Office of General Services

396

The proposed design for a gallery on 57th Street showing the work of contemporary painters and sculptors emphasizes the street-level visibility of a smaller gallery and its connection by means of an open staircase to a larger gallery on the floor below. A nine-square hung grid in the smaller gallery provides a flexible lighting system.

The absence of urban planning in Colorado Springs, as in the West generally, necessitated an attempt to influence and order the further growth of the downtown area. The projected buildings—including a convention center, municipal office building, two-hundred-room hotel, bank headquarters, public parking garage, and connecting elements to shops—are arranged so as to frame the view of Pike's Peak, and the different functions are unified by a circulation spine, which helps to fill the urbanistic vacuum now existing. The access to the complex is by way of a seventy-foot "galleria" with a glass roof, stretching across Pike's Peak Avenue and envisioned as a monumental gateway. A large urban plaza is created at the intersection of the two axes linking the planned new construction with existing buildings. The extension of these axes indicates a future course of expansion.

For the Cooper-Hewitt Museum's opening exhibition, organized by Hans Hollein and titled "Man TransForms," a ten-foot cubic lattice was created out of a commercially produced interlocking metal grid system normally used for shelving. The pure Cartesian geometry of the cube was then transformed into a kind of three-dimensional crossword puzzle by the visitors' hanging of cardboard alphabet letters on the grid, producing a changing labyrinth of spatial connections. The conceptual environment of the transformed alphabet block became a map of the metamorphosis from ideal form into concrete poetry—a metaphor for the architectural process itself.

"Architect Richard Meier undertook the task of carving some order out of the cavernous areas assigned to the moderns. His solution is a grid of windowed rooms, streets, avenues, colonnades, and long walls which both tie the raw volumes down to human scale and offer a chance to display giant paintings at their best. Strolling through his pristinely white constructions is like exploring an Aegean village built by Euclid-crazed Hellenes. The order is Classic in its relationship to spectators, yet amazingly Baroque in the variety of its changing sizes and shapes. Everything is simultaneously consistent (height of ceilings, rhythm of axes, perpendicularity of joints) and ambiguous—logical and theatrical. Meier's walls are suited to the New York School paintings; they bring out the almost sacred principle of murality that so many artists cherished as a secret dream or announced as combative dogma."—Thomas B. Hess, "Art: The Big Picture," New York Magazine, 24 October 1977

Aye Simon Reading Room
The Solomon R. Guggenheim Museum, New York, New York
1978

House in Palm Beach
Palm Beach, Florida
1980

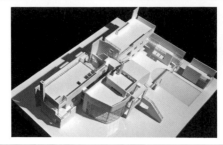

Apartment for Mr. and Mrs. Philip Suarez
New York, New York
1978

1978
Awarded the Residential Design Award Citation by the American Institute of Architects

Clifty Creek Elementary School
Columbus, Indiana
1982
Bartholomew Consolidated School Corporation

Hartford Seminary
Hartford, Connecticut
1981

Furniture for Knoll International
1982

398

"Mr. Meier has proven here that he both understands and loves the work of Frank Lloyd Wright, and the room he has designed stands as a loving tribute to both Wright himself and to the Guggenheim Museum of which it is a part. It is not imitation Wright, though it is Wrightian in spirit; it is not like the rest of Mr. Meier's work, though it is similar to that in spirit, too. . . . But what is most impressive of all here is how Mr. Meier has managed to keep Wright's spirit and mood without ever directly imitating his forms. The Guggenheim is a study in the use of natural light and the interplay of curving spaces against one another; this is exactly what Mr. Meier is exploring himself, in his own way, in the Simon reading room. The Meier room is sleeker and more refined than any of Wright's sections of the building, but it is no less respectful of Wright for its adherence to Mr. Meier's own stylistic tenets. Indeed the room stands in sharp contrast to the unsubtle, heavy addition to the Guggenheim's 89th Street side completed to the designs of William Wesley Peters, inheritor of Wright's practice, in 1968. The addition is full of Wright's ornamental motifs and decorative forms without being at all responsive to the underlying spirit of the Guggenheim. Mr. Meier's room does just the opposite—it uses none of Wright's forms directly, but by responding so well to the building's spirit it pays Wright the highest tribute of all."—Paul Goldberger, "New Room at the Guggenheim," *The New York Times*, 15 June 1978

The transformation of this Gramercy Park apartment was intended to define and enhance the scale of the existing non-descript, non-specific rooms, and give a sense of light-filled enclosure. Each room required both spatial and functional modification. Flying beams and fascias, a punctuating column, and the metamorphosis of the dining room into a soft pillbox by means of a poché curve along the window wall all helped create a kind of large-scale decoration, a modern version of moldings and dadoes. Natural light penetrates to the center of the apartment through a succession of transparent planes, making radiant walls that open yet preserve important boundaries. The apartment, which is on the ground floor, is at the level of the trees in the park, and the pale green of the living room reflects and deepens this outdoor verdure, making the room an extension of the exterior landscape.

"The principal reason why Richard Meier pays such great attention to the cladding in his work is the need to ensure that the building will withstand the test of time by protecting the materials. This is an aspect which modern architects, and Le Corbusier in particular, frequently disregard. Here, the examples of Villa Stein and Villa La Roche are a sufficient reminder that the constructive translation of the 'purist' architecture in the 'archaic' language imposed by the traditional worksite methods led to a betrayal of the ideal of modernism which Le Corbusier intended to project also into the world of the production. The prismatic purity of the external appearance of the villas in reality hides the fact that there are load-bearing walls made of concrete blocks and plaster. In the Columbus school, on the other hand, Richard Meier clearly places these same blocks in evidence when using them as cladding. The fact that these blocks are used, and the way in which they are employed, does not depend solely upon graphic requirements. The way in which the two layers, one white and the other gray, are positioned in the facade is indicative of reversal of position in respect of the physical characteristics of the materials themselves. Whereas a wall constructed according to traditional criteria would employ the stronger material—the concrete block—in the lower part of the building, in this school the facade gives the impression of a concrete wall suspended upon a delicate surface of glazed bricks—an impression emphasized even more by the difference in the relative thicknesses of the two materials employed."—Pierre-Alain Croset, "Elementary School in Columbus," *Casabella*, May 1984

"More than any other practicing architect in the U.S., Richard Meier presents himself as the heir to a didactic modernism framed on the one hand by the tenet 'a house is a machine for living in,' and on the other by the paradigm of the Dom-ino House, Le Corbusier's attempt to weld classicism to reinforced-concrete technology. . . . The utilization of such a purist aesthetic has provided a consistent vocabulary for Meier, in most of his private houses and many of his public institutions: the themes run clearly from the Smith House (1967) to the Hartford Seminary. Such a self-consciously lived debt to modernism places a special burden on criticism: his works cannot be entirely detached from the Corbusian canon, from which they derive much of their aesthetic force and conceptual unity; nor can they be totally separated from a 'post-modernist' context, where the operative criteria call for them to be seen as so many consumable examples of a dated and already eclectic style. Neither 'authentically' modern in an age that is nostalgic for roots, however tenuous these might be, nor completely 'post-modern'—insofar as the term refers to an unabashed historicism—Meier's buildings stand equivocal and hallucinatory, suspended between past and present. Their dreamlike quality is enhanced by their very perfection; untouched by time, and technically perfect; even, as in the case of the Seminary, divided from the ground by a thin black line. They seem to ask for special consideration in an age preoccupied by the ruin, the fantastic past."—Anthony Vidler, "Deconstructing Modernism," *Skyline*, March 1982

"There are echoes in all these pieces of the great furniture of Charles Rennie Mackintosh, the Art Nouveau architect of Glasgow, and to a lesser extent of the not so great furniture of Frank Lloyd Wright. What is absent, surprisingly, is a close tie either to the furniture of Le Corbusier, whose architecture has so influenced Mr. Meier's own, or to that of the other important designers of early modern furniture such as Marcel Breuer. Mr. Meier's attentions are somewhere else altogether from the International Style. He is preoccupied not with the making of light, tensile forms but with solid, molded ones. These are objects that feel constructed by hand, not by machine; it is no accident that they are of wood and not of the metal that was so crucial to most International Style furniture. The use of wooden grids or of a series of vertical slats, like little fences, is what calls Mackintosh to mind; Mr. Meier has used such fence-like forms as the central supports for his tables, and similar vertical tiers support the stool. But these pieces are crisper than the Mackintosh furniture, less romantic, more disciplined. . . . Meier's furniture is beautiful in a way that seems to sum up the different aspirations of the modern movement, from Wright's emphasis on materials to Mackintosh's sense of proportion and scale to the International Style's air of cool self-assurance."—Paul Goldberger, "Furniture by Architects: Vitality and Verve," *The New York Times*, 14 October 1982

1979
Elected to the American Arts Alliance and
the National Academy of Design

Giovannitti House
Pittsburgh, Pennsylvania
1983

Museum for the Decorative Arts
Frankfurt am Main, West Germany
1984
Stadt Frankfurt am Main

Irwin Union Bank and Trust Company
Columbus, Indiana

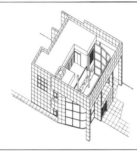

1980
Eliot Noyes Visiting Critic in Architecture at
Harvard University
Awarded the Medal of Honor by the New
York Chapter of the American Institute of
Architects

Somerset Condominiums
Beverly Hills, California
The Somerset Company

East 67th Street Housing
New York, New York
Sheldon Solow

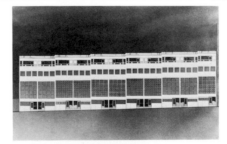

High Museum of Art
Atlanta, Georgia
1983
Atlanta Arts Alliance

"In Richard Meier's design for an Arts and Crafts Museum in Frankfurt am Main—the winning entry in a limited competition—we witness a phenomenon without precedent in his earlier work: a passionate engagement with the problem of context. To be sure, Meier's buildings have often been notably site-specific; but with the single exception of the Twin Parks Housing project, they seem to have proceeded from the premise that as works of architecture it is their obligation as well as their right to occupy center stage, to assert an autonomous presence, to be, in a word, self-sufficient. And the acknowledgment of context, in Twin Parks notwithstanding, this Museum is surely the first project in which Meier has felt obliged to defer, with an intensity of purpose that permeates every aspect of the design, to the preexisting building and landscapes within and around his site. It is his first essentially contingent building. . . . There is clearly another purpose as well: to reaffirm a domestic scale. And this is not just a matter of sympathy for the external context. It equally reflects a concern for the quality of the museum experience, especially in an institution dedicated to the collection and exhibition of objects which were made to be lived *with. One senses that to approach, to enter, to move through the interior spaces of this building will be an experience evoking everywhere a mood of domesticity. Thus from an architect whose private houses have often seemed to assert themselves as public acts, we now have a public building which aspires above all to suggest the pleasure of privacy."*—Henry N. Cobb, "Richard Meier's Museum für Kunsthandwerk," *Express*, April 1981

A sense of identity and quality of place are expressed in the architectural form of a projected drive-in branch bank in a suburban shopping center. The square, metal-paneled building is designed to address both those using the bank and those passing by on the highway.

This row of eleven luxury townhouses was designed for a mid-block Manhattan site above an existing subterranean parking structure. The eighteen-foot width and five-story height of each townhouse were specified by the program. The institutional image of the neighboring high-rise residential and commercial buildings was diminished by progressively breaking down the scale of the facades and by following the sloping plane of the street with the primary facade. The windows within windows and the fenestration pattern give identity to each townhouse and develop a scale and design relationship with aspects of the surrounding neighborhood and the typical Manhattan street. A covered stoop provides a degree of enclosure for entrance to each townhouse. Inside, the house is organized to provide spatial continuity between public and private zones. The family-use spaces are located on the lower two-and-one-half floors, and open to an interior private garden. This garden links the main volume of the townhouse with a two-story garden pavilion, open to the courtyard as well as to a communal exterior terraced garden. Solariums on the roof terrace provide additional outdoor space for each unit, and their configuration reflects the point of entry to each house below.

"Where the Atheneum remained, despite its ostensibly public program, a brilliantly exfoliated and overscaled 'residence'—permeated by rotational axes, intersecting planes, and serpentine walks—the Frankfurt Museum brought Meier face to face with the German classical tradition and shifted him off the main line of American Romanticism. . . . One senses a swerve in Meier's work at this juncture, away from what was surely a Gravesian affinity for Neo-Cubist Baroque toward a more rigorous structural method closer to the work of Mathias Ungers. The High Museum of Art takes reversion to formal order a stage further, for Meier's generic gallery type has now become unequivocally four-square with one corner removed. . . . The perimeter ramps to the four-story, high-quadrant volume (a foyer concept patently derived from Frank Lloyd Wright's Guggenheim Museum) are compositionally fixed in place by radial beams extending from the apex of the quadrant toward the circumference. It is important to note from a typological point of view that this top-lit 'space of public appearance' is nonetheless intended to be largely free of wall exhibits, unlike the Guggenheim, so that the four towers are naturally illuminated only by a single slot in glass brick. These opaque bastions house the main body of the collection. This typological shift away from the romantic avant-gardism of the Guggenheim is in itself a confirmation of Meier's creative return to a classical form. . . . More than ever one appreciates the value of Meier's sensuous stoicism, his determination to mediate his youthful modernism in a rational way, his capacity to remain committed to the realities of the epoch without falling into either historicist reaction or avant-gardist excess."—Kenneth Frampton, "High Museum of Art at Atlanta," *Casabella*, November 1982

Objects for Alessi Designs
Alessi Fratelli

Meier/Stella Collaboration
(With Frank Stella)

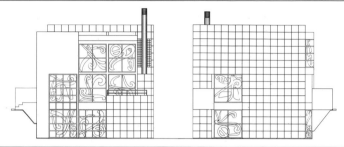

1981
Elected to the Board of Directors of the
International Center for Advanced Studies in
Art

Renault Administrative Headquarters
Boulogne-Billancourt, France
La Régie Nationale des Usines Renault

1982
Awarded the Distinguished Architecture
Award by the New York Chapter of the
American Institute of Architects

Des Moines Art Center Addition
Des Moines, Iowa
1984
Edmundson Art Foundation

Internationale Bauausstellung Housing
Berlin, West Germany
Gesellschaft für Anlagebeteiligung and
Klingbeil Gruppe GmbH

Parc de la Villette
Competition entry
Paris, France
Etablissement Public du Parc de la Villette

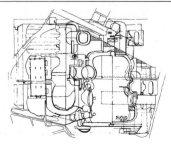

The design of a coffee and tea service for Officina Alessi, part of the manufacturer's program to offer designers and architects an opportunity to reinterpret industrially produced, functional objects with more experimental methods and innovative forms expressive of their own aesthetics, was conceived as an abstract composition in purist geometries and flat and curved highly reflective surfaces. Each object has its own identity as well as being part of a larger composition; thus every arrangement produces a new ensemble. The material of this three-dimensional still-life, which includes a coffeepot, teapot, creamer, sugar bowl, and tray, all designed to function serviceably, is polished sterling silver, with ivory handles on the coffeepot and teapot.

Frank Stella's window decorations for a one-story suburban house design consist of aluminum-foil outlines on tinted roll-up window shades. Contemporary reinterpretations of stained glass, they serve as both an inexpensive form of applied architectural decoration and a protection from the sun. The collaboration of the architect and artist here demonstrates a way of combining the two art forms without sacrificing the independence or abstractness of either. Architect and artist were able to work together without getting in one another's way or compromising their respective conceptions.

The proposal for the design of the Parc de la Villette is intended to be seen as both a microcosm of the city—employing such urbanistic ordering devices as axial vistas and spatial sequences derived from the adjacent Parisian city fabric and the memory of other cities—and a critique of the city, a special place that offers a naturalistic landscape as a contrast to and refuge from the city around it. Views of and vistas from the built forms within the park are manipulated to establish correspondences and create order among all the disparate elements that the La Villette site comprises. The primary axis of circulation connects a pedestrian bridge from the Parc des Buttes Chaumont to the south with the National Museum of Science and Industry to the north. Perpendicular to this the Canal de la Villette forms a major cross-axis. Vistas along these paths extend one's perception of space and give an immediate sense of orientation. A dialogue is then established between this axial system and the curvilinear form of the open spaces. These open spaces are defined by dense rows of planting that provide a contrasting sense of scale and enclosure related to traditional garden design. The overall composition of the park is conceived as a collage in which the layering of individual elements provides a framework of spatial variety.

1983
Elected to the American Academy and
Institute of Arts and Letters
Awarded the National Honor Award by the
American Institute of Architects

Office Building for Siemens
Munich, West Germany
Siemens AG

Opéra Bastille
Competition entry
Paris, France
Mission Opéra Bastille

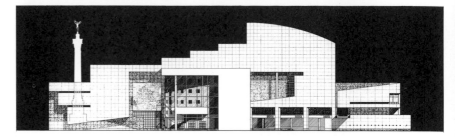

Tableware for Swid-Powell Designs
Swid-Powell Designs
1984

Lingotto Factory Conversion
Turin, Italy
Fiat S.p.A.

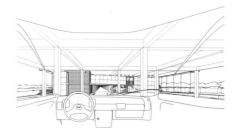

1984
Awarded the National Honor Award by the
American Institute of Architects, and the
Distinguished Architecture Award by the New
York Chapter of the American Institute of
Architects; named Officier de l'Ordre des Arts
et des Lettres by the Ministry of Culture of
France
Recipient of the Pritzker Architecture Prize

House in North Salem
North Salem, New York

Helmick House
Des Moines, Iowa

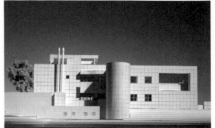

One aspect of the competition project for the Opéra is its relationship to the circular Place de la Bastille, which generated the curvilinear elevational forms on the facing facade. The scale is that of a monumental opera house with seating for twenty-five hundred people and the requisite ancillary functions. In retrospect, it seems somewhat overscaled for its site.

Tableware—including glassware and ceramic dishes, and silver bowls, candlesticks, and platters—is being designed for a new company specializing in functional decorative-arts products designed by architects. Most of the objects have either an applied or cut-out square motif in varying dimensions.

The house is located on a large, sloping site with magnificent views. It is more elaborate than previous houses in terms of both materials—combining metal panels, stucco, and glass—and form. While earlier notions of the separation of the public and private zones of the house are retained, they are articulated here in a more complex way.

This is a linear house of six thousand square feet for a flat site. The unusually flamboyant program called for a large number of recreational facilities.

Selected Bibliography

General

Abercrombie, Stanley. "Richard Meier's Sculptures for Living." *House & Garden*, November 1976, pp. 168–71, 196.

"Architektur: Dramatischer Dialog." *Der Spiegel*, 26 May 1980, pp. 237–41 (passim).

Bode, Peter M. "Im Bauhaus zu Hause: Richard Meier und sein Räume-Theater." *Frankfurter Allgemeine Magazin*, 3 June 1983, pp. 8–14.

Dal Co, Francesco. "The 'Allusions' of Richard Meier." *Oppositions* 9 (1977), pp. 6–18.

Davis, Douglas. "Designs for Living: Five Frontiersmen." *Newsweek*, 6 November 1978, pp. 82–91 (passim).

Diamonstein, Barbaralee. *American Architecture Now*. New York: Rizzoli, 1980, pp. 105–22.

Filler, Martin. "Modernism Lives: Richard Meier." *Art in America*, May 1980, pp. 123–31.

Five Architects: Eisenman/Graves/Gwathmey/Hejduk/Meier. Introductions by Kenneth Frampton and Colin Rowe. New York: Wittenborn, 1972, pp. 11–13, 111–34.

Five Architects NY. Introduction by Manfredo Tafuri. Rome: Officina Edizioni, 1976, pp. 24–28, 133–73.

"Five on Five." Articles by Romaldo Giurgola, Alan Greenberg, Charles Moore, Jaquelin Robertson, and Robert Stern. *Architectural Forum*, May 1973, pp. 45–57 (passim).

40 under 40: An Exhibition of Young Talents in Architecture. New York: Architectural League of New York and American Federation of Arts, 1966, pp. 19–20.

Frampton, Kenneth. "*Five Architects: Eisenman/Graves/Gwathmey/Hejduk/Meier*." *Lotus International* 9 (1975), pp. 147–61.

Goldberger, Paul. "Ad-Meier-ing." *Vogue*, June 1983, pp. 196–203, 256.

———. "Architecture's Big Five Elevate Form." *The New York Times*, 26 November 1973, sec. 2, pp. 1, 34.

———. "City Reaches Pinnacle as Architectural Leader." *The New York Times*, 4 April 1983, pp. B1, 4 (passim).

———. Review of *Richard Meier, Architect*. *The New York Times Book Review*, 5 December 1976, p. 10.

———. "Richard Meier: Form and Function." *Goodlife*, March 1984, pp. 34–41.

———. "Richard Meier Gets the Pritzker Prize." *The New York Times*, 18 April 1984, p. C20.

———. "Should Anyone Care about the 'New York Five'? . . . or about Their Critics, the 'Five on Five'?" *Architectural Record*, February 1974, pp. 113–16 (passim).

Hanson, Bernard. "Architecture in the Abstract." *Hartford Courant*, 4 May 1980, p. 2G.

Holmes, Ann. "Meier Admired Designer and a Major Architect." *Houston Chronicle*, 25 April 1981.

Hubbard, William. *Complexity and Conviction: Steps toward an Architecture of Convention*. Cambridge, Mass.: MIT Press, 1980, pp. 7–9, 221–26.

Hughes, Robert. "U.S. Architects: Doing Their Own Thing." *Time*, 8 January 1979, pp. 52–59 (passim).

Huxtable, Ada Louise. "Architectural Drawings as Art." *The New York Times*, 12 June 1977, p. 25 (passim).

———. "Is Modern Architecture Dead?" *New York Review of Books*, 16 July 1981, pp. 17–20 (passim).

———. "The Gospel according to Giedion and Gropius Is under Attack." *The New York Times*, 27 June 1976, pp. 1, 29 (passim).

———. "The Troubled State of Modern Architecture." *New York Review of Books*, 1 May 1980, pp. 22–25 (passim).

Kay, Jane Holtz. "Right Angles, White Lines." *The Christian Science Monitor*, 9 May 1984, pp. 29–30.

Keens, William. "Dialogue and Fantasy in White: An Interview with Richard Meier." *American Arts*, September 1983, pp. 16–21.

Kupper, Eugene. "Book Review: *Richard Meier, Architect*." *LA Architect*, February 1977, p. 2; reprinted in *Progressive Architecture*, July 1977, pp. 55–57.

Lewin, Susan Grant, and Schraub, Susan Hope. "The Structure of Space." *House Beautiful*, April 1978, pp. 79–91.

Marvel, Bill. "Architecture as Seen by the Eyes of the 'Whites.'" *National Observer*, 22 June 1974, p. 20.

Meier, Richard. "Cultural Congress." *Skyline*, April 1983, p. 7.

———. "Design Strategies: Eight Projects by Richard Meier and Associates—Systematic Self-Description of the Compositional Process." *Casabella*, May 1974, pp. 17–38.

———. "Dialogue." With Arata Isozaki. *A plus U*, August 1976, pp. 21–38.

———. "Guest Speaker: On the Spirit of Architecture." *Architectural Digest*, June 1981, pp. 156, 160, 162, 164.

———. "Lecture in Japan." *Spazio*, 20 December 1976, supplement.

———. "Les Heures Claires." In "Le Corbusier: Villa Savoye, Poissy, France, 1929–31." Edited by Yukio Futagawa. *Global Architecture* 13 (1973), pp. 2–7.

———. *On Architecture*. Text of Eliot Noyes Lecture. Cambridge, Mass.: Harvard University Graduate School of Design, 1982.

———. "Planning for Jerusalem." *Architectural Forum*, April 1971, pp. 56–57.

———. "Remembering Breuer." *Skyline*, October 1981, p. 11.

———. *Richard Meier, Architect: Buildings and Projects 1966–1976*. Introduction by Kenneth Frampton. Postscript by John Hejduk. New York: Oxford University Press, 1976.

———. "Thoughts on Frank Stella." In *Shards* by Frank Stella. London and New York: Petersburg Press, 1983, pp. 1–4.

Ministry of Culture and Sciences. *Trends in Contemporary Architecture*. Introduction by Kenneth Frampton. Athens: National Gallery, Alexander Soutzos Museum, pp. 17–18, 72–87.

Papier, Deborah. "Richard Meier: Young Master of Space." *The Washington Times*, sec. B, pp. 1–2.

Pettena, Gianni, et al. *Richard Meier*. Venice: Marsilio, 1981.

Richard Meier: Matrix 58. Exhibition catalogue. Hartford: The Wadsworth Atheneum, 1980.

Richard Meier: The Art of Architecture. Exhibition catalogue. Atlanta: The High Museum of Art, 1980.

"Richard Meier: Zeitströmungen in der Architektur—Einige Bauten." *Deutsches Architektenblatt*, 1 September 1981, pp. 1251–60.

Siola, Uberto, and Bonicalzi, Rosaldo. "Architettura e razione: Appunti sulla Internazionale di Architettura della XV Triennale." *Controspazio*, December 1973, pp. 16–24 (passim).

"Spatial Structure of Richard Meier." Includes the following: "Lyricism in Whiteness" by Arata Isozaki; "My Statement" by Richard Meier; "Analysis: Richard Meier's Work" by Mario Gandelsonas; "Recent Work of Richard Meier" by Rosemarie Bletter; "Meier's Whiteness" by Ching-Yu Chang; "Five Projects"; "Bibliography." *A plus U*, April 1976, pp. 45–120.

Stephens, Suzanne. "The Individual: Richard Meier." *Progressive Architecture*, May 1977, pp. 60–62.

Tafuri, Manfredo. " 'European Graffiti': Five × Five = Twenty-five." *Oppositions* 5 (1976), pp. 35–74 (passim).

———. "L'Architecture dans le Boudoir." *Oppositions* 3 (1974), p. 52.

———. "The Ashes of Jefferson." *L'Architecture d'Aujourd'hui*, August–September 1976, pp. 53–69 (passim).

Thorndike, Joseph. Jr., ed. *Three Centuries of Notable American Architects*. Essay by Paul Goldberger. New York: American Heritage, 1981, pp. 338–41.

Trescott, Jacqueline, and Forgey, Banjamin. "White on White." *The Washington Post*, 16 May 1984, pp. B1, B13.

Waisman, Marina. "Richard Meier: Del objecto al entorno." Introduction by Kenneth Frampton. Interview with and comments by Richard Meier. *Summarios*, April 1977, pp. 2–32.

"White Existence: Richard Meier, 1961–77." Includes the following: "A Word from Richard Meier"; "Dialogue: On Architecture" by Richard Meier and Fumihiko Maki; "A Personal View on R. Meier" by Yukio Futagawa; "Expression Crisis—the Implications of the Formation of Richard Meier" by Yuzuru Tominaga; "Architecture of Pleasure" by Hiromi Fujii; "Works: Private Buildings and Projects"; "Richard Meier's Works Chronologically Scanned." *Space Design*, January 1978, pp. 3–158.

The Atheneum

Abercrombie, Stanley. "A Vision Continued." *AIA Journal*, mid-May 1980, pp. 126–37.

"The Architecture of the Promenade: The Atheneum." *International Architect* 3 (1980), pp. 13–24.

Cassarà, Silvio. "Richard Meier: Intrinsic Qualities of Remembrances. The Atheneum at New Harmony, Indiana." *Parametro*, July–August 1976, pp. 16–19, 59.

Cohen, Arthur. "Richard Meier, Creator of a New Harmony: An Architect Builds a Classic Meeting Hall for the Nation's Heartland." *United Mainliner*, March 1980, pp. 69–71.

Futagawa, Yukio, ed. "Collage and Study Sketches for the Atheneum"; "Meier's Atheneum" by Kenneth Frampton; "Richard Meier, An American Architect" by Arthur Cohen; "The Atheneum, New Harmony, Ind. (First Scheme)"; "The Atheneum (Executed Scheme)." *GA Document* 1 (1980), pp. 25–65.

———. "The Atheneum, New Harmony, Indiana. 1975–1979." Text by Paul Goldberger. *Global Architecture* 60 (1981). Reprinted in *Global Architecture Book 6: Public Buildings*. Tokyo: A.D.A. Edita Co., 1981, n.p.

Goldberger, Paul. "The Atheneum: Utopia Lives." *Vogue*, February 1980, pp. 250–51, 296.
Haker, Werner. "New Harmony und das Athenaeum von Richard Meier." *Werk, Bauen und Wohnen*, December 1980, pp. 44–53.
"Harmonious Museum for New Harmony." *Life*, February 1980, pp. 60–62.
Huxtable, Ada Louise. "A Radical New Addition for Mid-America." *The New York Times*, 30 September 1979, sec. 2, pp. 1, 31.
Klotz, Heinrich, ed. "Das Athenaeum." Text by Richard Meier. *Jahrbuch für Architektur: Neues Bauen 1980–1981* (1981), pp. 53–64.
Magnago Lampugnani, Vittorio. *Architecture of Our Century in Drawings: Utopia and Reality*. Stuttgart: Verlag Gerd Hatje, 1982, pp. 106–107.
Marlin, William. "Dissonance in New Harmony." *Inland Architect*, December 1981, pp. 20–28.
———. "Revitalizing Architectural Legacy of an American 'Camelot.' " *The Christian Science Monitor*, 16 April 1976, p. 26.
Meier, Richard. "The Atheneum, New Harmony, Indiana; Manchester Civic Center, Manchester, New Hampshire—Comments." *Harvard Architecture Review*, spring 1981, pp. 176–87. Reprinted in French in *Les Cahiers de la Recherche Architecturale*, November 1982, pp. 66–73.
Rykwert, Joseph. "New Harmony Propylaeon." *Domus*, February 1980, pp. 12–17.
Shezen, Roberto. "La via storica: L'Atheneum di New Harmony nell' Indiana di Richard Meier." *Gran Bazaar*, January–February 1982, pp. 128–35.
Stephens, Suzanne. "Emblematic Edifice: The Atheneum, New Harmony, Indiana." *Progressive Architecture*, February 1980, pp. 67–75.
Zevi, Bruno. "Un UFO nel campo de grano." *L'Espresso*, 6 April 1980, p. 124.

Aye Simon Reading Room
Filler, Martin. "Splendid Spin-off." *Progressive Architecture*, October 1978, pp. 68–71.
Goldberger, Paul. "New Room at the Guggenheim." *The New York Times*, 15 June 1978, p. C17.

Bronx Developmental Center
"Bronx Developmental Center." Includes the following: "Bronx Developmental Center" by Paul Goldberger; "A Comparative Study—Bronx Developmental Center and Gunma Prefectural Museum of Modern Art" by Arata Isozaki; "The Modern Language of Architecture and Richard Meier" by Francesco Dal Co. *A plus U*, November 1977, pp. 3–29.
"Bronx State School." *A plus U*, June 1973, pp. 55–68.
Cassarà, Silvio. "Bronx Developmental Center." *Parametro*, May 1977, pp. 37–39.
Futagawa, Yukio, ed. "Bronx Developmental Center." *GA Document Special Issue: 1970–1980* (1980), pp. 240–43.
Goldberger, Paul. "Bronx Developmental Center: Is It a Masterwork or a Nightmare?" *The New York Times*, 3 May 1977, pp. 43, 46.
Huxtable, Ada Louise. "A Landmark before Its Doors Open." *The New York Times*, 8 May 1977, sec. 2, p. 1.
———. "The Latest Style Is Jeweler's Mechanical." *The New York Times*, 27 June 1976, pp. 1, 29 (passim).
Kulterman, Udo. *Architecture of the Seventies*. Boston: Architectural Book Publishing Co., 1980, pp. 4–7.
"Rieducazione a New York." *Domus*, April 1977, pp. 6–9.
Rykwert, Joseph. "The Very Personal Work of Richard Meier and Associates." *Architectural Forum*, March 1972, pp. 30–37.
Stephens, Suzanne. "Architecture Cross-examined." *Progressive Architecture*, July 1977, pp. 43–54.
Stevens, Mark. "Living in a Work of Art." *Newsweek*, 30 May 1977, p. 59.
Turner, Judith. *Five Architects*. New York: Rizzoli, 1980, pp. 107–27.
"Two New York Schools for the Retarded." *L'Architecture d'Aujourd'hui*, February–March 1971, pp. 96–97.

Charles Evans Industrial Buildings
Rykwert, Joseph. "The Very Personal Work of Richard Meier and Associates." *Architectural Forum*, March 1972, pp. 30–37.

Clifty Creek Elementary School
Croset, Pierre-Alain. "Elementary School in Columbus." *Casabella*, May 1984, pp. 4–13.
Futagawa, Yukio, ed. "Clifty Creek Elementary School, Columbus, Ohio." *GA Document* 9 (February 1984), pp. 114–21.

Cornell University Undergraduate Housing
Hoyt, Charles. "4 Projects by Richard Meier: Change and Consistency." *Architectural Record*, March 1975, pp. 111–20.
Meier, Richard. "Tre recenti progetti." *Controspazio*, September 1975, pp. 38–47.

Des Moines Art Center Addition
Demetrion, James T. "Des Moines Art Center." *Iowa Architect*, March–April 1984, pp. 16–25.

Douglas House
Davis, Douglas, and Rourke, Mary. "Architecture: Real Dream Houses." *Newsweek*, 4 October 1976, pp. 66–69 (passim).
Futagawa, Yukio, ed. "Douglas House." *GA Document Special Issue: 1970–1980* (1980), pp. 106–109.
———. "Douglas House, Harbor Springs, Michigan. 1974." Text by Paul Goldberger. *Global Architecture* 34 (1975). Reprinted in *Global Architecture Book 3: Modern Houses*. Tokyo: A.D.A. Edita Co., 1981, n.p.
Goldberger, Paul. "Honors for Uncertainty." *The New York Times Magazine*, 2 May 1976, pp. 68–69.
———. "Purism on the Lake." *The New York Times Magazine*, 22 September 1974, pp. 72–74.
"House in Harbor Springs." *A plus U*, November 1972, pp. 27–30.
Hoyt, Charles. "Richard Meier: Public Space and Private Space." *Architectural Record*, July 1973, pp. 89–98.
"L'Ultima Villa from the U.S.A." *Domus*, January 1975, pp. 19–22.
Morton, David. "Douglas House." *Progressive Architecture*, July 1975, pp. 58–61.
"Vorsicht Glashaus." *Häuser* 3 (1980), pp. 71–75.
"Wohnhaus am Michigan-See, U.S.A." *Baumeister*, July 1977, pp. 617–19.

Fredonia Health and Physical Education Building
"Fredonia's Athletic Center: Legible Design in Steel." *Architectural Record*, August 1971, pp. 105–107.
"Health and Physical Education Facility at S.U.N.Y., Fredonia, New York." *A plus U*, April 1975, pp. 57–64.

Furniture for Knoll International
Abercrombie, Stanley. "Furnishings." *AIA Journal*, December 1980, pp. 62–63.
Emery, Marc. *Furniture by Architects*. New York: Harry N. Abrams, pp. 204–207.
"Everything for the House: Furniture Drawings." *Express*, December 1980, p. 9.
Goldberger, Paul. "Furniture by Architects: Vitality and Verve." *The New York Times*, 14 October 1982, pp. C1, 8.
Halliday, Sarah. "Inside Furniture: Meier and Gwathmey/Siegel at Knoll." *Skyline*, April 1983, pp. 1, 21.
Klotz, Heinrich, ed. "Möbelentwürfe." *Jahrbuch für Architektur: Neues Bauen 1980–1981* (1981), pp. 85–86.
Phillips, Lisa. *Shape and Environment: Furniture by American Architects*. New York: Whitney Museum, 1982, pp. 19, 42–43.
"Richard Meier's Furniture Collection." *Domus*, February 1983, p. 64.
Wintour, Anna. "Design: Reserved Seating." *New York Magazine*, 27 September 1982, pp. 56–57.

Giovannitti House
"Private Residence: Pittsburgh, Pennsylvania." *Casa da Vendere/Ready Houses*. Mendrisio, Switzerland, and Old Westbury, N.Y.: Spazioarte Mendrisio and New York Institute of Technology, 1983, pp. 83–97.

Hartford Seminary
Arriola, Ricardo Contreras. "Richard Meier: Dos proyectos recientes." *ARS* (Revista del Centro de Estudios de la Arquitectura, Santiago), August 1981, pp. 75–79.
Brenner, Douglas. "A Progression into Light: The Hartford Seminary by Richard Meier & Partners." *Architectural Record*, January 1982, pp. 65–73.
———. "Two Projects in Context." *Architectural Record*, April 1981, pp. 87–97.
Canty, Donald. "Shining Vessel of Religious Thought." *AIA Journal*, mid-May 1982, pp. 124–33.
Davern, Jeanne. *Architecture 1970–1980: A Decade of Change*. New York: McGraw-Hill, 1980, pp. 254–55.

Doubilet, Susan. "Seminary, Hartford, Connecticut." *Architectural Review*, May 1982, pp. 25–31.

Fumagalli, Paolo. "Hartford Seminary, Hartford, Connecticut, 1978–1981." *Werk, Bauen und Wohnen*, January–February 1983, pp. 12–17.

Futagawa, Yukio, ed. "The Hartford Seminary Foundation." *GA Document* 1 (1980), pp. 66–69.

————. "The Hartford Seminary, Hartford, Connecticut"; "First Sight: The Hartford Seminary" by Theodore Gill. *GA Document* 4 (1981), pp. 50–67.

"Hartford Seminary." *A plus U*, February 1983, pp. 31–46.

Hoyet, Jean-Michel. "Made in U.S.A.: Trois conceptions récentes de Richard Meier & Associés." *Techniques & Architecture*, November 1982, pp. 140–47.

Huxtable, Ada Louise. "Architecture View: Moving into a New Realm." *The New York Times*, 27 September 1981, sec. 2, p. 33.

Kay, Jane Holtz. "Echo of the 1920's: Architect Richard Meier Teams Up with the Sun." *The Christian Science Monitor*, 22 January 1982, p. 15.

Margolies, Linda. "The Hartford Seminary Gets a New Look." *Hartford Courant Magazine*, 13 January 1980, pp. 4–6, 13.

Pettena, Gianni. "A Whiter Shade of Pale." *Domus*, June 1982, pp. 2–12.

"Richard Meier at Hartford and Atlanta." *L'Architecture d'Aujourd'hui*, February 1982, pp. 59–68.

Vidler, Anthony. "Deconstructing Modernism." *Skyline*, March 1982, pp. 21–23.

High Museum of Art

Balfour, Alan. "High Museum, Atlanta, Georgia." *Architectural Review*, February 1984, pp. 26–27; project documentation, pp. 20–25.

Campbell, Robert. "Forms 'Exploding' from a Drum." *Architecture: The AIA Journal*, May 1984, pp. 222–29.

Cassarà, Silvio. "Richard Meier: The New Museum of Atlanta. 'Ratio' and 'Inclusive Dimensions.'" *Parametro*, August–September 1982, pp. 44–51.

Davis, Douglas. "Making Museums Modest." *Newsweek*, 26 July 1982, pp. 66–67 (passim).

"Ein Kunstmuseum als Kunst der Museums-Architektur." *Werk, Bauen und Wohnen*, April 1984, pp. 4–10.

Filler, Martin. "Sneak Preview of a Dazzling New Museum." *House & Garden*, August 1980, p. 6.

Fox, Catherine. "A New High for Atlanta." *Artnews*, November 1983, pp. 102–106.

————. "The New High 'A Work of Art.'" *The Atlanta Journal/Constitution*, 7 October 1983, pp. 1A, 13A.

Fox, Catherine, et al. "A New High: An Introduction to Atlanta's Museum." *The Atlanta Journal/Constitution*, 9 October 1983, supplement.

Frampton, Kenneth. "High Museum of Art at Atlanta." *Casabella*, November 1982, pp. 50–61.

Futagawa, Yukio, ed. "The High Museum of Art, Atlanta, Georgia." *GA Document* 6 (1983), pp. 78–85.

————. "The High Museum of Art, Atlanta, Georgia." *GA Document* 9 (February 1984), pp. 100–13.

Gaskie, Margaret. "Atlanta High." *Architectural Record*, January 1984, pp. 118–31.

Goldberger, Paul. "Architecture: New Atlanta Museum." *The New York Times*, 5 October 1983, p. C21.

————. "Designing a Proper Environment for Art." *The New York Times*, 4 July 1982, sec. 2, pp. 19–20 (passim).

Griffith, Helen C. "Atlanta's New Museum of Art—A Striking Balance between Architecture and Art." *Southern Accents*, March–April 1984, pp. 112–18.

"High Museum of Art." *A plus U*, February 1983, pp. 47–50.

"High Museum of Art, Atlanta, Georgia, 1983." *A plus U*, February 1984, pp. 19–32.

Irace, Fulvio, and Fox, Catherine. "Art Games/Atlanta High Museum." *Domus*, May 1984, pp. 14–19.

Mettler, Alexandra. "Reaching for a New High." *Atlanta*, January 1981, pp. 31–34.

Pettena, Gianni. "A Whiter Shade of Pale." *Domus*, June 1982, pp. 2–12.

"Richard Meier at Hartford and Atlanta." *L'Architecture d'Aujourd'hui*, February 1982, pp. 59–68.

Russell, John. "Atlanta's New Museum Has Spaces to Fill." *The New York Times*, 13 November 1983, sec. 2, p. 29.

Searing, Helen. "New American Art Museums." *Skyline*, June 1982, pp. 16–21 (passim).

————. *New American Art Museums*. Statements by Gudmund Vigtel and Richard Meier. New York: Whitney Museum/University of California Press, 1982, pp. 106–13.

Tighe, Mary Ann. "A New High for Atlanta." *House & Garden*, November 1983, pp. 148–53.

Vaudou, Valérie. "Une Architecture de Synthèse." *Techniques & Architecture*, February–March 1984, pp. 124–36.

Vigtel, Gudmund; Meier, Richard; Ames, Anthony. *High Museum of Art. The New Building: A Chronicle of Planning, Design and Construction*. Atlanta: High Museum of Art, 1983.

Wernick, Robert. "Atlanta's New High Museum Is a Jewel for a Queenly City." *Smithsonion*, January 1984, pp. 38–47.

Hoffman House

"Hoffman House." *A plus U*, November 1983, pp. 128–33.

Plumb, Barbara. "White on White." *The New York Times Magazine*, 23 March 1969, pp. 96–97.

"Record Houses of 1969." *Architectural Record*, mid-May 1969, pp. 76–79.

"Top 20 House Designs Emphasize 'Great Spaces.'" *The New York Times*, 22 June 1969, sec. 8, p. 1 (passim).

House in Old Westbury

"The Arts in America—the Forgotten Home." *Newsweek*, 24 December 1973, p. 76.

Davern, Jeanne. *Architecture 1970–80: A Decade of Change*. New York: McGraw-Hill, 1980, pp. 56–57.

Futagawa, Yukio, ed. "House in Old Westbury." *GA Document Special Issue: 1970–1980* (1980), pp. 46–49.

————. "House in Old Westbury, Long Island, New York, 1971." *Global Architecture Detail* 2 (1976), pp. 26–59.

————. "House in Old Westbury, Long Island, New York, 1971." Text by David Morton. *Global Architecture* 22 (1973). Reprinted in *Global Architecture Book 3: Modern Houses*. Tokyo: A.D.A. Edita Co., 1981, n.p.

————. "Houses in U.S.A." *Global Interiors* 6 (1974), pp. 72–80.

"Habitation Old Westbury, Long Island." *L'Architecture d'Aujourd'hui*, August–September 1971, pp. 68–69.

"House on Long Island." *Domus*, December 1972, pp. 14–16.

Morgan, James D. "A House that Glows with Crystalline Transparency." *Architectural Record*, April 1972, pp. 97–104.

"A Sculptured Machine for Living." *House & Garden*, March 1972, pp. 68–77, 115.

House in Pound Ridge

"House in Pound Ridge." *A plus U*, November 1972, pp. 31–34.

Rykwert, Joseph. "The Very Personal Work of Richard Meier and Associates." *Architectural Forum*, March 1972, pp. 30–37.

Internationale Bauausstellung Housing

Futagawa, Yukio, ed. "Housing Project, Berlin." *GA Document* 9 (February 1984), pp. 122–25.

Lingotto Factory Conversion

"Consultazione internazionale per la fabbrica FIAT–Lingotto: Meier." *L'Architettura*, May 1984, pp. 338–39.

Venti Progetti per il futuro del Lingotto. Milan: Etas Libri, 1984, pp. 120–27.

Maidman House

Futagawa, Yukio, ed. "House in Sands Point." *Global Architecture Houses* 5 (winter 1978), pp. 116–23.

Lewin, Susan Grant, and Schraub, Susan Hope. "The Structure of Space." *House Beautiful*, April 1978, pp. 79–91.

"Meiers Meisterwerk." *Häuser*, February 1981, pp. 14–19, 54.

Manchester Civic Center

"Manchester Center, Manchester, U.S.A." *L'Architecture d'Aujourd'hui*, September 1978, pp. 68–69.

Meier, Richard. "The Atheneum, New Harmony, Indiana; Manchester Civic Center, Manchester, New Hampshire—Comments." *Harvard Architecture Review*, spring 1981, pp. 176–87. Reprinted in French in *Les Cahiers de la Recherche Architecturale*, November 1982, pp. 66–73.

Museum for the Decorative Arts

"Architektur: Ein 'Juwel' für Frankfurt." *Der Spiegel*, 20 July 1981, pp. 132–34.

"Arts and Crafts Museum, Frankfurt." *Architectural Review*, October 1980, pp. 196–97.

Brenner, Douglas. "The Frankfurt Museum for the Decorative Arts: Theme and Variations." *Architectural Record*, April 1981, pp. 87–95.

Cobb, Henry N., and Meier, Richard. "Richard Meier's Museum für Kunsthandwerk." *Express*, April 1981, p. 7.

"Die Erste Skizze/The First Sketch." *Daidalos*, 15 September 1982, pp. 46–47.

Futagawa, Yukio, ed. "Winning Scheme, Museum for the Decorative Arts Competition, Frankfurt am Main, West Germany." *Global Document* 2 (1981), pp. 66–71.

Hoyet, Jean-Michel. "Made in U.S.A.: Trois conceptions récentes de Richard Meier & Associés." *Techniques & Architecture*, November 1982, pp. 140–47.

Klotz, Heinrich, ed. Includes "Der Wettbewerb für das Museum für Kunsthandwerk in Frankfurt am Main" by Frank Werner. *Jahrbuch für Architektur: Neues Bauen 1980–1981* (1981), pp. 22–29, 30–39.

Knobel, Lance. "Meier Modules." *Architectural Review*, July 1981, pp. 34–38.

Magnago Lampugnani, Vittorio. *Architecture of Our Century in Drawings: Utopia and Reality.* Stuttgart: Verlag Gerd Hatje, 1982, p. 108.

———. "The Jewel with All Qualities." *Lotus International* 28 (1980), pp. 95–110.

Ministry of Culture and Sciences. *Trends in Contemporary Architecture.* Athens: National Gallery, Alexander Soutzos Museum, 1982, pp. 76–83.

"Musée des Arts Décoratifs, Francfort." *L'Architecture d'Aujourd'hui*, September 1980, pp. XI–XII.

"Museum für Kunsthandwerk in Frankfurt." *Baumeister*, August 1980, pp. 767–73.

Ruthenfranz, Eva. "Nobler Kultur-Park für die Bürger." *Art, das Kunstmagazin*, September 1983, pp. 68–74.

Museum of Modern Art at the Villa Strozzi

"Dortmunder Architekturausstellung 1979. Museumsbauten: Entwürfe und Projekte seit 1945." *Dortmunder Architekturhefte* 15 (1979), n.p.

Hoyt, Charles. "4 Projects by Richard Meier: Change and Consistency." *Architectural Record*, March 1975, pp. 111–20.

Meier, Richard. "Tre recenti progetti." *Controspazio*, September 1975, pp. 38–47.

Morton, David. "MOMA, Italian Style." *Progressive Architecture*, March 1975, pp. 58–61.

"Museum in der Villa Strozzi, Florenz." *Baumeister*, May 1975, pp. 416–17.

New York School Exhibition

Hess, Thomas B. "Art: The Big Picture." *New York Magazine*, 24 October 1977, pp. 68, 71.

Murphy, Jim. "An Artful Streetscape." *Progressive Architecture*, May 1978, pp. 72–75.

Office Building for Siemens

Futagawa, Yukio, ed. "Siemens Office Building, Munich." *GA Document* 9 (February 1984), pp. 126–31.

Olivetti Projects

Allen, Gerald. "Traditional Image for Olivetti." *Architectural Record*, February 1974, pp. 117–24.

Moneo, Rafael. "Proyectos no realizados para Olivetti." *Arquitecturas Bis*, July 1975, pp. 10–14.

"Olivetti." *Architecture Plus*, September 1973, pp. 20–27 (passim).

"Olivetti Dormitory in Tarrytown." *A plus U*, March 1974, pp. 40–43.

"Olivetti Prototype, Olivetti Washington & Olivetti Tarrytown." *A plus U*, August 1974, pp. 29–50.

"Prototyp für Olivetti." *Bauen und Wohnen*, February–March 1976, pp. 56–58.

Schwarting, Jon Michael. "Richard Meier & Associates: quattro progetti per la Olivetti in U.S.A." *Domus*, March 1974, pp. 2–8.

Renault Administrative Headquarters

Brenner, Douglas. "An American in Paris." *Architectural Record*, October 1982, pp. 116–23.

Futagawa, Yukio, ed. "Renault Administrative Headquarters, Boulogne-Billancourt, France." *GA Document* 6 (1983), pp. 86–93.

Hoyet, Jean-Michel, "Made in U.S.A.: Trois conceptions récentes de Richard Meier & Associés." *Techniques & Architecture*, November 1982, pp. 140–47.

La modernité: Un projet inachevé. Exhibition Catalogue. Paris: Editions du Moniteur, 1982, pp. 102–107.

"L'Image d'une entreprise: Renault." *Architecture Intérieure/Crée*, October 1982, pp. 90–91.

"Projet pour le Nouvel Immeuble Administratif de la Régie Renault." *L'Architecture d'Aujourd'hui*, September 1982, pp. 23–27.

"Renault." *A plus U*, February 1983, pp. 51–54.

Saltzman House

"Bianca e spettacolare." *Domus*, June 1970, pp. 16–17.

Futagawa, Yukio, ed. "Houses in U.S.A." *Global Interiors* 1 (1971), pp. 152–69.

"House in East Hampton." *A plus U*, November 1972, pp. 107–14.

Raggi, Franco. "Templi e roulottes." *Casabella*, October 1974.

"Villa bei New York, U.S.A." *Bauen und Wohnen*, December 1970, pp. 448–49.

"Villa Saltzman." *Progressive Architecture*, April 1970, pp. 100–105.

Shamberg House

Futagawa, Yukio, ed. "House in Mount Kisco, New York." *Global Architecture Houses* 1 (1976), pp. 92–97.

Goldberger, Paul. "Architecture: Richard Meier." *Architectural Digest*, September 1978, pp. 150–55, 180.

Hoyt, Charles. "4 Projects by Richard Meier: Change and Consistency." *Architectural Record*, March 1975, pp. 111–20.

Meier, Richard. "Tre recenti progetti." *Controspazio*, September 1975, pp. 38–47.

"Record Houses of 1977." *Architectural Record*, mid-May 1977, pp. 68–71.

"Shamberg Pavilion." *A plus U*, April 1975, pp. 57–64.

Smith House

Blake, Peter. "Movement, Space, Direction." *Daily Telegraph Magazine*, October 1973, pp. 102–105.

Demoriane, Hélène, "Chaque soir fuir la ville." *Connaissance des Arts*, March 1970, pp. 90–91.

Eisenman, Peter. "Letter to the Editor: Meier's Smith House." *Architectural Design*, August 1971, p. 52.

Futagawa, Yukio, ed. "Houses in U.S.A." *Global Interiors* 1 (1971), pp. 144–51.

———. "Smith House, Darien, Connecticut. 1967." *Global Architecture Detail* 2 (1976), pp. 7–25.

———. "Smith House, Darien, Connecticut. 1967." Text by David Morton. *Global Architecture* 22 (1973). Reprinted in *Global Architecture Book 3: Modern Houses.* Tokyo: A.D.A. Edita Co., 1981, n.p.

"Habitation à Darien, Connecticut." *L'Architecture d'Aujourd'hui*, February–March 1968, pp. 92–94.

"House in Darien." *Toshi-Jutaku*, April 1969, pp. 65–70.

"House Opens 180 Degrees." *Architectural Forum*, December 1967, pp. 66–71.

Kulski, Julian. *Architecture in a Revolutionary Era.* Nashville: Aurora, 1971, pp. 295, 298.

"Le due Americhe." *Abitare*, October 1969, pp. 14–19.

Lee, Sarah Tomerlin. "Transparent Geometry." *House Beautiful*, September 1968, pp. 106–12.

"Mit der Aussicht wohnen." *Bauen und Wohnen*, November 1968, pp. 392–94.

Plumb, Barbara. "Taking the Long View." *The New York Times Magazine*, 23 March 1969, pp. 96–97.

"Record Houses of 1968." *Architectural Record*, mid-May 1968, pp. 52–57.

"Un sogno americano." *Domus*, April 1968, pp. 20–23.

Zevi, Bruno. "Un sogno americano." *L'Espresso*, 10 March 1974.

Suburban House Prototype

Meier, Richard. "College Suburb." *La Biennale di Venezia 1976.* Venice: Edizioni La Biennale di Venezia, 1978, vol. 2, pp. 134–40.

Twin Parks Northeast Housing

Cliff, Ursula. "U.D.C. Scorecard." *Design and Environment*, September 1972, pp. 54–63.

Cohen, Stuart. "Physical Context/Cultural Context: Including It All." *Oppositions* 2 (1974), pp. 14–21, 30–37.

Davern, Jeanne. *Architecture 1970–1980: A Decade of Change.* New York: McGraw-Hill, 1980, pp. 92–93.

Frampton, Kenneth. "Twin Parks as Typology." *Architectural Forum*, June 1973, pp. 56–61.

Goldberger, Paul. "Twin Parks, an Effort to Alter the Problem of Public Housing." *The New*

York Times, 27 December 1973, p. 39.

————. "Two Cheers for Eight Winners." The New York Times Magazine, 2 June 1974, pp. 62–64.

————. "U.D.C.'s Architecture Has Raised Public Standard." The New York Times, 5 March 1975, p. 43 (passim).

Hoyt, Charles. "Richard Meier: Public Space and Private Space." Architectural Record, July 1973, pp. 89–98.

"Learning from Twin Parks." Architectural Forum, June 1973, pp. 62–64.

Mackay, David, and Sherwood, Roger. "La obra de Richard Meier en Bronx." Arquitecturas Bis, May 1974, pp. 1–7.

Pommer, Richard. In "The Architecture of Urban Housing in the U.S. during the Early 1930s." Journal of the Society of Architectural Historians, December 1978, p. 263.

"Twin Parks Northeast." A plus U, June 1973, pp. 55–68.

"U.D.C. Twin Parks Northeast." L'Architecture d'Aujourd'hui, August–September 1976, pp. 4–7.

Weintraub, Myles, and Zicarelli, Mario. "Tale of Twin Parks." Architectural Forum, June 1973, pp. 54–55.

Westbeth Artists' Housing

"Artists: Lofty Solutions." Time, 18 August 1967, p. 60.

Berkeley, Ellen Perry. "Westbeth: Artists in Residence." Architectural Forum, October 1970, pp. 44–49.

Blake, Peter. "Downtown Dakota." New York Magazine, 3 August 1970, pp. 54–57.

Fowler, Glenn. "Low Budget Buildings Fare Well in AIA Awards." The New York Times, 30 May 1971, sec. 8, p. 1 (passim).

Huxtable, Ada Louise. "Bending the Rules." The New York Times, 10 May 1970, sec. 2, p. 23.

"Westbeth." The New Yorker, 8 June 1968, pp. 26–28.

"Westbeth Artists' Housing." Space Design, June 1972, pp. 17–28.

"Westbeth's Rehabilitation Project: A Clue to Improving Our Cities." Architectural Record, March 1970, pp. 44–49.

Other Projects

"Beach House, Fire Island, New York." Arts and Architecture, January 1964, pp. 22–23. (Lambert Beach House)

Borg, Alan. "Ten Lessons from a Superb House." American Home, March 1967, pp. 82–87. (House for Mr. and Mrs. Jerome Meier)

Diamonstein, Barbaralee, ed. Collaboration: Artists and Architects. New York: Whitney Library of Design, 1981, pp. 104–108 and passim. (Stella/Meier Collaboration)

Futagawa, Yukio, ed. "Apartment in New York." Global Architecture Houses 6 (1979), pp. 90–92. (Apartment for Mr. and Mrs. Philip Suarez)

————. "New York Apartment Renovation." Global Architecture Houses 5 (winter 1978), pp. 110–15. (Apartment for Richard Meier)

Genauer, Emily. "New Styles in Synagogues." The New York Times, 5 October 1963, p. 22. ("Recent American Synagogue Architecture")

Giovannini, Joseph. "Design Notebook: Tea Services with the Touch of an Architect." The New York Times, 17 November 1983, p. C18. (Objects for Alessi Designs)

Goldberger, Paul. "A Meeting of Artistic Minds." The New York Times Magazine, 1 March 1981, pp. 70–80 (passim). (Stella/Meier Collaboration)

————. "Architecture: Townhouse Rows." The New York Times, 16 June 1980, p. C15. (East 67th Street Housing)

Gueft, Olga. "House with Sky Inside." Interiors, August 1964, pp. 58–62. (House for Mr. and Mrs. Jerome Meier)

————. "Sona the Golden One." Interiors, September 1965, pp. 150–53.

"Habitation à Essex Falls, New Jersey." L'Architecture d'Aujourd'hui, September–October 1965, pp. 82–83. (House for Mr. and Mrs. Jerome Meier)

Huxtable, Ada Louise. "Designs for American Synagogues." The New York Times, 5 October 1963, p. 22. ("Recent American Synagogue Architecture")

Meier, Richard. Recent American Synagogue Architecture. New York: The Jewish Museum, 1963.

Michelson, Annette. "An Art Scholar's Loft." Vogue, 15 March 1967, pp. 136–42, 154–55. (Rubin Loft)

"New Jersey House of Contrasts Wins a Design Award." The New York Times, 4 July 1965, sec. 8, p. 1. (House for Mr. and Mrs. Jerome Meier)

O'Brien, George. "Living in an Art Form." The New York Times Magazine, 22 March 1964, pp. 94–95.

Pica, Agnoldomenico. "Sona: Un centro di artigianato indiano a New York." Domus, December 1966.

Plumb, Barbara. "One of a Kind." The New York Times Magazine, 24 September 1967. (Stella Studio)

————. "Remodeling on a Grand Scale." The New York Times Magazine, 24 September 1966, pp. 170–72. (Renfield House)

"Record Houses of 1964." Architectural Record, mid-May 1964, pp. 68–71. (House for Mr. and Mrs. Jerome Meier)

Stephens, Suzanne. "Design Deformed." Artforum, January 1977, pp. 44–47. (Opening Exhibition, Cooper-Hewitt Museum)

"Stirling e Meier: costruire a Manhattan." Domus, July 1980, p. 32. (East 67th Street Housing)

Sverbeyeff, Elizabeth. "For the New Horizon: A Sculptured Profile." House Beautiful, September 1967, pp. 140–45. (Renfield House)

Photographers

Photographs of buildings and
models are by Ezra Stoller
© ESTO, Mamaroneck,
New York, except as follows:
Dorothy Alexander, New York, pp.
120, 121, 122 *bottom*
Mario Carrieri, Milan, pp. 232,
236, 237
Louis Checkman, Jersey City, pp.
160, 168 *bottom*, 169, 182 *top*,
183, 184, 188, 189
Paul Crocker, New York, p. 115
top
Wolfgang Hoyt © ESTO,
Mamaroneck, New York, pp. 82,
222, 225, 226, 227, 230, 231
Balthazar Korab, Troy, Michigan,
pp. 262, 266, 267
Roberto Schezen, New York, pp.
208, 209
Photograph of Richard Meier by
Irving Penn, courtesy *Vogue*
© 1983 Condé Nast
Publications Inc., p. 380

Collaborators

The people listed here are among those who have worked in the office and assisted on the buildings and projects in this book.

Appreciation is due to the many engineers and consultants who have collaborated with this office, especially Ed Messina and the office of Severud-Perrone-Szegezdy-Sturm; John L. Altieri and his staff; the office of P. DeBellis; Flack and Kurtz; and Cosentini Associates.

Paul Aferiat
Dorothy Alexander
Stanley Allen
Philip Babb
Margaret Bemiss
Susan Berman
Karl Born
Michel Bourdeau
Andrew Buchsbaum
Anne Luise Buerger
Christopher Chimera
John Chimera
Mark Cigolle
Miles Cigolle
John Colamarino
David Diamond
Pamela Donnelly
Bernd Echtermeyer
John Eisler
Murray Emslie
David Estreich
Donald Charles Evans
Manfred Fischer
Frank Fitzgibbons
Steven Forman
Jonathan Friedman
Laurent Gilson
Hans Christoph Goedeking
Gerald Gurland
Marc Hacker
Ireneus Harasymiak
Frank Harmon
Douglas Kahn
George Kewin
Sherman Kung
Stephen Lesser
Hans Li
Barbara Littenberg
Jean Mas
Era Malewitsch
Joachim Mantel
Carl Meinhardt

Ada Karmi Melamede
Jean Michel Meunier
Edward Mills
Richard Morris
Katsu Muramoto
Bruce Nagel
Richard Oliver
Alfonso Peña
Michael Palladino
Vincent Polsinelli
Stephen Potters
J. Woodson Rainey, Jr.
Alan Schwabenland
Jon Michael Schwarting
Sandra Schwartz
Suzanne Sekey
Henry Smith-Miller
Gunter Standke
Peter Szilagyi
Leland Taliaferro
Jean-Christophe Tougeron
Valerie Vaudou
Greta Weil
Tod Williams
David Woolf